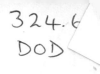

A Sylvia Pankhurst reader

In memory of Lillian Harman
(1893–1985), my grandmother

A
SYLVIA
PANKHURST
reader

edited by Kathryn Dodd

Manchester University Press
Manchester and New York

distributed exclusively in the USA and Canada by St. Martin's Press

Copyright © Kathryn Dodd 1993

Published by Manchester University Press
Oxford Road, Manchester M 13 9PL, UK
and Room 400, 175 Fifth Avenue, New York, NY 10010, USA

Distributed exclusively in the USA and Canada
by St. Martin's Press, Inc., 75 Fifth Avenue, New York, NY 10010, USA

British Library Cataloguing-in-Publication Data
A catalogue record for this book is available from the British
Library

Library of Congress Cataloging-in-Publication Data applied for
Pankhurst, E. Sylvia (Estelle Sylvia), 1882–1960.
  A Sylvia Pankhurst reader / edited by Kathryn Dodd.
    p.   cm.
  Includes bibliographical references and index.
  ISBN 0–7190–2888–4 (hardback).—ISBN 0–7190–2889–2 (paperback)
  1. Feminism—Great Britain.   2. Socialism—Great Britain.
3. Women—Suffrage—Great Britain.   I. Dodd. Kathryn, 1950–   .
II. Title
HQ1597.P36   1993
305.42'0941—dc20   92–31627
                                                              CIP

Typeset by J&L Composition Ltd, Filey, North Yorkshire
Printed in Great Britain
by Bell & Bain Limited, Glasgow

Contents

Contents

Acknowledgements

As always, a book of this kind depends on the assistance of many people. I am especially grateful to Richard Pankhurst for his continuous support for the project and for allowing me to publish his mother's work. I am also indebted to particular librarians. I would especially like to thank Mieke Ijzermans, in charge of the Pankhurst Papers at the International Institute of Social History at Amsterdam, not only for her meticulous attention to locating the papers and photocopying them, but also for her generous hospitality. David Doughan, at the Fawcett Library, provided invaluable help and enlightening conversation, and several assistants at the London School of Economics were helpful in locating newspapers and pamphlets. I want to thank Professor Jane Lewis, Dr Liz Stanley and Dr Pankhurst for their helpful comments on the Introduction, and Dr Julia Brannen and Professor Ann Oakley for their more general support. I would also like to acknowledge the editorial staff at Manchester University Press who have patiently supported the project through its long gestation.

A lot more than thanks are owed to Philip Dodd, who throughout the project has given unstinting personal and intellectual support; without his criticisms I would never have found out what I wanted to do with the mountain of photocopies of Pankhurst's writing that littered the house for months on end. Lastly a word to Matthew, who spent so many weekends wondering when he would stop having to listen to conversations about dead suffragettes.

Finally, I need to thank the publishers of Sylvia Pankhurst's books for their kind permission to reprint extracts from her published work: the Longmans Group UK for *The Suffragette Movement*; the Random Century Group for *The Home Front* and *The Life of Emmeline Pankhurst*; HarperCollins for *Save the Mothers*; and the International Institute of Social History for extracts from the manuscripts In the Red Twilight, Women's Citizenship, and Fascism As It Is. Every effort has been made to trace other possible copyright holders, but anyone claiming copyright who has not been acknowledged should get in touch with the publisher.

Abbreviations

BSP	British Socialist Party
CP-BSTI	Communist Party – British Section of the Third International
CPGB	Communist Party of Great Britain
ELFS	East London Federation of the Suffragettes
ILP	Independent Labour Party
NAC	National Administrative Council (ILP)
NUWSS	National Union of Women's Suffrage Societies
PP	Pankhurst Papers at the International Institute of Social History, Amsterdam
SLP	Socialist Labour Party
SWSS	South Wales Socialist Society
WFL	Women's Freedom League
WIL	Women's International League for Peace and Freedom
WSF	Workers' Suffrage Federation (1916–18)
WSF	Workers' Socialist Federation (1918–20)
WSPU	Women's Social and Political Union
(. . .)	words omitted from a passage
* * *	pages omitted

NOTE: In the extracts from Sylvia Pankhurst's writings, her original punctuation and style (in such matters as use of italics and capitals) have largely been preserved, though a few misspellings have been silently corrected.

Introduction

The politics of form in Sylvia Pankhurst's writing

Sylvia Pankhurst's achievements as a political leader and as a prolific writer are as substantial as they are rare in English history, and yet the extraordinary range of both her political affiliations and her publications has tended to diminish rather than establish her reputation. This may be because there is simply no available way within the dominant definitions of politics and culture, still too often seen as mutually exclusive categories, to make sense of and value a woman who was, in the course of a long life (1882–1960), an accomplished artist who wished to practise a political art; a politically committed writer who wanted to experiment with literary forms; a militant suffragist who acknowledged class as well as gender oppression; a revolutionary communist who fought for feminism, democracy and freedom of speech within a Communist Party that insisted on central control; and a tireless anti-fascist campaigner and writer, who focused her attention unfashionably on Africa.[1]

The historical record for the most part ignores her as an artist, writer and founder-editor of four newspapers, and acknowledges her primarily as a character in the militant suffrage movement.[2] Her better-known mother, Mrs Emmeline Pankhurst, the founder of the Women's Social and Political Union (WSPU) and her sister, Christabel, the Union's most charismatic leader and main policy-maker, have somewhat obscured Sylvia's contribution to socialist–feminism within the movement. Her formation of the socialist–feminist East London Federation of the Suffragettes, a semi-independent group within the WSPU, and her subsequent excommunication from the Union by Christabel for working with the socialist Herald League, which Christabel considered to be a men's organisation and a class

I

organisation,[3] have been regarded by several historians as her only important contribution to the women's movement. Her subsequent years in the East End as a socialist and pacifist are seen more in terms of social work than as an extension of her feminism, and her years as a communist tend to be totally marginalised or forgotten.[4]

Pankhurst's socialist–feminism, which was later transformed into 'left-wing' communist–feminism, has not helped her reputation, especially as the history of early twentieth-century feminism and the history of socialism and communism in Britain have usually been constructed as separate intellectual discourses – and often as antagonistic ones. For mainstream historians of British communism, Pankhurst's East London Federation, renamed the Workers' Suffrage Federation (WSF) in 1916, and renamed yet again in 1918 as the Workers' Socialist Federation, which campaigned first as a socialist group, then as a communist organisation, was simply irrelevant in the history of British communism or, as one commentator has glossed it, was 'an infantile tributary flowing into the Leninist mainstream, later to emerge as an effluent which disappears into the void'.[5] That Lenin personally took the trouble to criticise Pankhurst's 'left-wing' communism, which included among other things a rejection of the policies of running candidates for Parliament or affiliating to the Labour Party, has tended to cloud Pankhurst's arguments for the development of democracy within communism, revolutionising domestic labour and representing women as mothers through community-based household soviets.[6] That she refused to hand over the editorship of her widely read communist newspaper, the *Workers' Dreadnought*, to the increasingly centralised (male) leadership of the Communist Party, or stop her left-wing criticism, for which she was expelled by the Party in 1921, only confirms her 'bourgeois' origins, according to the leading historian of communism, Stuart Macintyre.[7]

Perhaps even more curious than this kind of historical condescension is the attempt to reduce Pankhurst's politics to a form of psychological disorder. According to Patricia Romero, Pankhurst's most recent and most unsympathetic biographer, the inexplicable and 'incongruous' switch from suffrage politics to revolutionary communism can be accounted for only by claiming that Pankhurst had 'a less secure hold on reality' at this time, was suffering from 'inner tension and overwork', and perhaps even indulging in 'a desire for notoriety'.[8] Romero simply cannot take Pankhurst seriously as a political writer or activist; her commitments throughout her life are consistently belittled as 'extremist', 'maverick', 'eccentric', 'hysterical' or 'antics', words that themselves echo Pankhurst's obituary in The Times.[9] It is depressing to see how certain political beliefs and activities which fundamentally threaten received ideas about what women should be thinking or doing can be translated into abnormal psychological behaviour; as Ann Morley and Liz Stanley have shown in the case of Emily Wilding Davison, self-sacrificing feminist militancy could be similarly demoted to the hysterical action of a lunatic.[10]

Despite a record of almost sublime personal and political in-dependence, Romero concludes that Pankhurst's life was merely driven by a 'succession of dependencies on men'.[11] And this is the verdict on a woman who as a suffrage campaigner was constantly imprisoned and tortured for her belief in the right to fight for women's freedom; was one of the handful of women leaders in the revolutionary communist movement in Europe; and who lived out her beliefs in sexual freedom: she had a long affair with Keir Hardie, and refused to marry Silvio Corio, her second partner, even when she gave birth to their child at the age of forty-five.

The final phase of Pankhurst's political life has compounded the general unease about her 'wayward' career: as a fervent anti-fascist campaigner she gave Haile Selassie, the Emperor of Ethiopia, unstinting support after the invasion of Mussolini's Italian troops in 1935. She founded and edited a campaigning newspaper, the New Times and Ethiopia News, in 1936, and ran it for twenty years, with the aim of obtaining freedom for the only independent black state in Africa, for which she was supported by African nationalists such as Jomo Kenyatta, Wallace Johnston, George Padmore and T. R. Makonnen.[12] But the Euro-centric historical verdict appears to be that the erstwhile communist ended her life hero-worshipping an African dictator.[13] Her final emigration to Ethiopia in the mid-1950s only confirms the received opinion about her eccentric unbelonging.

In order to begin to reclaim both Pankhurst's politics and her writing, it may be helpful to start by suggesting some analogies between Pankhurst and William Morris, someone whom she acknowledged as a formative influence.[14] Like him, she was committed to art and decorative crafts and saw them as integral to her socialist politics.[15]

Again paralleling Morris, she was a middle-class socialist who worked against the grain of the liberal and Fabian–socialist gradualism of her class, and who finally took the 'un-English' revolutionary path as the only way to bring about the necessary radical social, political and cultural changes. Morris's way of producing his literary–political writings offers an even closer parallel; his work, like Pankhurst's, was often 'occasional', appearing first in periodical form, only subsequently and occasionally gathered in volumes, and written in a wide variety of forms. When Perry Anderson says of Morris that his ways of writing and of publishing may have made it difficult to weigh his achievement, the fate of Pankhurst too comes to mind.[16]

Now to make these comparisons is not to suggest any direct inheritance, nor to imply that a woman needs a male precedent to establish her credibility. But it is to recognise that a certain kind of figure within English culture may be marginalised as a result of her failure to fit into existing practices, institutions and categories. Pankhurst's problems were exacerbated by a radical reconstruction of intellectual ideas and categories which took place from the 1880s to the 1920s, the years during which she forged her politial beliefs. For example, ethical and Utopian-socialism was marginalised by those who saw themselves as 'scientific' socialists; English literature was established as a university subject and an authorised male-dominated canon constructed; and economics, politics and social science began to be taught as academic disciplines at the London School of Economics.[17] It was a sign of the times when the expert academic emerged as the authoritative intellectual figure.[18] In these circumstances, to cling to Utopian beliefs in the wholeness of knowledge and experience, as Pankhurst did, to be a political activist *and* an artist *and* a writer – of history, *and* politics, *and* poetry – was a good way to be at best ignored, or at worst derided. Pankhurst was anything but a scientific or specialist writer; she was an exceptionally productive and restless writer who was ready to experiment with a very wide range of forms. Only by ignoring traditional genre boundaries could she begin to make some sort of sense of her radical politics, and at the same time clarify and organise the history within which she lived.

However surprising a starting-point this may be in the attempt to establish Pankhurst's importance, the approach demands, at the very least, a recognition that writing was one of her principal activities and that she remained a writer throughout her life. Even more crucial is

4

the analysis of Pankhurst's actual work, its vocabulary, its form and conventions, since, as Raymond Williams has argued, the concentration on the general conditions of production of a cultural practice often leads to 'the partial or total neglect of the practice itself' and, as a result, the works become appropriated only 'in terms of their manifest or presumed social content . . .'. Earlier Williams had argued for the need to acknowledge the much more complex work that is necessary to understand a practice of writing and its conditions of production: 'Significant facts of real relationships are thus included or excluded, assumed or described, analysed or emphasised by variable conventions which can be identified by formal analysis, but which can be understood only by social analysis.'[19]

I want to apply Williams's approach to argue that the forms of Pankhurst's writing were not merely incidental to or reflections of her life or her ideas, but constitutive of her politics and the social formation of which she was a part; and that if we want to understand her politics and her heroic attempts to forge new social and political relationships, we need to attend to the writing – to the stance, the language, the form and conventions – and not see it as some unproblematic repository of her thoughts.

To provide a full explanation of the reasons for the general indifference towards her writing is beyond the scope of this brief introduction, but it is important to identify some of the causes because otherwise they may continue to block our recognition not only of Pankhurst's achievement but of that of other women writers.[20] The first point to note is that because Pankhurst's non-fictional writing often has 'historical' interest, it is historians and biographers, rather than literary critics, who have made use of the texts, with the consequence that a few selected works, most particularly the 1931 autobiography *The Suffragette Movement*,[21] are used over and over again as sources of evidence. Historians have differed as to their assessment of the use of Pankhurst's autobiography; for example, Andrew Rosen says that 'regarding all family matters, Sylvia's strong biases must be taken into account, in particular her idealisation of her father'. Martin Pugh on the other hand sees it as more generally reliable when compared to the memoirs of other militants, which he considers 'largely fantasy'. Patricia Romero, after extensively using the book as source material, later declares that it is not 'objective history', but self-serving propaganda, full of exaggerations of her political importance and of 'bitter recriminations' against her mother and sister Christabel.[22]

Now there is no reason why Pankhurst's works should not be used by historians and biographers as repositories of more or less factual information, testing them for their reliability by comparing the accounts with other independent sources. But historians who address the works only insofar as they provide documentary evidence of the period about which they are written, ignoring the need to situate them in the moment at which they were produced (which also requires a consideration of the significance of the form of writing for that particular moment) drastically reduce what 'evidence' they really could provide. For example, *The Suffragette Movement* was published three years after Ray Strachey's *The Cause*,[23] and though both were ostensibly concerned with the history of the women's movement, they are in fact narratives written from two conflicting political positions in the present, revealing, as I shall show in detail later, as much about the politics at the moment of production (that is, the late 1920s, when universal suffrage had been granted, but in the wake of the defeat of the Labour movement) as they do about the pre-war women's movement. But such issues are rarely addressed by historians and biographers intent on extracting from the works, reliable content from subjective bias.

These limitations should not apply to literary critics, whose approach to texts usually alerts them to such conditions of production, as well as to the rhetoric of writing. Yet they too have failed to accommodate Pankhurst's work, for a different set of reasons. One problem is the very definition of the word 'literature', which, during the period when Pankhurst was writing, was centred on a highly selective tradition of 'creative' work in drama, poetry and the novel, to the exclusion of all 'non-fictional' prose.[24] With such a deep division, it has been difficult until relatively recently to gain a recognition that the various forms of non-fiction (a term which loosely accommodates most of Pankhurst's work) are *rhetorical*, with meaning forged not merely through their 'factual' subject-matter but also by their conventions and form, and the narrator's relationship to the inscribed reader.[25]

Take, for example, Pankhurst's book, *Save the Mothers*[26] which was published in 1930 and argued the case for establishing a national maternity service in order to reduce the enormous number of deaths in childbirth of women and children. Now such social reforming works are not generally regarded as having a form; their authority rests on their being supposedly transparent, allowing the reader to assess the objective evidence about a 'problem' and the administrative solutions on offer. But in one of the very few analyses of the form of such documents, Bryan Green suggests that such transparency is part of the form's rhetoric of 'reality effects', which facilitates the presentation of a social problem as an objective description, rather than a particular political construction of that problem.[27] Such 'reality effects' include the use of the 'evidence' of informed witnesses, experts, statistics, and the organisation of the material into administrative sections, with summaries and indexes, with the result that reforms are represented not as the political aspirations of a particular middle-class formation, but as the rational outcome of the measurement of an objective problem and the identification of a solution based on the consensus of 'society' at large. The political provenance of these conventions is traced by Green to the plethora of official Parliamentary Reports in the early and mid-nineteenth century which presented the findings of commissions set up by the state to enquire into the operation of, for example, the Poor Law, prisons, factories and schools.[28]

Save the Mothers, Pankhurst's feminist argument for the reform of the maternity services, shares many of these characteristics of the form. After the emotional appeal of the title, the long subtitle, 'A plea for measures to prevent the annual loss of about 3,000 child-bearing mothers and 20,000 infant lives in England and Wales and a similar grievous wastage in other countries', immediately declares its credentials: this is going to be an argument for reform to prevent inefficient 'wastage', backed up with reliable statistics. The book thus predictably opens with an address to its readers using the rhetoric of facts and figures, and the observations of 'expert' medical commentators on the persistently high maternal and infant mortality rates, establishing the 'crisis' that any reformer needs to create in order to press for change. Pankhurst organises the text, again conventionally in terms of the form, by dividing the problem into administrative chapters, presenting the problems associated with the mother herself, with the attitudes and practices of doctors, and with the training of midwives. The last section is a summary of the reforms needed to establish a national maternity service and thus solve the problem she has described.

None of this is merely the recitation of facts. It is the skilled use of an authorised, rhetorical convention of writing to appeal to a middle-class audience which might otherwise regard *Save the Mothers* as feminist special pleading. An examination of another book on a related theme of women's poverty, Eleanor Rathbone's *The Disinherited Family*,[29] written a few years earlier, would reveal exactly the same conventions of writing. Pankhurst's choice of subject and method of writing about it should thus be seen as neither accidental nor merely personal: Romero insists Pankhurst wrote the book to keep herself in the public eye, after the publicity she enjoyed after the birth of her only son as an unmarried mother.[30] Much more important was the need to present feminist arguments in a conventionalised form, legitimised by its political provenance, to a middle-class readership who had to be persuaded if any government reform was ever to take place.

As lack of space prevents a commentary on the forms of all Pankhurst's work included in this *Reader*, I shall devote the rest of this Introduction to an examination in detail of three of the forms of writing used by her. It should be noted that each section of the *Reader* is prefaced by a brief editorial introduction which extends the discussion a little further. By examining two of Pankhurst's very early texts, 'The Potato-Pickers' (1909) and *The Suffragette* (1911), together with her most influential work, *The Suffragette Movement* (1931), all of which provide a representation of women's politics, I hope to illuminate the ways in which the forms of writing – the essay, history and autobiography – do not merely reflect a political or historical content, but permit and condition specific political and historical meanings. I go on to show how Pankhurst continually struggled to embrace new ideas about politics – the importance of class within feminism, the strategic importance of the militant women within the suffrage struggle, the intimate connection between ethical socialism and the pre-war women's militant movement – and explicate how those struggles were permitted, conditioned and inflected through the forms of her writing.

EARLY WRITING ON WOMEN

Among Pankhurst's first attempts at journalism was a series of occasional essays written for *Votes for Women*, the newspaper of the

WSPU, on the lives of labouring women.[31] They derive from an extraordinary year-long journey she embarked on in the summer of 1907 to the north of England and Scotland, which was prompted by the desire to witness the lives of women who worked in a variety of industries and in agriculture, and to record their struggle. She did not go equipped with a 'scientific' questionnaire as Charles Booth or Rowntree might have done, but with her paintbrushes and paper, intent on recording the lives of women, as a sympathetic chronicler, in both her painting and her writing. She worked continually, travelling to the pottery factories and chainmakers in Staffordshire, the shoemakers in Leicester, the pit-brow women in Wigan, the fisherwomen in Scarborough, the agricultural workers of Berwickshire, and the millwomen in Glasgow, producing some of her best pictorial work in gouache, watercolour and charcoal, depicting women in their working environment.[32] And yet there is no record of their being exhibited or sold and only a few essays she wrote about the women appeared in *Votes for Women*. The ones that were published were spread over a long period, thus minimising any impact they might have had.

One of the essays, 'The Potato-Pickers', opens and closes with quotations from the nineteenth-century rural writer Richard Jefferies, in which he implores the reader to have hope in a better life, which will not be a constant struggle of ceaseless labour but a sweet accommodation with the natural world.[33] Pankhurst takes up the theme contrasting the beautiful countryside and the 'well-groomed horses' with the 'hideous' women workers – 'miserable creatures, clad in vile, nameless rags' – who have come to pick the potatoes by hand. Pankhurst is struck by the women's physicality: their gnarled skin, swollen, shapeless and purple lips, and their red eyes. They squatted on the ground to eat, and had the harsh voices and the 'awful laughter' of 'degraded creatures lower than the beasts of the field'. She deplores their subhuman condition and finishes by urging all women of whatever class to answer the call of 'the great Woman's Movement' and take up the work waiting for them.

Pankhurst was writing this essay at a time in the history of the WSPU when the relationship of class and gender was being remade. If in 1903, at its inception, the WSPU was a northern provincial organisation aimed at educating the working-class members of the socialist ILP, the Union from 1906 gradually became metropolitan-led and rapidly began to attract educated, professional, middle-class women. *Votes for Women*, set up as a monthly by Emmeline and Frederick Pethick-Lawrence, embodied the new metropolitan orientation, with its focus on solidarity based on gender, whatever the class of women.[34] Yet Pankhurst's essay continues to articulate the tension between classes of women:

All the hush and awe of the evening was around me, but still my thoughts were busy with these poor, dreadful women, and my heart ached. . . .

Oh, can it be that we women would have let so many things go wrong in this world, and should we have let it be so hard a place for the unfortunate, if we had had the governing power that men have had?

But the tension is not only in the explicit content, it is there in the form of the writing, which is a rural variant of the late nineteenth-/ early twentieth-century 'into unknown England' tradition that Peter Keating has described.[35] The tradition of writing which stretches back to the beginning of the nineteenth century (and incidentally, though Keating does not make this point, is continuous with writing such as George Orwell's *The Road to Wigan Pier*[36]) was used by a fraction of the middle class who were able to articulate their anthropological explorations of the dangerous territory of the slums, and represent and remake the urban working class, often through meticulous documentation, for the rest of their class, whom they often saw as blind and uncaring. Lower-class lives were no longer simply abominated as the inevitable result of personal improvidence or degeneration, but seen as a pathetic spectacle to be recognised and understood by those with power to change such conditions. George R. Sims, one such writer, described his purpose in 1889:

I propose to record the result of a journey into a region which lies at our own doors – into a dark continent that is within easy walking distance of the General Post Office. . . . the wild races who inhabit it will, I trust, gain public sympathy as easily as those savage tribes for whose benefit the Missionary Societies never cease to appeal for funds.[37]

However powerful this representation of one class by another was to move the conscience of the middle-class reader, it also had other political implications. What is established by the tradition is a class separation defined by physical and cultural difference, in which, in 'The Potato-Pickers', 'we, women' are marked out from the 'unfortunate'. The critic, Gill Davies, has noted that practitioners of this mode of writing were particularly prone to using animal metaphors when describing working people, with an undue emphasis on repellent physical attributes, concentrating, especially in the case of women, on the mouth.[38] Pankhurst's essay uses precisely this vocabulary: her potato-pickers have 'purple, shapeless lips' from which is emitted an 'awful laughter'. So while she was reaffirming class within a new gendered feminist politics, the form within which she expressed her affiliation and solidarity was actually articulating separation and difference: 'the unfortunate' suffer and 'we' must pity and act on their behalf. To say this is not to suggest any sense of superiority towards Pankhurst, but to register how the available form of writing conditioned what she was could express and in certain ways ran counter to her political purpose. What we see in 'The Potato Pickers' is Pankhurst straining to find ways of articulating women's solidarity across class, and being held within a received language, which expresses separation.

THE SUFFRAGETTE (1911)

If Pankhurst's early attempts at writing were an effort to re-establish class as an issue within the politics of militant suffrage, the aim of her first book, The Suffragette, a 500-page history of the WSPU, was to show how the Union ranked 'amongst the great reform movements of the world'.[39] Despite the fact that the frontispiece of the book depicts Pankhurst painting a mural to decorate the 1909 WSPU Exhibition, the artist's life had been permanently abandoned in order to meet the demands of 'the great struggles to better the world for humanity', as she was to describe her painful translation many years later.[40] However, she did not so much abandon art for political action, as substitute one form of artistic representation for another: The Suffragette was the first attempt at history-writing which both represented and legitimated the militant woman suffragist.

The reason why the WSPU leadership decided to commission the writing of its own history as it was unfolding is not clear, though in the Preface to the book, Mrs Emmeline Pankhurst speaks of the 'coercion, repression, misrepresentation and insult' heaped upon the militant movement and the need to celebrate the persistence, courage and vision of the suffragette women. *The Suffragette* was published at a transitional period in the politics of the WSPU, when there was a change in tactics towards more individual acts of disobedience, as public demonstrations were abandoned in the face of the systematic physical abuse and violence from police and the torture of force-feeding of militant prisoners.[41] Sylvia in her Preface notes that despite the 'glorious' deeds of the 'pioneers and martyrs . . . their work lacks completion' and that their followers will have to suffer even greater 'social ostracism, violence, and hardship of all kinds' to see the struggle triumph. It would thus appear that the publication of her text was itself an act of provocation, not only in declaring the need for even greater militancy, but also in glorifying the militant movement by providing it with a legitimate history.[42]

But how could Pankhurst legitimate a movement which had been increasingly represented by its opponents as at best hysterical and at worst unconstitutional, lawless and subversive?[43] Her solution (which as we shall see was only a partial one) was to inflect, for her own radical purposes, the dominant form of nineteenth-century English Whig history, which had presented a continuous, chronological procession of past events which glorified the present state of pro-gressive (male) achievement, and had presumed that history, to paraphrase Carlyle's dictum, was the biography of great men.[44] *The Suffragette* uses a form of writing which had traditionally legitimated bourgeois male political, military and economic power and turns the logic of this narration on its head: instead of celebrating the achievement of progress, Pankhurst uses the historical form to describe the women's militant fight against the systematic denial of it to women; instead of a continuous, completed history, she recounts an unfinished struggle up to the present which expresses discontinuity, discontent and change; and she celebrates the qualities not only of women, but of 'great' militant women, who were in the process of changing history.

Pankhurst represents a discontinuous history by jettisoning the history of the nineteenth-century suffrage pioneers, and by omitting practically all events prior to the formation of the WSPU in Manchester in 1903, even though the main source for *The Suffragette* lay in a series of around fifty articles which Pankhurst published in *Votes for Women* over a two-year period, half of which were concerned with the description of the campaigns in the nineteenth century.[45]

Pankhurst thus selectively edits one narrative to create another, with the effect of obscuring the political roots of the WSPU, and constructing a history which appears to be still in the making, a living history about a completely new political force. The narrative strongly evokes a sense of the time and the place by providing a detailed account of the experiences of the women participants to which only an insider would have access.

Yet the mode of address is the omniscient third person narrator who speaks in the past tense, the conventional 'objective', legitimating historical stance. Only at moments does Pankhurst break out of the traditional convention and claim the positive affiliation of 'we' and the present tense which provides a more direct, subjective reactualisation of the women's struggle.[46] Her difficulty with sustaining an 'objective' narrative stance can be seen in the following passage:

On Friday, October 20, *a crowded demonstration was held* to welcome the ex-prisoners in the Free Trade Hall from which they had been flung out with ignominy but a week before, and now, as they entered, the audience rose with raised hats and waving handkerchiefs and greeted them with cheers. Christabel Pankhurst and Annie Kenney did not speak of their imprisonment. *We knew* that they had been treated as belonging to the third and lowest class of criminals . . . and, losing their own names, had answered only to the number of their cell. These things *we know*, but they refused to speak of them then, wishing that all attention should be concentrated upon the cause of the enfranchisement for women for which they had been willing to endure all. (*pp. 35–6, my emphases*)

Pankhurst moves from the passive tense to describe the welcoming party of which she herself was a part, to the active past 'we knew', and finally in the space of four sentences to the active present 'we know'. There is a tension in the work between an inherited mode of objective history writing and what appears to be something new: a modernist form of history writing which requires a more mobile subjective narrator who can legitimate an oppositional, radical movement by giving an insider's account of the participants' heroism and moral conviction.

Pankhurst both uses and subverts the dominant historical narrative form in her presentation of 'great' militant women through the presentation of their exceptional moral character. There is no space here to discuss in detail the significance to nineteenth-century English political individualism of the development of moral character, but suffice it to say that it became a positive function of the state to create the social conditions in which a very particular class-based moral character could develop: one characterised by self-reliance, independence, rationality, sobriety, self-restraint, duty and philanthropic service. It is in these conventionalised terms that Pankhurst describes the moral courage of the women of the WSPU, thus implicitly arguing that women were the moral equals if not superiors of men, with the ensuing right to enter the body politic.[47]

I have suggested how Pankhurst begins her history of militant women by evoking their spiritual and moral qualities of courage and self-restraint in the face of physical violence and imprisonment. Now I want to turn to a central chapter in the middle of the text, which in terms of pages takes up ten per cent of the book and which serves to stress the self-reliance and sober rationality of militant women. The chapter re-enacts the trial of Mrs Pankhurst, Christabel Pankhurst and Mrs Drummond in October 1908 for inciting a 'rush' on Parliament, by presenting it as a drama in direct speech, with Christabel Pankhurst as lead actress, defending herself with rational and incisive arguments, and expertly cross-examining her Government witnesses, Lloyd George and Herbert Gladstone:

Mr Herbert Gladstone, the Home Secretary, was then called and took his place in the witness box. . . . As soon as he had been sworn, he placed his elbows on the ledge in front of him and looked smilingly around the court, as much as to say, 'Nothing of this kind can disturb me, I intend to enjoy myself.' . . .

Miss Pankhurst began [reading from Gladstone's own speech] . . . 'Did you say men had to struggle for centuries for their political rights?' 'Yes.' 'Did you say that they had to fight from the time of Cromwell and that for the last 130 years the warfare had been perpetual?' 'Yes.' 'Did you say that on this question, experience showed that predominance of argument alone was not enough to win the political day? Did you say that?' 'Yes.' . . . 'Then you cannot condemn our methods any more,' she said triumphantly. (*pp. 293, 298–9*)

It is perhaps surprising to those who have read Sylvia Pankhurst's *The Suffragette Movement*, and found Christabel Pankhurst vilified as an autocratic leader, to discover that in *The Suffragette* she is seen, as here, as an inspiring leader. For example, about Christabel's decision in 1906 to campaign against the government Liberal candidates in by-elections rather than actively to support Labour, even though the Pankhursts were then still members of the socialist ILP, Sylvia is here entirely supportive, declaring that the policy showed her 'keen political insight and that indomitable courage and determination which are so essential to real leadership' (p. 96). This stance towards leadership is an integral element of the inherited form. Pankhurst, in establishing the credentials of the WSPU as a legitimate women's political organisation, uses the conventions of biographical history of 'great' leaders, which she could not transform, but could only try to inflect.

For example, Pankhurst's foregrounding of 'great' women leaders makes it difficult to present the movement as a whole; the rank-and-file members of the Union appear as worthy disciples, the backcloth for the presentation of the principal actors, with the effect of creating another kind of invisibility by apparently endorsing the view that 'ordinary' women could not make their own history, without charismatic leadership.[48] This problem of representation is also suggested in Mrs Pankhurst's Preface, mentioned earlier, where she talked of the experience of militant feminism in terms of 'the joy of battle, the exaltation that comes of sacrifice of self for great objects and the prophetic vision that assures us of the certain triumph of this twentieth-century fight for human emancipation'. Here is suggested the combination of womanly strength in battle and womanly spirituality that Lisa Tickner has described as the dominant representation of the 'Militant Woman' within the WSPU from 1911.[49] Joan of Arc, Boadicea, the Virtues (Justice, Liberty, Truth) were, as Tickner shows, the inspiring representations appropriated by the leadership, but ones which could not be applied to ordinary rank-and-file members; after all, there was only one St Joan whom the rest must follow.

While subverting the conventions of Whig history, by constructing a narrative about moral and rational *female* leadership, Pankhurst is nevertheless so held within the conventions of the form that she concludes that conflict must soon end, progressive harmony will be established and thus historical discontinuity will be healed. At the very end of the book the reader is told that the women's struggle for the vote is, after all, part of the process of inspiring the right moral character in women, so justifying their claim to citizenship, which itself will be the herald for social harmony:

So the gallant struggle for a great reform draws to its close. Full of stern fighting and bitter hardship as it has been, it has brought much to the women of our time – a courage, a self-reliance, a comradeship, and above all a spiritual growth, a conscious dwelling in company with the ideal, which has tended to strip the littleness from life and to give to it the character of an heroic mission. May we prize and cherish the great selfless spirit that has been engendered and applying it to the purposes of our Government – the nation's housekeeping – the management of our collective affairs, may we, men and women together, not in antagonism, but in comradeship, strive on till we have built up a better civilisation than any that the world has known. (*p. 505*)

Believing, prematurely, that the women's struggle is about to end in triumph, Pankhurst immediately puts the women's fight for reform in the past, stressing the legacy of women's idealism and spiritual growth which both reinforces their right to enter the body politic and promises to increase the quality of the nation's 'housekeeping'. She continues with a plea for national unity over the sectional claims of gender or class, appealing to the family of the nation, to work together for the common good. Pankhurst, although brilliantly evoking women's resourcefulness, courage and solidarity within the militant movement, which challenged not only the apparatus of the state but the whole notion of what it was to be a woman, finally was not able to transcend the politics of a dominant form of history writing which sees progress as the end of conflict and just within grasp. As a result she is forced to cancel the idea of a continuing feminist political struggle.

However, Pankhurst's difficulty in inflecting a gendered and classed historical form of narration should not lessen the significance of the cultural breakthrough the publication of *The Suffragette* represents. By placing militant feminists in a historical narrative about great leaders of strength and character and occupying a form of writing dominated throughout the nineteenth century by male historians, Pankhurst delivered what Martha Vicinus has described as 'the most revolutionary aspect' of the militant women's movement: 'its insistence upon a female presence – even leadership – in male arenas.'[50] Vicinus of course was talking about the physical presence that women established in the public domain of the streets, but the disruption of male space and male discourse was no less established from this point onwards in the cultural sphere – in the writing of women's history and autobiography.

Introduction

Within two years of completing *The Suffragette*, Pankhurst was openly confronting the increasingly anti-socialist policy of the WSPU leadership, by setting up alliances between women's suffrage and working-class organisations.[51] Only then was she able to find a working-class constituency for both her socialist–feminist politics and for her writing, and move towards a class-based feminist mode of address. The first paper she founded and edited, *The Woman's Dreadnought*, which began publication in 1914, was the flagship of Pankhurst's East London Federation of the Suffragettes (ELFS), which after the outbreak of the First World War became the site of a long and vigorous anti-war campaign. The paper first highlighted the appalling conditions of local women brought about the failure of both national and local government to provide adequately for those made destitute by the war and went on to fight against a whole mass of injustices including the passing of the Defence of the Realm Act, the National Register Act, and the Contagious Diseases Act, all of which attacked civil liberties; military and industrial conscription, women's sweated war work, and the treatment of conscientious objectors. The campaigns on specific issues were linked to more general arguments for socialism (which included support for James Connolly and the Irish struggle and for John Maclean and the shop stewards' movement in Scotland), pacifism, and the political goal of 'human suffrage'.[52]

After the enormous effort to set up a rudimentary system of social services in the East End (which included two cost-price restaurants, four baby clinics, a day nursery and a toy factory), and her revulsion from the slaughter of soldiers that the Government insisted was necessary for victory, Pankhurst was to welcome the possibility of social and political revolutionary change that the 1917 Russian Revolution seemed to present: 'To me this was life. From the drab and limitless poverty of the East End . . . from the monstrous miseries which were a typical by-product of the war, from a social system which caused this poverty – I saw escape into a life founded on justice and equality.'[53] Within a year she had set up the People's Russian Information Bureau, a publishing outlet for communist literature, and gradually emerged as a revolutionary communist leader of the Workers' Socialist Federation, spreading her ideas by forming branches throughout Great Britain and making several hazardous journeys to make contact with the international movement, including speaking at the 1919 Congress of the Italian Socialist Party, going to meet the German revolutionary feminist Clara Zetkin, and in 1920 debating with Lenin in Moscow about the strategy of European communism.[54]

But her revolutionary politics, which made her an immediate and firm supporter of the Russian Bolsheviks, led her to despair when she saw their early experiments in workers' control and sexual liberation abandoned in favour of what she saw as a 'reversion to capitalism' with the pronouncements of the New Economic Policy on efficiency and centralised party control.[55] Her persistent criticism led to her expulsion from the Communist Party in 1921 and to her almost complete political isolation after 1924, when the Dreadnought finally closed down and she left the East End for good. Now politically isolated, she became a prolific writer, producing several books (and a child) before publishing The Suffragette Movement (1931), her autobiographical history of the militant women's movement. Given her political transformation in the twenty years between 1911 and 1931, it is unsurprising that her second history was a very different narrative from that of The Suffragette.

Pankhurst's use of autobiography in The Suffragette Movement, rather than the more orthodox and authorised third-person historical narrative, to re-tell the history of the militant women's movement was a particular response to the times through which she was living. The text was one of a large number of autobiographies which were published from around the mid-1920s to the mid-1930s, in which writers began to narrate their lives in order to reconstruct and assess the pre-war and war years in and for the present. The male autobiographies, according to the cultural critics Robert Wohl and Paul Fussell,[56] were remarkably consistent: there had been massive social and political disruption, marked by a profound sense of discontinuity between the pre- and post-war period; all was desolation and loss; masculinity had been totally compromised with the best men destroyed in the war, so that England now belonged to the women and domesticity; there was 'failure and calamity in every department of human life'.[57] The title of Robert Graves' autobiography Goodbye to All That (1929) suggests the structure of feeling of the time which found later expression in 1935 with George Dangerfield's influential history, The Strange Death of Liberal England.[58] That Dangerfield would identify the women's militant movement as one of the sources of the decline, and exact revenge by belittling and making a comic 'drama' of their politics, as Jane Marcus has described,[59] should be seen in the context of the near-fatal blow to masculinity that male writers felt had been delivered in the post-war period.

Though this male sense of desolation and disruption has persisted as the dominant representation in autobiography of the inter-war period, women's autobiographies (particularly those written by ex-suffragists) were no less in evidence, even if they have now been completely written out of the tradition. But where male autobiography focused on the pre-war period with a private sense of loss, women autobiographers such as Sylvia Pankhurst generally focused on their public and collective gains. Once women found they had a story to tell about their public lives, there was an explosion of such writing: Millicent Garrett Fawcett, Annie Kenney, Emmeline Pethick-Lawrence, Helena Swanwick, Cecily Hamilton, Evelyn Sharp, Elizabeth Robins, Dame Ethel Smyth, Viscountess Rhondda, were among the many ex-suffrage activists who wrote about their lives during this period.[60]

Yet even contemporary feminist accounts of women's writing of the inter-war period overwhelmingly focus on fictional writing, either totally ignoring the autobiographical volumes or, as in one commentary, dismissing them as inadequate because they lack insight of private or intimate life, and offer only a 'repressed feminist consciousness' and a 'limited' feminist analysis to the contemporary reader.[61] Taking a contrary line, Jane Marcus, in a much more sophisticated analysis of selected autobiographies of 'women of genius' in the period, identifies in them a deliberate process of minimising and making ordinary their extraordinary professional achievements, as they allow the work to take second place to the 'life' of personal relationships.[62] Both approaches assume that the essential characteristic of women's autobiography is its focus on the private rather than on the public self.[63]

Through the nineteenth century, published auto/biography had been predominantly a male form, defining in crucial ways what masculinity should be about.[64] As Virginia Woolf commented in *Three Guineas* (1938), the form often served as a major outlet for the public expression and confirmation of masculinity, particularly of militarism.[65] It was thus quite rare to find women publishing autobiographies in the nineteenth century: without a vote, without citizenship, women were not 'individuals' as defined by the body politic and their stories were not generally told in this form.[66] It is all the more interesting therefore to find an explosion in women's published autobiography from the mid-1920s, which, as Elizabeth Winston who has noted, are much less apologetic about their subject's public achievements than those written prior to this point.[67]

The Suffragette Movement (hereafter SM) and other women's autobiographies written around the same time are not private and confessional, so intimate or sexual experience is generally ignored. Women claimed a right to enter a cultural space and occupy it unapologetically on the same terms as men: they were public women providing an account of their successful professional and/or political, collective struggles. If Pankhurst does not mention her long affair with Keir Hardie, or if Viscountess Rhondda explicitly denies that her marriage has any bearing on the story she has to tell,[68] it does not necessarily follow that the subjects were repressed or lacked psychological insight. They could be merely stressing a preference for not discussing the personal in public, though Ethel Smyth certainly had no such reservations in her *Female Pipings in Eden* (1933). However, it seems equally likely that they were using a form of writing to question women's ascribed position within the personal, the sexual, the non-political, and the a-historical domestic world and attempting to make sense of their lives as a group of women who had collectively entered the male territories of professional life or politics and who needed to construct a new idea of what it was to be a woman in the public domain.[69] It is in the exhilaration of coming to terms with a new women's public identity which had been collectively constructed that the 'personal' within the texts gets re-defined. Annie Kenney went so far as to deny that there was any distinction in her life while a WSPU militant between the personal and the public: 'we were taught never to give vent to our desires, feelings, or ideas, but to stand firm on one question, which was "Will you give women the vote?"'[70] But in all the texts the personal is transformed by public life.

But I do not want to suggest that the narratives within this group of women's autobiographies were a single or uniform-gendered discourse. Women were not united within a single politics either before or after the First World War, and the women's autobiographies of the period under discussion take up a position in an uncertain present where, after the rise and fall of the Labour Party, followed by the defeat of the General Strike, stark choices were being made about the nature of inter-war politics. Mrs Pankhurst's declaration in

1927, when she was adopted as a Conservative Party Parliamentary candidate, expresses the choice in characteristically robust terms: 'today there are only two parties – the Constitutional Party, represented by Mr Baldwin and the Conservatives, and the Revolutionary Party.'[71] A similar 'constitutional' anti-socialist argument was put forward forcibly in The Cause (1928), the first women's biographical history to be published since women had got the vote, by Ray Strachey, who had been instrumental in defeating the pre-war campaign within the non-militant NUWSS to support the Labour Party and who later became the Parliamentary secretary for the conservative MP, Lady Astor.[72]

I want to argue that SM was a specific socialist challenge to such conservative politics, especially as articulated in The Cause, which had represented the WSPU as undemocratic and 'uncivilised', not, as in Dangerfield's Strange Death, a slightly risible side-show, but as something altogether more sinister – one of the subversive sources for the 'unconstitutional' activities of the labour and socialist movements in the post-war period. Strachey had presented the militants as non-rational, using 'sensational', 'aggressive', 'headlong' and 'autocratic' methods to force change precipitately and undemocratically by 'moral violence' (p. 310). She even went so far as to suggest that force-feeding was a reasonable punishment for such unruly elements.[73]

Pankhurst chose not to write a 'history' in reply to The Cause, perhaps already aware that Strachey's construction of the non-militant women's movement, as the culmination of progressive politics and the defeat of socialism, was already the authorised version; Pankhurst's review of The Cause was the only unfavourable one.[74] Instead, she wrote about the experience of being a socialist-feminist, from below, in the conventions of an 'oppositional' autobiography, one of the several traditions of autobiographical writing, which stretches back at least to the seventeenth century, when men and women in a variety of Puritan sects wrote of their conversions, religious experiences and persecution.[75] The resulting power and coherence of Pankhurst's witnessing for a marginalised belief lies in her ability to use the conventions of a potent politico-religious vocabulary, already appropriated by the socialist movement, and inflect it in a new socialist-feminist direction.

Pankhurst's socialist inheritance gave her access to an ethical political vocabulary of popular struggle based on solidarity, co-operation

21

and mutual aid, whose origins can be found in what Stephen Yeo has glossed as the 'religion of socialism' movement, which permeated many socialist groupings in the late nineteenth century, including the ILP, to which Pankhurst had given her first allegiance.[76] Pankhurst's family knew many of the key figures of the movement including Keir Hardie, Bruce Glasier, Katherine St John Conway, Enid Stacy, Caroline Martyn, Tom Mann and Robert Blatchford (SM, pp. 126–8), whose politics presented, according to Yeo, 'a certain ground for hope, a convincing analysis of what had gone before, a morally impeccable challenge, and as an organised movement demanding commitment, sacrifice, and missionary activity by the newly converted.' (p. 10) Socialist conversion narratives became common, and Yeo documents how autobiography was a prime means of expressing the quality of the experience, which was more akin to joining a religious 'sect' than a church; individuals were required to commit their lives to social redemption and individual regeneration, a process that could mean ostracism and even separation from relatives and friends.

The evangelical basis of Pankhurst's socialist commitment can be observed in SM from the first chapter, where she describes her childhood in a household which was a 'shrine . . . of earnest and passionate striving' where the children were almost daily exhorted by their father, who was himself 'vilified and boycotted, yet beloved by a multitude' for his socialist beliefs, to be workers for 'social betterment' and thus be worth the upbringing (p. 3, my emphases). But the language of the religion of socialism finds its most potent expression once Pankhurst has found her vocation as a socialist feminist among the labouring classes of the East End. Her license under the conditions of the 'Cat and Mouse' Act having expired, and still weak from hunger-striking, Pankhurst describes how she nevertheless decided to speak at a public meeting and risk re-arrest, imprisonment and forcible feeding:

A crowd of stalwarts shut and guarded the main door. I had torn off the dark coat and hat; the air was rent with cheers. While I was waiting to speak, a paper was passed to me – a note from Zelie Emerson that she had found me a hiding-place in the hall. I shook my head. She knew that I was determined to go out amongst the people as before. . . . To me it was a great struggle, not for the vote alone; for the upliftng of these masses, the enlarging of their horizons. I spoke to them as I felt: 'They say that life is sweet and liberty is precious; there is no liberty for us so long as the majority of our people lead wretched lives. Unless we can free them from the chains of poverty, life, to us, is not worth preserving, and I, for one, would rather leave this world.' (*p. 481*)

There follows a frantic chase through the streets with the police in pursuit: 'Like trapped wild things, we thrust ourselves against every door: one of them gave. We found ourselves in a dark, disused stable' (p. 482). Perhaps finding refuge in a stable is not a direct biblical reference, but there is nevertheless a messianic quality to the passage, with the martyr-prophet risking her freedom, if not her life, to 'go out amongst the people' and to 'uplift' them. The political critique, such as it is, seeks to put an end to the immorality of 'wretched lives' caught in the 'chains of poverty'. But the precise wording of the message is less important than the example made by the prophet who is seen to be willing to make enormous personal sacrifices for the cause of social betterment. The long and horrifying description of one of her hunger and thirst strikes (Book VII, Chapter III) is written in this context: 'I was always convinced that the element of *martyrdom* provided the highest and keenest incentive to our movement. I knew that the hallowing influence of *sacrifice* cemented the *comradeship* of the great mass movement which had grown up' (p. 505, my emphases).

This witnessing of a shared spiritual fellowship through autobiography is reminiscent of that much earlier moment in the seventeenth century when the beliefs in religion, in the form of puritanism, and revolution had not become separate. Both men and women in Baptist and Quaker sects, according to Paul Delany, wrote an enormous body of autobiographical writing after 1648 describing their democratic sense of a shared, sometimes visionary religious experience and preaching to the unconverted.[77] The most celebrated was John Bunyan's *Grace Abounding to the Chief of Sinners* (1666) which followed the convention of describing the author's conversion, his calling and ministry, including in Bunyan's case his experiences in prison when he was persecuted for his beliefs.[78] The parallels continue. As Bunyan wrestled with childhood sin and the temptations of early manhood, so Pankhurst describes her anxiety about not reaching the perfection required of her during childhood, which was torn by 'the anguish of ethical struggles, and depression descending into agony and despair for trivial failings' (p. 100). Later, she renounces her career as an artist to take up the political cause of women when she could no longer face her damning self-accusation: 'As a speaker . . . you are wanted; as an artist the world has no real use for you; in that capacity you must fight a purely egotistical struggle.' (p. 218). Her fight against the sins of egoism is vindicated as she experiences persecution in prison for the women's cause and then begins her 'ministry' in the East End slums.

Before leaving the analogy to Puritan autobiography, I want to suggest that the temptation to renounce God and become a Judas-like betrayer, which Bunyan tells us racks sinners like him before they are saved,[79] has a parallel in SM, in the construction of Christabel Pankhurst. She is the damned, the betrayer of socialist feminism, who as the autocratic 'incipient' Tory (p. 221), defeats a potentially national mass movement to bring about the socialist-feminist trans-formation of society, by her desire to marginalise class in the politics of the WSPU, by recruiting non-socialist, middle-class women, by her autocratic methods, and by her later promotion of a separatist feminist sex war. She compounds her political betrayal with personal betrayal in her self-imposed exile in Paris, which is presented in SM as the final act of cowardice and the absolute negation of moral leadership: urging others to greater and greater sacrifice and asking nothing of oneself. 'A thousand times easier to be in the struggle, and share its anguish' than 'giving the orders leading to the imprisonment and torture for other women!' is Sylvia's judgment (p. 518). One effect of this presentation is to show how Sylvia resists such egotistical leadership, becomes the socialist–feminist true believer, and expresses her faith as the evangelist to the masses.

I am conscious in providing this particular reading of a tiny fraction of Pankhurst's writing that many questions remain. For example, how did her years as a communist affect the forms in which she represented class and gender? What was the significance of Pankhurst's engage-ment in her writing with economically under-developed nations such as India and Ethiopia? What is the significance of the use by her of the forms of travel writing and poetry? Despite leaving so many questions unanswered, I hope I have indicated a fruitful method of approaching Sylvia Pankhurst's writing which shows how she politically addressed specific audiences at different historical moments in a variety of forms of writing, whose conventions permitted and conditioned political meaning. Her early attempts to address one class about another gave way to a history which established the 'greatness' of the women militant leaders of the WSPU, within the conventions of a historical narrative which had always excluded women. Not until *The Suffragette Movement* did Pankhurst find a socialist–feminist autobiographical mode of address which overcome the contradictions of other gendered and classed forms of writing. At last her politics and the form of writing did not strain against one another: she had discovered a socialist way of expressing her feminism, even if the cost was to pitch the movement in an oppositional and persecuted mould.

Kathryn Dodd
London, 1992

NOTES TO INTRODUCTION

1 Although the style 'E. Sylvia Pankhurst' was adopted for all her published books, a convention I have retained, I have used the less formal 'Sylvia Pankhurst' to refer to her as an individual throughout. There are a number of biographies of Sylvia Pankhurst that have been drawn on for the Introduction: Patricia W. Romero, *E. Sylvia Pankhurst. Portrait of a Radical* (Yale University Press, New Haven and London, 1987); R. K. P. Pankhurst, *Sylvia Pankhurst, Artist and Crusader. An Intimate Portrait* (Paddington Press, New York and London, 1979); David Mitchell, *The Fighting Pankhursts. A Study in Tenacity* (Macmillan, New York, 1967); Barbara Castle, *Sylvia and Christabel Pankhurst* (Penguin Books, Harmondsworth, 1987). Ian Bullock and Richard Pankhurst (eds), *Sylvia Pankhurst. From Artist to Anti-Fascist* (Macmillan Academic, Basingstoke, 1992) is an important book of essays, which came to the editor's notice only at the time of going to press

2 For a list of Pankhurst's published books and the newspapers she edited, see the Appendix. The historical account of women's suffrage has been drawn from: Andrew Rosen, *Rise Up Women! The Militant Campaign of the Women's Social and Political Union 1903–1914* (Routledge and Kegan Paul, London, 1974); Richard Evans, *The Feminists: Women's Emancipation Movements in Europe, America and Australasia 1840–1920* (Croom Helm, London, 1977); Roger Fulford, *Votes for Women: The Story of a Struggle* (Faber and Faber, London, 1957); Sandra Stanley Holton, *Feminism and Democracy. Women's Suffrage and Reform Politics in Britain, 1890–1918* (Cambridge University Press, Cambridge, 1986); David Morgan, *Suffragists and Liberals: The Politics of Woman Suffrage in England* (Blackwell, Oxford, 1975); Martin Pugh, *Women's Suffrage in Britain 1867–1928* (pamphlet) (The Historical Association, London, 1980); Antonia Raeburn, *The Militant Suffragettes* (Michael Joseph, London, 1973); Constance Rover, *Women's Suffrage and Party Politics in Britain, 1866–1914* (Routledge and Kegan Paul, London, 1967)

3 Rosen, *Rise Up Women!*, p. 219

4 The emphasis on social work can be seen explicitly in R. K. P. Pankhurst's biography, *Sylvia Pankhurst*, and in Anne Wiltsher, *Most Dangerous Women. Feminist Peace Campaigners of the Great War* (Pandora, London, 1985), p. 134. An exception however is the recently published essay by Barbara Winslow, 'Sylvia Pankhurst and the Great War', in Bullock and Pankhurst (eds), *Sylvia Pankhurst*

5 Mark Shipway, *Anti-Parliamentary Communism. The Movement for Workers' Councils in Britain, 1917–45* (Macmillan, Basingstoke, 1988), p. xii. Shipway is glossing other historians' rather than his own position here. See also Ian Bullock, 'Sylvia Pankhurst

and the Russian Revolution: the making of a "left-wing" communist', in Bullock and Pankhurst (eds), *Sylvia Pankhurst*

6 V. Lenin, *Left-Wing Communism. An Infantile Disorder* (Foreign Language Press, Peking, 1975/1920). Pankhurst published Lenin's 'Infantile sickness of "left" communism' in *The Workers' Dreadnought*, 31 July 1920, but, rather than reply herself, allowed Herman Gorter space to reply over a number of weeks. For a general discussion of the debate about Lenin's influence on the CPGB and Sylvia Pankhurst's contribution to feminist communist thinking, see Martin Durham and Bill Schwarz, *Constitutionalism and Extra-Parliamentary Action: Socialism and the Definition of Politics, 1910–20* (Occasional Paper, History Series, Centre for Contemporary Cultural Studies, University of Birmingham, 1984), pp. 48–67

7 Stuart Macintyre, *A Proletarian Science. Marxism in Britain 1917–1933* (Cambridge University Press, Cambridge, 1980), p. 28

8 Romero, E. *Sylvia Pankhurst*, pp. 125–6, 137. Romero appears to mistake Pankhurst's repudiation of the CPGB, of which she was always critical, for left-wing communism, which she championed. In a letter to Mrs Walsh (n.d., but probably 1930) she says: 'I am a Communist too, but not of the Communist Party.' (Autograph Collection, Militants, 20A, 1928–56, number 185, Fawcett Library). On the systematic downgrading of Pankhurst's achievements and the numerous inaccuracies in Romero's biography, see Rita Pankhurst, 'Sylvia Pankhurst in perspective. Some comments on Patricia Romero's biography' (*Women's Studies International Forum*, XI, 1988, pp. 245–62)

9 Romero, E. *Sylvia Pankhurst*, pp. 4, 72, 136, 191. *The Times* obituary, 28 September 1960

10 Ann Morley with Liz Stanley, *The Life and Death of Emily Wilding Davison. A Biographical Detective Story* (Women's Press, London, 1988), pp. 155–8

11 Romero, E. *Sylvia Pankhurst*, p. 287

12 R. K. P. Pankhurst, *Sylvia Pankhurst*, p. 196. Richard Pankhurst has since published a much more detailed examination of his mother's campaign for Ethiopia in an essay, 'Sylvia and New Times and Ethiopia News' in Bullock and Pankhurst, (eds), *Sylvia Pankhurst*

13 Romero, E. *Sylvia Pankhurst*, pp. 247, 275, 287–8

14 Lisa Tickner, *The Spectacle of Women. Imagery of the Suffrage Campaign 1907–14* (Chatto and Windus, London, 1987), pp. 27, 32. Tickner describes how Pankhurst was brought up in the 'richly blended politico–aesthetic ambience' of her parents' home with its William Morris wallpapers and reproductions of Walter Crane, a socialist arts-and-crafts disciple of Morris's and later Pankhurst's tutor in art. Pankhurst reprinted William Morris's 'The socialist ideal in art' in almost the last editon of the *Workers' Dreadnought*, 3 May 1924, and wrote of his influence on her in the mid-1920s, in the 'World That I Want' series for the *Daily Express*, quoted by Mitchell, *The Fighting Pankhursts*, p. 239. In Pankhurst's autobiography, *The Suffragette Movement. An Intimate Account of Persons and Ideals* (Virago reprint, London, 1977/1931), p. 21, she talks of her father, whom she greatly admired as a communist 'in the broad sense which would cover William Morris, Peter Kropotkin and Keir Hardie'

15 E. P. Thompson, *William Morris, Romantic to Revolutionary* (Pantheon Books, New York, 1976/1955), pt. 2 chapter 1

16 Perry Anderson, *Arguments Within English Marxism* (New Left Books and Verso, London, 1980), chapter 6

17 For an account of these intellectual shifts see Thompson, *William Morris*, pp. 785–99; Philip Abrams, *The Origins of British Sociology 1834–1914* (University of Chicago Press, Chicago, 1968), chapters 6–8; R. Colls and P. Dodd (eds), *Englishness: Politics and Culture 1880–1920* (Croom Helm, London, 1986), *passim*

18 The Fabian socialist intellectuals Sidney and Beatrice Webb were clear about the necessity of creating a pool of experts: 'Above all, we want the ordinary citizen to feel that reforming society is no light matter and must be undertaken by experts specially trained for the purpose', Beatrice Webb, quoted in Sir Sidney Caine, *The History of the*

Introduction

Foundation of the London School of Economics and Political Science (G. Bell & Son, London, 1963), p. 2

19 Raymond Williams, *Culture* (Fontana Paperbacks, London, 1981), p. 139, and *Marxism and Literature* (Oxford University Press, Oxford, 1977), p. 176

20 It is not just Pankhurst, of course, who is ignored in the account of inter-war writing. For the dominance of male literary figures in the period see Peter Widdowson, 'Between the acts? English fiction in the thirties', in Jon Clarke, Margot Heinemann, David Margolies and Carole Snee (eds), *Culture and Crisis in Britain in the Thirties* (Lawrence and Wishart, London, 1979); Samuel Hynes, *The Auden Generation. Literature and Politics in England in the Thirties* (The Bodley Head, London, 1976)

21 E. Sylvia Pankhurst, *The Suffragette Movement*

22 See Rosen, p. 15 note, Martin Pugh, *Women's Suffrage in Britain*, p. 40, and Romero, *E. Sylvia Pankhurst*, pp. 186–7, 190

23 Ray Strachey, *The Cause. A Short History of the Women's Movement in Great Britain* (Virago reprint, London, 1978/1928)

24 Raymond Williams, *Keywords* (Fontana, London, 1973)

25 The rhetoric of history for example is the focus of Hayden White's *Metahistory. The Historical Imagination in Nineteenth-Century Europe* (The Johns Hopkins University Press, Baltimore and London, 1973), where historical narratives are seen as having four types of 'plot', the Romantic, Tragic, Comic, and Satirical. More recent analyses include Dominick LaCapra, *History and Criticism* (Cornell University Press, Ithaca, 1985), and Richard Johnson *et al.* (eds), *Making Histories. Studies in History-Writing and Politics* (Hutchinson and CCCS, London, 1982)

26 E. Sylvia Pankhurst, *Save the Mothers. A Plea for Measures to Prevent the Annual Loss of about 3,000 Child-Bearing Mothers and 20,000 Infant Lives in England and Wales and a Similar Grievous Wastage in other Countries* (Alfred A. Knopf, London, 1930)

27 Bryan S. Green, *Knowing the Poor. A Case Study in Textual Reality Construction* (Routledge and Kegan Paul, London, 1983), *passim*

28 Green, *Knowing the Poor*, pp. 92, 99, 101

29 Eleanor Rathbone, *The Disinherited Family. A Plea for the Endowment of the Family* (Edward Arnold, London, 1924)

30 Romero, *E. Sylvia Pankhurst*, p. 165

31 Three essays appeared in *Votes for Women*: 'The Potato-Pickers', 28 January 1909, 'Women Farm Labourers in the Border Counties', 26 August 1910, and 'Pit Brow Women', 11 August 1911

32 For an account of the journey see Pankhurst, *The Suffragette Movement*, pp. 270–1. For reproductions of the paintings she produced as a result see R. K. P. Pankhurst, *Sylvia Pankhurst*

33 'The Potato-Pickers' is reprinted in this volume

34 Pankhurst, *The Suffragette Movement*, pp. 222–7. For a good account of Pankhurst's struggle to maintain the socialist–suffrage alliance within the WSPU, see Les Garner, 'Suffragism and socialism: Sylvia Pankhurst 1903–1914' in Bullock and Pankhurst (eds), *Sylvia Pankhurst*. For a discussion of the force and independence of the 'freelance', non-metropolitan members of the rank-and-file in the WSPU, as a balance against the commonly accepted view, that the Union was led from the front by an autocratic leadership, see Morley and Stanley, *Emily Wilding Davison*, pp. 118, 153–5, 174–5

35 Peter Keating (ed.), *Into Unknown England 1866–1913* (Fontana, London, 1976). For an account of the tradition in the early nineteenth century see F. S. Schwarzbach '"Terra Incognita" – an image of the city in English literature, 1820–1855' in *Prose Studies*, V, 1982, pp. 61–84

36 See Kathryn Dodd and Philip Dodd, 'From the East End to *EastEnders*' in Stephen Wagg and Dominic Strinati (eds), *Come on Down?* (Routledge, London, 1992)

37 Keating, *Into Unknown England*, pp. 65–6

38 Gill Davies, 'Foreign bodies: images of the London working class at the end of the

nineteenth century' (*Literature and History*, XIV, 1988), pp. 69–70. It should be noted that the art Pankhurst produced at the time represented working-class women not as victims but as independent, self-contained, sometimes defiant working women. See Tickner, *The Spectacle of Women*, pp. 28–9

39 Preface to E. Sylvia Pankhurst, *The Suffragette. The History of the Women's Militant Suffrage Movement 1905–1910* (Sturgis and Walton, New York, 1911), n.p.

40 E. Sylvia Pankhurst in Countess of Oxford and Asquith, *Myself When Young* (Frederick Miller, London, 1938), p. 284

41 Pugh, *Women's Suffrage*, p. 22; Evans, *The Feminists*, chapter 4

42 As Dale Spender describes, there was no equivalent history of British women to match the six volumes produced in the US by Elizabeth Cady Stanton, Susan B. Anthony, Matilda Joslyn Gage and Ida Husted Harper, *History of Women's Suffrage*, produced between 1881 and 1922. See Dale Spender, *Women of Ideas and What Men Have Done To Them* (Pandora, London, 1988), pp. 257–70. English volumes that appeared around the same time as *The Suffragette* include: Teresa Billington Greig, *The Militant Suffragette Movement* (Frank Palmer, London, 1911), reprinted in Carol McPhee and Ann FitzGerald (eds), *The Non-Violent Militant. Selected Writings of Teresa Billington-Greig* (Routledge and Kegan Paul, London, 1987); Bertha Mason, *The Story of the Women's Movement* (Sherratt and Hughes, London, 1912); Millicent Garrett Fawcett, *Women's Suffrage: A Short History of a Great Movement* (T. C. & E. C. Jack, London, 1912); Ethel Snowden, *The Feminist Movement* (Collins, London, 1913)

43 Brian Harrison, *Separate Spheres: the Opposition to Women's Suffrage in Britain* (Croom Helm, London, 1978, pp. 187–99); Margherita Rendel, 'The contribution of the Women's Labour League to the winning of the franchise' in Lucy Middleton (ed.), *Women in the Labour Movement. The British Experience* (Croom Helm, London, 1977), p. 79

44 Carlyle spoke of history as 'the essence of innumerable biographies', quoted in White, *Metahistory*, p. 68. Carlyle is seen by White as part of the Romantic tradition of history where the will of the individual is seen as 'the sole agent of causal efficacy'

45 *Votes for Women*. October 1907–September 1909. The serial mode of publication was a feature of Pankhurst's writing, e.g. 'Soviet Russia As I Saw It' in the *Workers' Dreadnought*, 1921, and 'Fascism As It Is' in *New Times and Ethiopia News*, 1936

46 For one discussion of the narrator's stance in historiography see Gianna Pomata, 'Versions of narrative: overt and covert narrators in nineteenth-century historiography' (*History Workshop Journal*, XXVII, 1989)

47 For the role of 'character' in liberal politics see Stefan Collini, *Liberalism and Sociology. L. T. Hobhouse and Political Argument in England 1880–1914* (Cambridge University Press, Cambridge, 1979), pp. 28–9. For the arguments around women's morality see Olive Banks, *Faces of Feminism* (Martin Robertson, Oxford, 1982), chapters 5, 6

48 For a discussion of writing biography from the point of view of the rank-and-file through tracing the 'webs of friendship' within the WSPU see Morley and Stanley, *Emily Wilding Davison*, pp. 174–6. The history of working-class radical suffragism is told in J. Liddington and J. Norris, *One Hand Tied Behind Us. The Rise of the Suffrage Movement* (Virago, London, 1978)

49 Tickner, *The Spectacle of Women*, pp. 205–13

50 Martha Vicinus, *Independent Women: Work and Community for Single Women 1850–1920* (Virago, London, 1985), p. 264

51 See Garner, 'Suffragism and socialism', pp. 70–8, where he argues, using Barbara Winslow's unpublished PhD (see Bibliography), that Pankhurst was radicalised by her two lecture tours in the USA in 1911 and 1912, which also gave her the confidence to act independently. Pankhurst, in concentrating on the activities of her organisation, the East London Federation of Suffragettes, gives the impression in *The Suffragette Movement* that hers was the only successful socialist–feminist movement operating at this time (see pp. 563–77). For a good discussion of the whole development of 'democratic feminism' in the period see Holton, *Feminism and Democracy, passim*

52 It is difficult to convey the vitality and range of political subjects tackled by *The Woman's Dreadnought*. The few articles reprinted in this volume can be supplemented by those in Jane Marcus (ed.), *Suffrage and the Pankhursts* (Routledge and Kegan Paul, London, 1987). For a comprehensive analysis of the activities of the ELFS during the war, see Winslow, 'Sylvia Pankhurst and the Great War', where she explicates the organisation's anti-war activities, its social work, and its campaigns for working women, adult suffrage and socialism

53 In the Red Twilight, (n.d., approx. 1933), handwritten notebook of fragments towards the third volume of her autobiography about her revolutionary years (PP, Folder 83, p. 9)

54 Pankhurst's meeting with Lenin is described in *Soviet Russia As I Saw It*; the journey to see Clara Zetkin and her story of Rosa Luxemburg's political life and death is described in In the Red Twilight (pp. Folder 80, pp. 135 onwards). It should also be noted that Pankhurst published the writing of leading European political writers in the *Workers' Dreadnought*, including: Trotsky (13 December 1919), Gorki (27 December 1919), Lukácz (21 August 1920), Bukharin (4 December 1920), Alexandra Kollontai (11 June 1921, 27 August 1921, 13 May 1922), Kropotkin (17 December 1921, 27 May 1922), Rosa Luxemburg (serialised from 13 May 1922)

55 As early as September 1921, Pankhurst began writing in the *Workers' Dreadnought* about the betrayal by the Russian revolutionaries of their communist principles. From then on she focused in particular on their apparent abandonment of the support for soviets and the 'reversion to capitalism'. See articles reprinted in the *Reader*

56 Robert Wohl, *The Generation of 1914* (Weidenfeld and Nicolson, London, 1980); Paul Fussell, *The Great War and Modern Memory* (Oxford University Press, Oxford, 1975)

57 Wohl, *The Generation of 1914*, p. 113

58 George Dangerfield, *The Strange Death of Liberal England* (MacGibbon and Kee, London, 1935)

59 See Jane Marcus, 'Re-reading the Pankhursts and women's suffrage', introduction to Marcus (ed.), *Suffrage and the Pankhursts* (Routledge and Kegan Paul, London, 1988), pp. 2–5

60 Autobiographies include: Annie Kenney, *Memories of a Militant* (Edward Arnold, London, 1924); Millicent Garrett Fawcett, *What I Remember* (T. Fisher Unwin, London, 1924); Elizabeth Robins, *Ibsen and the Actress* (Hogarth Essays, Hogarth Press, London, 1928); Viscountess Rhondda, *This Was My World* (Macmillan, London, 1933); H. M. Swanwick, *I Have Been Young* (Victor Gollancz, London, 1935); Cecily Hamilton, *Life Errant* (J. M. Dent, London, 1935); Emmeline Pethick-Lawrence, *My Part in a Changing World* (Victor Gollancz, London, 1938); Evelyn Sharp, *Unfinished Adventure. Selected Reminiscences from an Englishwoman's Life* (John Lane, London, 1933); Ethel Smyth, *Female Pipings in Eden* (Peter Davies, London, 1933)

61 Tricia Davis et al., '"The public face of feminism": early twentieth-century writings on women's suffrage', in Richard Johnson et al. (eds) *Making Histories. Studies in History-Writing and Politics* (Hutchinson and CCCS, Birmingham University, London, 1982), p. 311. For the dominance of Virginia Woolf in feminist cultural analysis of the period see Elaine Showalter, *A Literature of Their Own. British Women Novelists from Bronte to Lessing* (Virago, London, 1982), chapters IX and X

62 Jane Marcus, 'Invincible mediocrity: the private selves of public women', in Shari Benstock (ed.), *The Private Self. Theory and Practice of Women's Autobiographical Writings* (Routledge, London, 1988), pp. 121–3

63 See discussions of the 'private' in women's autobiographies in Estelle Jelinek (ed.), *Women's Autobiography: Essays in Criticism* (Indiana University Press, Bloomington, 1980), passim, and in the essays in Benstock (ed.), *The Private Self*

64 See Linda Peterson, *Victorian Autobiography: the Tradition of Self-Interpretation* (Yale University Press, New Haven, 1986), p. 120. For a discussion of male working-class autobiographies and the paucity of working-class women's writing see David Vincent, *Bread, Knowledge and Freedom. A Study of Nineteenth-Century Working-Class Autobiography*

(Methuen, London, 1981), pp. 8–9, and chapter 1; on the construction of such a woman's autobiography see Carolyn Steedman's Introduction to Kathleen Woodward's *Jipping Street* (Virago, London, 1983)

65 Virginia Woolf, *Three Guineas* (Chatto and Windus, The Hogarth Press, London, 1984/ 1938), p. 177

66 For one exception see Florence Nightingale's autobiographical essay, written in 1852 but first published as *Cassandra* as an appendix to Strachey, *The Cause*, in 1928

67 Elizabeth Winston, 'The autobiographer and her readers: from apology to affirmation', in Jelinek (ed.), *Women's Autobiography*, p. 93. It should also be noted that studies of women's eighteenth-century Quaker commonplace writing, which were part of a highly conventionalised public religious discourse, belie the notion that women's autobiographical writings are uniquely private and fragmented: see Felicity A. Nussbaum, 'Eighteenth-century women's autobiographical commonplaces' in Benstock (ed.), *The Private Self*, p. 153

68 Rhondda, *This Was My World*, p. vi

69 See discussion of the personal in women's autobiography in Celia Lury, 'Reading the self: autobiography, gender and the institution of the literary' in Sarah Franklin, Celia Lury and Jackie Stacey (eds), *Off-Centre. Feminism and Cultural Studies* (Harper Collins Academic, London, 1991), pp. 98–100

70 Annie Kenney, *Memories of a Militant* (Edward Arnold, London, 1924), p. 127

71 Quoted in Mitchell, *The Fighting Pankhursts*, p. 175. Christabel Pankhurst's writing in the 1920s was focused on the heralding of the Second Advent of Christ and was anti-communist, anti-democratic, proto-fascist and racist. Applauding the new strength of the Latinate, 'Roman' empire, led by Italy's Mussolini, which she sees as a bulwark against an 'oriental rising against the occident' and 'Bolshevist world-activity . . . a menace even greater', she sees dictatorship as 'good and necessary' until the imminent return of Christ. See *The World's Unrest. Visions of the Dawn* (Morgan and Scott, London, 1926), pp. 32, 92; *Seeing the Future* (Harper, New York, 1929), pp. 204–212

72 Strachey, *The Cause*, pp. 392–3 and *passim*; Holton, *Feminism and Democracy*, pp. 138–42

73 Strachey, *The Cause*, p. 314. For the politics of *The Cause*, see Kathryn Dodd, 'Cultural politics and women's historical writing' (*Women's Studies International Forum*, XIII, 1990), pp. 127–37

74 Copy of Pankhurst's review (PP, File 200(5), 32 (e)), n.d.

75 Elspeth Graham, Hilary Hinds, Elaine Hobby and Helen Wilcox (eds), *Her Own Life. Autobiographical Writings by Seventeenth-Century Englishwomen* (Routledge, London, 1989)

76 Stephen Yeo, 'The new life: the religion of socialism in Britain 1883–1896' (*History Workshop Journal*, IV, Autumn 1977)

77 Paul Delany, *British Autobiography in the Seventeenth Century* (Routledge and Kegan Paul, London, 1969), pp. 81–5

78 Delany, p. 89

79 Delany, pp. 91–2

Part I

Women, class and politics
1907–16

Sylvia Pankhurst began writing regularly in 1907. By then, she was 25 and had recently completed her training as a fine artist at the Royal College of Art, having already attended Manchester School of Art and won a travelling scholarship to Venice and Florence as best student of the year. She was a member of the Independent Labour Party, of which her parents, Emmeline and Richard Pankhurst, had been staunch supporters since 1896, and a founder member of the Women's Social and Political Union (WSPU), which was inaugurated in 1903 by Mrs Pankhurst as a ginger group in Manchester to awaken the socialist movement to feminist issues. The Union received enormous publicity in 1905 when Christabel Pankhurst, Sylvia's sister, and Annie Kenney, a textile worker and one of the first working-class recruits to the WSPU, disrupted a speech by Sir Edward Grey at the Manchester Free Trade Hall by their repeated shouts for 'Votes for Women', and were manhandled out of the hall, arrested and sentenced to seven days' imprisonment in the Third Division, after refusing to pay their fines.

Sylvia, then living in London, received instructions from her mother to begin the militant women's campaign in the capital and with the help of her lover, Keir Hardie, and Annie Kenney she set about arranging a demonstration of East End women in the unemployed workers' movement and establishing a London Committee of the WSPU. But for reasons that are not immediately apparent, Sylvia relinquished the secretaryship of the Committee, and by 1906, Mrs Pankhurst and Christabel, with the help of two progressive and well-connected supporters, Emmeline and Frederick Pethick-Lawrence, had taken over the running of the WSPU in London and set up an office at Clements Inn.

31

At this point, Sylvia seems to have become detached from the day-to-day organisation of the WSPU, as she concentrated her energies on trying to establish herself as an artist and illustrator 'in the cause of progress'. She was singularly unsuccessful, lived extremely spartanly, and received very few commissions. The Union seemed incapable of integrating her as an artist into their political work and only used her sporadically to design a membership card, or to provide murals to decorate the halls in which the WSPU held exhibitions. In 1907, after a six-month journey around the North of England and Scotland painting and sketching working women, she gradually abandoned her vocation and committed herself full-time to the women's cause. From this moment she began to write regularly, first, between October 1907 and September 1909, publishing a long serialised history of the campaign for women's suffrage in the WSPU campaigning journal, *Votes for Women*, which became the basis of her first book, *The Suffragette* (1911), and also contributing a few occasional essays on the conditions of working-class women in the North of England, two of which are reprinted here. The significance of this early work is discussed in detail in the Introduction.

Pankhurst's life was now that of a political campaigner, organising, writing, and speaking on women's suffrage all over the country and later, in 1911 and 1912, in the United States. Her tour of the US seems to mark a turning-point in Pankhurst's political development; she began to carve out a place within the Union for her long-held belief in the need to develop a socialist–feminist mass movement, and by 1913 she had established the East London Federation, a working-class base for the WSPU in the East End districts of Bow, Hackney and Stepney. Sylvia had found her political home, but, as she describes in 'Our Paper' (reprinted), she was continually persecuted by the authorities as a political outlaw under the provisions of the Prisoners' Temporary Discharge for Ill Health Act (more usually known as the 'Cat and Mouse' Act), whereby as a hunger- and thirst-striker in gaol, she could be let out on license for a short period to regain her strength and then re-arrested to serve her term. Sentences could thus be extended indefinitely unless the prisoner went underground and evaded re-arrest.

Despite Sylvia's heroic martydom, Christabel, by then in exile in Paris, could not tolerate her open association with socialist groups and forced Sylvia out of the WSPU. Immediately the East London

Federation of the Suffragettes was formed, becoming one of a number of women's groups within the militant and constitutional suffrage organisations which were forging alliances between feminism and socialism. In March 1914, Pankhurst edited the first edition of the Federation's newspaper, *The Woman's Dreadnought*, which immediately after the outbreak of the First World War became the focus for numerous campaigns to alleviate the appalling conditions of women and children at the 'home front' caused by the failure to provide adequately for those made destitute. Coverage later widened to such an extent that the *Dreadnought* became a major anti-war publication, campaigning against a huge range of injustices, including the Defence of the Realm Act and the National Register Act, both of which threatened civil liberties; women's sweated war-work; the revival of the Contagious Diseases Act to control prostitution; the death rate of mothers; war profiteering; pacifism; military conscription, and the treatment of conscientious objectors. Politically, the paper increasingly supported the socialist demand for universal, 'human suffrage', and by setting up branches in Birmingham, Nottingham, Glasgow and Wales, its political base was widened. By March 1916, the Federation of Suffragettes was renamed the Workers' Suffrage Federation in protest against the Government's Franchise Bill, which blatantly discriminated against younger propertyless women, and Pankhurst's translation from the suffrage feminist into the socialist–feminist was complete.[1]

---

1 Pankhurst provides her own account of this period of her life in her autobiographical histories, *The Suffragette Movement* (1931) and *The Home Front* (1932), a section from each of which is reprinted in Part IV of this volume

'The potato-pickers'

[*Votes for Women*, 28 January 1909]

Let us not look at ourselves, but onwards, and take strength from the leaf and the signs of the field. He is indeed despicable who cannot look onwards to the ideal life of man. Not to do so is to deny our birthright of mind.—*Richard Jefferies*

It was a fresh, bright, autumnal morning, with the sun shining, and the patches of strong, clear, blue sky showing bravely between the driving clouds. A lark was singing overhead, and the ploughman was driving his team across the field. The man whistled, and the sides of fat, well-groomed horses glistened, and every time they went up and down the field the ploughshare cut straight through the heart of one of the weed-covered ridges where the withered stalks of the potato plants were growing, and left behind it in their place an open furrow, where the potatoes could be seen lying amid the moist dank earth.

And following in the wake of the plough there was a long line of women stooping and bending, bending and stooping, over the furrows, groping with their hands in the loose soil, and gathering up the potatoes as they came.

There were three or four men in the field also, the overlookers, who stood talking and smoking by the hedge, and from time to time carried away the filled potato baskets that the women had placed ready, and emptied them into the potato 'pit'.

Hour after hour the women went on toiling with bent backs and eyes fixed on the ground, until at last one of the men shouted to them to stop, for it was half-past twelve.

Then the potato pickers rose, and straightened themselves, and came towards me where I sat watching them, and I saw them clearly for the first time. They were poor, miserable creatures, clad in vile, nameless rags, sometimes pinned, sometimes tied round them with other rags or bits of string. There were old, old women, with their skin all gnarled and wrinkled, and their purple lips all cracked. There were young women with dull white sullen faces, many with scars or black bruises round the eyes, and swollen, shapeless lips. Their hair was all matted and neglected, and every woman's eyes were fiery red.

They came and squatted on the piles of straw laid ready for covering the potatoes, and began each one to eat her meal of bread and jam or bread and cheese, or of dry bread alone. As they did so they shouted to each other, in loud harsh voices, coarse, ribald jokes and oaths, and then laughed at them with awful laughter. When they had finished eating, the elder women sat talking together more quietly, and smoking short clay pipes, whilst the younger women either lay about half-asleep in the straw or chased each other across the field with rough horseplay.

At one o'clock the men called them back to their work again, and so they went on till five, when they gathered together their ragged shawls and outer garments, and noisily left the field.

Beside the three straw-covered lorries on which they were driven back to their homes in Berwick-on-Tweed, I saw them standing huddled together, these poor, degraded creatures lower than the beasts of the field.

I left them, and turned away down the quiet lane between the woods, where the red light of the setting sun shone upon the tree trunks and the moss and the pine needles at their feet, but as I came upon the open road again they overtook me and drove away past me shouting and singing as though to make the sweet country-side around them hideous with their noise.

The sky was diffused with a glorious pale gold, and silhouetted against it the leaves and stems showed with delicate distinctness the beauty of their myriad shapes. All the hush and awe of the evening was around me, but still my thoughts were busy with those poor, dreadful women, and my heart ached.

They had gone back to the slums where they stay except when there is potato or fruit-picking or some other work of the kind for them to do. The town of Berwick is very sordid. It has more than its share of tramps and vagabonds. This is partly because it is a great centre for the potato merchants, who give casual employment to these poor waifs and strays, and partly too, they say, because it is a garrison town.

Oh, can it be that we women would have let so many things go wrong in this world, and should we have let it be so hard a place for the unfortunate, if we had had the governing power that men have had?

The light faded, and the stars began to show, and as I climbed up the steep hill between the dark and overhanging trees there came a swinging, marching tune with a wail behind it into my ears, and the words of an old folk-song:—

Oh, cursed be the cruel wars that ever they did rise,
And out of Merry England pressed many a lad likewise!
They pressed young Harry from me, they pressed my brothers three,
They took them to the cruel wars in high Germany.

The little house at the top of the hill looked warm and cosy as one came in out of the darkness, but the woman who sat knitting there by the fire was sad, because the children she had loved and worked for had gone out into the world, and left her. She was lonely, and had not enough to do to occupy her thoughts.

Yet if she could but realise it, the great Woman's Movement calls her as it calls all other women, and out in the world there is a work that waits for her,

And endless succession of labour, under the brightness of summer, under the gloom of winter. To my thought it is a sadness even in the colour and light and glow of this hour of sun, this ceaseless labour, repeating the furrow, reiterating the blow, the same furrows, the same stroke—shall we never know how to lighten it, how to live with the flowers, the swallows, the sweet delicious shade, and the murmur of the stream?—*Richard Jefferies.*

'Pit brow women'

[*Votes for Women*, 11 August 1911]

To the Editors of VOTES FOR WOMEN.
Dear Editors,—In view of the present attempt to prohibit the employment of women upon the brow of the coal mine, some description of the actual work performed by the pit brow lassies may be of interest to your readers.

The pit brow workers wear the usual Lancashire clogs, with

bonnets, or bonnets and shawls upon their heads and shawls over their shoulders. In the old days they always wore over their stout corduroy knickerbockers, not the ordinary skirt, but something called a 'coat'. The coat, usually made of blue print, is in reality a kind of apron, the fact that it is open at the back being disguised by wide looping folds. Its advantage over an ordinary short skirt is that should it catch in any of the machinery it would be easy to unbutton it and to allow it to slip off; whereas, in the case of a circular skirt, a woman would be unable to free herself, and would be drawn into the machinery and crushed, as has happened in some cases.

Now that the machinery about the mine is more adequately fenced the skirts are coming back, and the 'coat' is beginning to disappear; but its disuse is, I fear, also partly due to the criticisms which have been made of the pit brow lassies and their work.

The term Pit Brow Lassies includes the Bankswomen, the Pit Brow Lassies proper, and the Sorters or Screen Women. In some collieries all these three classes of women are employed; in others only the Pit Brow Lassies and the Sorters; and in others again only the sorters.

BANKSWOMEN

Let us deal first with the work of the bankswomen. They stand, two of them, at the mouth of the shaft that reaches down into the mine below. As the cage laden with coal-filled tubs (tubs are square boxes on wheels) comes to the surface and then stops, they enter it, and between them drag the tubs out one by one, and with a hard push send them rolling off along some railway lines. This work is sometimes done by men, sometimes by women, and one may sometimes see a banksman and bankswoman standing together at the shaft, working the same number of hours, and performing their equal share of the same task, but whilst a banksman is paid from 4s 9d to 5s a day a bankswoman gets only from 1s 10d to 2s 4d.

The tubs roll off at the push of the banksmen and bankswomen, and are met as they come by a group of pit brow lassies, who push and drag and guide them on their way to the sorting screens. The wages for pit brow lassies range from 1s 6d to 2s or 2s 2d a day. In some cases, one woman with a knowledge of coal is stationed at a point to which all the tubs must come and at which the lines leading to the various screens diverge. Here, according to the size and quality of the coal which it contains, she decides in which direction each tub must go, turning the points for it and pushing it on towards the receiver into which it is emptied, and from whence the coal falls to the sorting screen.

SORTERS

The sorting screens are in the form of long belts, which move continually and carry the coal along with them. They are usually some three feet wide, and about three feet from the ground. On either side of the belts rows of women stand picking out pieces of stone, wood, and other waste stuff from amongst the coal as it slowly moves past. Sometimes they pick out the waste pieces with their fingers, sometimes they catch at them with an iron hook or rake, and sometimes with a hammer they strike off those which may be adhering to the coal itself. Some collieries supply many more tools for coal sorting than others do, where most of the work is done with the fingers. Serious accidents on the pit brow are now rare, but minor accidents to fingers caused frequently by the slipping of large pieces of coal upon them, are not more common. The dust from the coal is constantly rising, and the women's faces, hands and clothing are soon blackened by it. Their heads are closely muffled in shawls to protect their hair. In some cases the belt is so arranged that it is necessary for two women to kneel on the ground at the end of it to attend to the aperture by which the coal passes off the belt, and to prevent its becoming clogged. The women who sort the coal are usually paid 1s 6d a day, though girls and those who are learning get less, and some get as much as 2s a day.

The sorting of coal entails practically no physical exertion, but the work of the bankswomen and pit brow lassies necessitates great muscular strength and power of endurance. Both of these things they possess in abundant measure. Indeed, when one sees them working side by side with men, they appear almost stronger than the men. They are many of them splendidly made, lithe and graceful, and, including the sorters, for all the coal dust, have clear, fresh complexions. Their rosy cheeks contrast strangely with the wan white faces of their sisters in the neighbouring cotton mills.

FROM MILL TO PIT BROW

'My father was pleased when I came to work on the pit brow, because it brought me out so,' a coal sorter told me a few years ago, there being at the time no talk of prohibiting the work. I asked what to be 'brought out' meant, and she said that since coming to the pit she had felt and looked stronger and brighter than before. I asked what her previous employment had been. She replied domestic service.

A young woman who formed part of the deputation to Mr Masterman last Friday told me that she had at one time worked in a cotton factory, and was then constantly in the doctor's hands, but that during five years on the pit brow she had ailed nothing. She had a sister who was still in the mill, but as she was delicate the doctor had said 'we should try and get her to t' pit.'

But, indeed, one cannot spend any time amongst the pit brow lassies without hearing stories of this kind. I will not give more of them, but will add a word of personal experience. For some time I was engaged in making a series of sketches of women at work in various trades. When, in order to make these sketches, I went for some weeks to a boot factory, I suffered from almost constant headache, owing to the heat and noise of the machines. When I went into a Glasgow cotton spinning mill I fainted after one hour in the 'mule spinning' room, and was literally unable to work in the 'ring spinning' room, where I was pained to see numbers of poor little half-timers—tiny, stunted creatures all of them, and a large proportion with bandy legs and curvature of the spine. When I went into the dipping house of a pottery I fainted twice during the first morning, and all the time I was going there continually felt a sensation of pressure and discomfort in the ears and throat, and a desire to swallow and to draw saliva into the mouth, and had after a time the nasty sweet taste of which the lead workers complain. In all these places I was struck by the leaden pallor of the workers.

When I went to the pit brow of a Wigan colliery my face was blackened like the faces of the workers, but that did me no harm, and I was perfectly well all the time that I was there. Certainly the work is not what many of us would choose, and the wages are lower than they should be, but one must regard it in comparison with the other trades that are open to women. One must remember, too, that there is no hardship so great, and no temptation so strong, as that of being without work and without means.

Amongst the reasons why the women themselves prefer the work on the pit brow to that in a factory is that in the factories the silent system is usually enforced, whilst there is considerable freedom at the pit, and the lassies laugh and call to each other as they pull the tubs about.

THE DUTIES OF THE AUTHORITIES

Those who desire to abolish the employment of women on the pit brow contend, amongst other things, that the work is carried on in cold and exposed places. Those who wish to retain the women assert that the buildings erected on the brow of the pit are well warmed and ventilated.

In any case, it is quite certain that those who work in the open air, even under conditions of some hardship, are always stronger and healthier than those employed in heated factories. Too much air is always better than too little. But the fact of the matter is that the conditions vary. I have been to collieries where the sorting, etc., took place under conditions admitting of warmth in winter and freshness in summer. At the same time, I know an exposed platform walled in on one side only—roofed overhead, it is true, but open on three sides to all the elements. I have seen the rain sweep across it and drench the women sorters again and again.

As however it has been proved, by their existence in certain collieries, that shelter and warmth for the workers on the pit-brow can be provided, and as the Factory Acts and factory inspectors are there to secure that they shall be provided in every case, it is unquestionably already the duty of all concerned to see that this is done. To put the law into force, by bringing into line the less satisfactory collieries with those that are well planned and well managed, and thus to secure proper conditions for all the workers, men and women alike, is surely the right course to take, especially when Parliament has always the power to make the amendments to the existing Acts which changing circumstances may render necessary.

But the chief reason for objecting to the attempt to prohibit the employment of women upon the pit brow is that the women themselves, who are fully developed adult human beings, wish to continue the work, and resent this officious and interested tampering with their liberty.

Twenty years ago a similar attempt was made to wrench their livelihood from them. The women then protested loudly, numbers of indignation meetings were held, and a deputation of workers in costume went up to the House of Commons to voice their own claims. It is much to be regretted that on last Friday's deputation, organised not by the women themselves, the women who formed a part of it were there merely as a show and were not allowed to speak. 'Why shouldn't we have something to say?' some of them asked.

NO POLITICAL POWER

Perhaps the saddest aspect of the situation is that the women whose trade is threatened have no shred of political power and little influence. They are allowed no voice in the decision of their fate. The real fight lies between the colliery owners, who wish to retain the cheap labour of women on the one hand, and on the other those who wish to gain power and popularity by snatching more work for men (the fact that the under-payment of women tends to bring down wages being their sole shadow of excuse), backed up by their responsible faddists and sentimentalists who wish to treat women as though they were children.

For many years a few isolated men, justly-minded enough to desire equal treatment and opportunities for men and women, have raised their protests in such crises. They have been as voices crying in the wilderness, but now the day of change is at hand, and already the organised forces of women battling for the fullest political freedom, have the power to render it increasingly difficult for the Legislature to deal unjustly towards their sisters.—Yours, etc.,

Sylvia Pankhurst.

Linden Gardens, Bayswater, W.

The Suffragette (1911)

PREFACE

IN writing this history of the Militant Women's Suffrage Movement I have endeavoured to give a just and accurate account of its progress and happenings, dealing fully with as many of its incidents as space will permit. I have tried to let my readers look behind the scenes in order that they may understand both the steps by which the movement has grown and the motives and ideas that have animated its promoters.

I believe that women striving for enfranchisement in other lands and reformers of future days may learn with renewed hope and confidence how the 'family party,' who in 1905 set out determined to make votes for women the dominant issue of the politics of their time, in but six years drew to their standard the great woman's army of to-day. It is certain that the militant struggle in which this woman's army has engaged and which has come as the climax to the long, patient effort of the earlier pioneers, will rank amongst the great reform movements of the world. Set as it has been in modern humdrum days it can yet compare with any movement for variety and vivacity of incident. The adventurous and resourceful daring of the young Suffragettes who, by climbing up on roofs, by sliding down through skylights, by hiding under platforms, constantly succeeded in asking their endless questions, has never been excelled. What could be more piquant than the fact that two of the Cabinet Ministers who were carrying out a policy of coercion towards the women should have been forced into the witness box to be questioned and cross-questioned by Miss Christabel Pankhurst, the prisoner in the dock? What, too, could throw a keener searchlight upon the methods of our statesmen than the evidence put forward in the course of that trial?

To many of our contemporaries perhaps the most remarkable feature of the militant movement has been the flinging-aside by thousands of women of the conventional standards that hedge us so closely round in these days for a right that large numbers of men who possess it scarcely value. Of course it was more difficult for the earlier militants to break through the conventionalities than for those who followed, but, as one of those associated with the movement from its inception, I believe that the effort was greater for those who first came forward to stand by the originators than for the little group by whom the first blows were struck. I believe this because I know that the original militants were already in close association with the truth that not only were the deeds of the old time pioneers and martyrs glorious, but that their work still lacks completion, and that it behoves those of us who have grasped an idea for human betterment to endure, if need be, social ostracism, violence, and hardship of all kinds, in order to establish it. Moreover, whilst the originators of the militant tactics let fly their bolt, as it were, from the clear sky, their early associates rallied to their aid in the teeth of all the fierce and bitter opposition that had been raised.

The hearts of students of the movement in after years will be stirred by the faith and endurance shown by the women who faced violence at the hands of the police and others in Parliament Square and at the Cabinet Minister meetings, and above all by the heroism of the noble women who went through the hunger strike and the mental and physical torture of forcible feeding.

A passionate love of freedom, a strong desire to do social service and an intense sympathy for the unfortunate, together made the movement possible in its present form. Those who have worked as a part of it know that it is notable not merely for its enthusiasm and courage, but also for its cheery spirit of loyalty and comradeship, its patient thoroughness in organisation which has made possible its many great demonstrations and processions, its freedom from bitterness and recrimination, and its firm faith in the right.

[FROM CHAPTER 1: EARLY DAYS (1905)]

WHILST the educational propaganda work of the Women's Social and Political Union was being quietly carried on, stirring events were in preparation. The resignation of the Conservative Government was daily expected. The Liberal leaders were preparing themselves to take office, and every newspaper in the country was discussing who the new Ministers were to be. A stir of excitement was spreading all over the country and now the organisers of the Liberal Party decided to hold a great revival meeting in that historic Manchester Free Trade Hall, which stands upon the site of the old franchise battle of Peterloo. The meeting was fixed for October 13, and here it was determined that the old fighting spirit of the Radicals should be revived, the principles and policy of Liberalism should be proclaimed anew and, upon the strength of those principles and of that policy, the people should be called upon to support the incoming Government with voice and vote.

When the evening of the thirteenth came, the great hall was filled to overflowing with an audience mainly composed of enthusiastic Liberals, for the meeting was almost entirely a ticket one, and the tickets had been circulated amongst the Liberal Associations throughout the length and breadth of Lancashire. The organ played victorious music, and then the Liberal men, whose party had been out of office for so long and who now saw it coming into power, rose to their feet and cheered excitedly as their leaders came into the hall. After a few brief words from the chairman, words in which he struck a note of triumphant confidence in the approaching Liberal victory, Sir Edward Grey was called upon to speak. The future Cabinet Minister, in a speech full of fine sentiments and glowing promises, named all the various great reforms that the Liberal Government would introduce, and appealed to the people to give the Liberal Party its confidence, and to return a Liberal ministry to power. Whilst he was speaking, Sir Edward Grey was interrupted by a man who asked him what the Government proposed to do for the unemployed. Sir Edward paused with ready courtesy to listen. 'Somebody said the unemployed', he explained to the audience; 'well, I will come to that', and he did so, saying that this important question would certainly be dealt with. Then he came to his peroration; he spoke of the difficulties of administration, difficulties which were especially great at the present time. 'We ask for the Liberal Party', he said, 'the same chance as the Conservative Party has had for nearly twenty years. There is no hope in the present men, but there is hope in new men. It is to new men with fresh minds, untrammelled by prejudice and quickened by sympathy, and who are vigorous and true, that I believe that the country will turn with hope. What I ask for them is generous support and a fair chance'. The thunder of applause that greeted his final words had scarcely died away when, as if in answer to Sir Edward Grey's appeal and promise, a little white cotton banner, inscribed with the words, 'VOTES FOR WOMEN', was put up in the centre of the hall, and a woman was heard asking what the Government would do to make the women politically free. Almost simultaneously two or three men were upon their feet demanding information upon other questions. The men were at once replied to, but the woman's question was ignored. She therefore stood up again and pressed for an answer to her question, but the men sitting near her forced her down into her seat, and one of the stewards of the meeting held his hat over her face. Meanwhile, the hall was filled with a babel of conflicting sound. Shouts of 'Sit down!' 'Be quiet!' 'What's the matter?' and 'Let the lady speak!' were heard on every hand. As the noise subsided a little, a second woman sitting beside the first got up and asked again, 'Will the

Liberal Government give women the vote?' but Sir Edward Grey made
no answer, and again arose the tumult of cries and counter cries. Then
the Chief Constable of Manchester, Mr William Peacock, came down
from the platform to where the women were sitting, and asked them
to write out the question that they had put to Sir Edward Grey, saying
that he would himself take it to the Chairman and make sure that it
received a reply. The women agreed to this suggestion, and the one
who had first spoken now wrote:

> Will the Liberal Government give votes to working women?
> Signed on behalf of the Women's Social and Political Union,
> ANNIE KENNEY,
> Member of the Oldham Committee of the
> Card and Blowing Room Operatives.

To this she added that as one of the 96,000 organised women cotton
workers, and for their sake, she earnestly desired an answer. Mr
Peacock took the paper on which the question had been written back
to the platform, and was seen to hand it to Sir Edward Grey, who,
having read it, smiled and passed it to the Chairman, from whom it
went the round of every speaker in turn. Then it was laid aside, and
no answer was returned to it. A lady, sitting on the platform, who had
noticed and understood all that was going on, now tried to intervene.
'May I, as a woman, be allowed to speak—?' she began, but the
Chairman called on Lord Durham to move a vote of thanks to Sir
Edward Grey. When this vote had been seconded by Mr Winston
Churchill, and when it had afterwards been carried, Sir Edward Grey
rose to reply. But he made no reference, either to the enfranchisement
of women, or to the question which had been put. Then followed the
carrying of a vote of thanks to the Chair, and by this time the meeting
showed signs of breaking up. Some of the audience had left the hall,
and some of the people on the platform were preparing to go. The
women's question still remained unanswered and seemed in danger of
being forgotten by everyone concerned. But the two women were
anxiously awaiting a reply, and the one who had first spoken now rose
again, and this time she stood up upon her seat and called out as loudly
as she could, 'Will the Liberal Government give working women the
vote?' At once the audience became a seething, infuriated mob.
Thousands of angry men were upon their feet shouting, gesticulating,

and crying out upon the woman who had again dared to disturb their meeting.

She stood there above them all, a little, slender, fragile figure. She had taken off her hat, and her soft, loosely flowing hair gave her a childish look; her cheeks were flushed and her blue eyes blazing with earnestness. It was Annie Kenney, the mill girl, who had gone to work in an Oldham cotton factory as a little half-timer at ten years of age. A working woman, the child of a working woman, whose life had been passed among the workers, she stood there now, feeling herself to be the representative of thousands of struggling women, and in their name she asked for justice. But the Liberal leaders, who had spoken so glibly of sympathy for the poor and needy, were silent now, when one stood there asking for justice; and their followers, who had listened so eagerly and applauded with so much enthusiasm, speeches filled with the praise of liberty and equality, were thinking now of nothing but Liberal victories. They howled at her fiercely, and numbers of Liberal stewards came hurrying to drag her down. Then Christabel Pankhurst, her companion, started up and put one arm around Annie Kenney's waist, and with the other warded off their blows, and as she did so, they scratched and tore her hands until the blood ran down on Annie's hat that lay upon the seat, and stained it red, whilst she still called, 'The question, the question, answer the question!' So, holding together, these two women fought for votes as their forefathers had done, upon the site of Peterloo.

At last six men, Liberal stewards and policemen in plain clothes, seized Christabel Pankhurst and dragged her away down the central aisle and past the platform, then others followed bringing Annie Kenney after her. As they were forced along the women still looked up and called for an answer to their question, and still the Liberal leaders on the platform looked on apparently unmoved and never said a word. As they saw the women dragged away, the men in the front seats—the ticket holders from the Liberal clubs—shouted 'Throw them out!' but from the free seats at the back, the people answered 'Shame!'

Having been flung out into the street, the two women decided to hold an indignation meeting there, and so, at the corner of Peter Street and South Street, close to the hall, they began to speak, but within a few minutes, they were arrested, and followed by hundreds of men and women, were dragged to the Town Hall. Here they were both charged with obstruction, and Christabel Pankhurst was also accused of assaulting the police. They were summoned to attend the Police Court in Minshull Street next morning.

Meanwhile, as soon as the women had been thrown out of the hall, there came a revulsion of feeling in their favour and the greater part of the meeting broke up in disorder. Believing that some explanation was expected of him, Sir Edward Grey now said that he regretted the disturbance which had taken place. 'I am not sure' he continued 'that unwittingly and in innocence I have not been a contributing cause. As far as I can understand, the trouble arose from a desire to know my opinion on the subject of Women's Suffrage. That is a question which I would not deal with here to-night because it is not, and I do not think it is likely to be, a party question.' He added that he had already given his opinion upon votes for women and that, as he did not think it a 'fitting subject for this evening', he would not repeat it.

Thus, within a few days of the fortieth anniversary of the formation of the first Women's Suffrage Society (perhaps even upon that very anniversary), and after forty years of persevering labour for this cause, Sir Edward Grey announced that Women's Suffrage was as yet far outside the realm of practical politics, and the two women who had dared to question him upon this subject were flung with violence and insult from the hall.

The next morning the police court was crowded with people eager to hear the trial. The two girls refused to dispute the police evidence as to the charges of assault and obstruction, and based their defence solely upon the principle that their conduct was justified by the importance of the question upon which they had endeavoured to secure a pronouncement and by the outrageous treatment which they had received. But though ignoring the violence to which they had been subjected and exaggerating the disturbance which they had made, the Counsel for the prosecution had dwelt at length upon the scene in the Free Trade Hall; the women were not allowed to refer to it and, though it was evident that but for what had taken place in the meeting they would not have been arrested for speaking in the street, they were ordered to confine their remarks to what had taken place after they had been ejected. Both defendants were found quilty, Christabel Pankhurst being ordered to pay a fine of ten shillings or to go to prison for seven days and Annie Kenney being fined five shillings with the alternative of three days' imprisonment. They both refused to pay the fines and were immediately hurried away to the cells.

'Our paper: *The Woman's Dreadnought*'

[*The Woman's Dreadnought*, 8 March 1914:
first issue published by the East London
Federation of the Suffragettes.]

The name of our paper, *The Woman's Dreadnought*, is symbolic of the fact that the women who are fighting for freedom must fear nothing. It suggests also the policy of social care and reconstruction, which is the policy of awakening womanhood throughout the world, as opposed to the cruel, disorganised struggle for existence amongst individuals and nations from which Humanity has suffered in the past.

This first advance number of our paper is to be sold at a penny, but when *The Woman's Dreadnought* begins to be published as a regular weekly newspaper, on Saturday, April 4th 20,000 copies will be issued freely each week in East London and as far as possible, the publishing expenses will be covered by the prices charged for the advertisements displayed in our columns. It is by the advertisements that every newspaper is made to pay its way.

The Woman's Dreadnought is published by the East London Federation of the Suffragettes, an organisation mainly composed of working women, and the chief duty of *The Dreadnought* will be to deal with the franchise question from the working woman's point of view, and to report the activities of the votes for women movement in East London. Nevertheless, the paper will not fail to review the whole field of the women's emancipation movement.

THE EAST LONDON FEDERATION OF THE SUFFRAGETTES

Some of our readers may ask, What is the East London Federation of the Suffragettes? And when and why was it formed?

These are the facts.

In October 1912, Mrs Drummond and I agreed that the work of arousing the working women of East London to fight for their own enfranchisement must be seriously and systematically attacked. Mrs Drummond was not able to give much time to the enterprise, but I went down to the East End daily, and between us we induced some of the West London Local Unions, who have money and leisured members, to help in breaking up the ground. Hence the Kensington WSPU opened a centre of work in Bethnal Green, the Chelsea WSPU worked in Stepney and Limehouse: the Paddington WSPU in Poplar, Lincoln's Inn House paid the rent of a shop in Bow Road, and I collected a body of workers for that district. A big procession and demonstration in Victoria Park was held on November 10th 1912.

Immediately after the demonstration came the Bow and Bromley by-election, caused by the resignation of Mr George Lansbury, the Labour Member of Parliament for the constituency. As all the world knows, Mr Lansbury resigned his seat in order that he might be free to put up an uncompromising fight against the Government on the question of Votes for Women. He felt that as a Member of the Parliamentary Labour Party he was not free to make that fight, and he therefore wished to represent the constituency as an Independent Member or not at all.

The Election Campaign, into which the WSPU threw itself vigorously, and in which every other Suffrage Society joined, made Bow and Bromley people think a good deal about Votes for Women, but Mr Lansbury was not returned.

Soon after the by-election and originally at my suggestion, preparations began to be made for the Working Women's Deputation to Mr Lloyd George. though volunteers for the Deputation were invited from all over the country, by far the largest number came from East London, and the various East London districts were the most systematically worked.

Of the thousands who had volunteered for the Deputation, only twelve were finally chosen to go to Downing Street. These included a Poplar laundress, a home-worker who made pinafores at sweated rates in Bow, a waste rubber worker from Poplar, and the wife of a labourer earning 22s a week, who had eight children and lived in a wretched two roomed tenement in Bethnal Green, for which she paid 5s a week in rent.

On the eve of the discussion of the Suffrage Amendments, the Deputation of Working Women waited on Mr Lloyd George and Sir Edward Grey. Mr Lloyd George assured the women that the prospect of the Votes for Women amendments being carried was so good as almost to amount to a certainty. Sir Edward Grey spoke to the same

49

effect: but that very night, whilst the women were assembled in various public halls, and fifty of them by special permission, were gathered together in the Grand Committee Room of the House of Commons, the Speaker let fall his bombshell. He announced that if any of the Women's amendments were carried, the whole Reform Bill would be out of order.

The House adjourned and Mr Asquith took time to consider the situation. On the following Monday he announced that the Reform Bill would be withdrawn, and that though the Liberal Government still intended to introduce Manhood Suffrage later on, women must rely on the efforts of Private Members to secure their Enfranchisement. Mr Asquith also withdrew his oft-repeated promise that the Government would make itself responsible for any Private Member's Bill to give Votes to Women after it had passed its second reading unaided.

When the Working Women's Deputation was over, most of the West London workers left the East End, and all financial aid from the WSPU headquarters was finally withdrawn.

I was determined that the East End work must go on. Lady Sybil Smith and I had collected some money for big popular open-air meetings during the summer and autumn, and as that money was not all spent, we had used it to further the East End campaign. A few pounds still remained and with them as a nucleus I decided to take the risk of opening a permanent East End headquarters in Bow.

Miss Emerson and I went down there together one frosty Friday morning in February to hunt for an office. The sun was like a red ball in the misty, whitey-grey sky. Market stalls, covered with cheerful pink and yellow rhubarb, cabbages, oranges and all sorts of other interesting things, lined both sides of the narrow Roman Road. The Roman, as they call it, was crowded with busy, kindly people. I had always liked Bow. That morning my heart warmed to it for ever. We decided to take a shop and house at 321, Roman Road, at a weekly rental of 14s 6d a week. It was the only shop to let in the road. The shop window was broken right across, and was only held together by putty. The landlord would not put in new glass, nor would he repair the many holes in the shop and passage flooring because he thought we should only stay a short time. But all such things have since been done.

Plenty of friends at once rallied round us. Women who had joined the Union in the last few weeks came in and scrubbed the floors and cleaned the windows. Mrs Wise, who kept the sweet shop next door, lent us a trestle table for a counter and helped us to put up purple, white and green flags. Her little boy took down the shutters for us every morning, and put them up each night, and her little girls often came in to sweep. A week after the shop was opened Miss Emerson and I were arrested. We went to prison on Friday night, February 14th, and our fines were paid on Saturday at noon. We had been hunger-striking, and as soon as we had broken our fast we went back to Bow. We found Mrs Lake scrubbing the table, and as many other members as the shop would hold talking about us, and wondering how we were getting on.

On the following Monday, February 17th we held a Meeting at the Obelisk, and after it was over Mrs Watkins, Mrs Moor, Miss Annie Lansbury, and I broke an undertaker's window. Mr Will Lansbury broke a window in the Bromley Public Hall, and Miss Emerson broke a Liberal Club window. We were all six arrested, and sent to prison without the option of a fine.

That was the beginning of Militancy in East London. Miss Emerson, Mrs Watkins and I decided to do the hunger-strike, and hoped that we should soon be out to work again. But though Mrs Watkins was released after ten days, Miss Emerson and I were forcibly fed, and she was kept in for seven weeks, although she had developed appendicitis, and I for five. When we were once free we found that we were too ill to do anything at all for some weeks.

But we need not have feared that the work would slacken without us. A tremendous flame of enthusiasm had burst forth in the East End. Great meetings were held, and during our imprisonment long processions marched eight times the six miles to cheer us in Holloway, and several times also to Brixton gaol, where Mr Will Lansbury was imprisoned. The people of East London, with Miss Dalglish to help them, certainly kept the purple, white and green flag flying.

Early in April the anti-Suffragist Government entered on a strenuous campaign of Suffragette persecution. Mrs Pankhurst was sentenced to three years' penal servitude on April 2nd. Miss Annie Kenney was summoned under a musty old Statute of Edward III, which was directed by that monarch and his Parliament against 'pillers and robbers from beyond the sea,' and was now raked up by the Liberal Government to prevent her speaking at the Albert Hall Meeting on April 10th. Mrs Drummond and Mr George Lansbury, who spoke at that Meeting, were summoned because of their speeches under the same old Act. Miss Kenney and Mrs Drummond were afterwards charged with conspiracy, but Mr Lansbury was ordered to either bind himself over in heavy sums of money to make no more such speeches, or to go to prison for three months. He appealed against the magistrates' decision. Meanwhile the Government had not only tried to prohibit the printing of The Suffragette newspaper, but had prohibited the WSPU meetings in Hyde Park. The police kept the Suffragette platforms out of the Park, but they could not prevent the women speaking. Nevertheless, anti-Suffragist hooligans and police together might have given the speakers a bad time but for the help of the East London dockers, who fought to protect the women. Sunday after Sunday.

On Sunday, May 25th, 1913 was held 'Women's May Day' in East London. The Members in Bow, Bromley, Poplar, and neighbouring districts had prepared for it for many weeks past and had made hundreds of almond branches, which were carried in a great procession with purple, white and green flags, and caps of Liberty flaunting above them from the East India Dock gates by winding ways, to Victoria Park. A vast crowd of people – the biggest ever seen in East London – assembled in the Hyde Park of East London to hear the speakers from twenty platforms.

A few days later the East London Federation of the Suffragettes, or East London Federation of the WSPU as it was then called was formally set up to unite for greater strength the local Unions that had been formed in Bow, Bromley, Poplar, Stepney and Hackney, Canning Town has since been added to the number. The Federation Council consists of the Hon. Secretary, the Hon. Treasurer, the Hon. Financial and Hon. Meetings Secretaries, the Hon. Advertisement Manager, the District Secretaries and Organisers, and two elected representatives of the Members in each district.

On Sunday, June 29th 1913 the East London Federation organised a big procession to Trafalgar Square, in which Suffrage Societies and Trades' Unions and Labour organisations joined. There was an immense crowd in the Square. But of what use was one more big Meeting where so many had been held? The 'Cat-and-Mouse' Act had just been passed and under it Mrs Pankhurst and a number of other hunger-strikers were being ruthlessly dragged back and back to prison. Their lives were at stake. Emily Wilding Davison, feeling their peril, had given her own life to make the nation think. On June 4th she had flung herself into the midst of the Derby racehorses and had been killed. In face of such happenings what was the use of talking? The need was for an emphatic public protest. I asked the people to go and hoot the Cabinet Ministers and if they were able to do more than hoot – to imprison the Cabinet Ministers in their official residences as they had imprisoned more than 2,000 women Suffragists until the Ministers would agree to give Women the Vote.

I had hardly finished speaking when the people were streaming off down Whitehall and soon they were hooting and shouting 'Votes for Women' outside Mr Asquith's house. Police reinforcements were immediately hurried across from Scotland Yard to force the people away and a sharp struggle took place in which five men were arrested.

The following Thursday, July 3rd I too was summoned under the antique Statue of Edward III to appear at Bow Street on July 5th. I did not consider it my duty to obey, and instead I went away for the weekend and then made my way to the Bromley Public Hall in Bow Road, where I had promised to speak. After the Meeting the people rallied unanimously, and fought to protect me from the detectives, who had come with a warrant for my arrest. Eventually I was taken prisoner with five others. One of these was Miss Mary Richardson who on July 4th had been struck with the flat of his sword by one of the King's equerries when she was trying to present a Petition to the King.

After remaining the night at Bow Street. I was sentenced next morning to three months imprisonment, because I would not promise not to make militant speeches. On reaching prison I started the hunger-and-thirst strike.

On being released the following Sunday I was received as a guest by Mr and Mrs Payne at 28, Ford Road, Bow. Letters of sympathy, flowers and presents of all kinds were showered on me by kindly neighbours. One woman wrote to say that she did not see why I should ever go back to prison when every woman could buy a rolling-pin for a penny.

I had tremendous welcomes, both in Bow and Poplar, when I spoke during my week's licence. On the Monday after the licence expired I got to the Bromley Public Hall Meeting in disguise, and so splendidly did the good people fight with me to forward Votes for Women, and smash the 'Cat-and-Mouse' Act that detectives and policemen were held at bay and I was rushed away into safety by the crowd.

On Sunday, July 27th the East London Federation organised another great March to Trafalgar Square. The Square was densely packed with people. It was said that no meeting so large had been held there since the eighties.

In spite of a veritable host of policemen and detectives, I was able to get there in disguise and just at the moment when the principal superintendent of police was asking if I had arrived and his lieutenants were replying in the negative I was taking my seat on the back of one of Landseer's lions. When I came undisguised from a sheltering group of friends, the people greeted me with cheers and eagerly agreed to go to Downing Street to carry our Women's Declaration of Independence to the Prime Minister's official residence.

I sprang from the plinth. Friends down below caught me and closed around me, forcing the police away. All the vast gathering swarmed behind.

At the top of Whitehall policemen on horseback met us. We rushed between them and pressed on.

A taxi-cab was standing in the middle of the road. The people opened the door and asked me to ride away thinking that thus I might elude the police. I said 'No. I am going with you to Downing Street.' The cab door was shut. We pressed on nearly to Downing Street but reinforcements from Scotland Yard – a great company – came upon us. I was dragged away by detectives, dragged off to Holloway. The crowd was beaten back and twenty-seven people were arrested.

Next day Mr Lansbury's appeal against the sentence imposed upon him under the Act of Edward III was decided against him and he was ordered to surrender to his bail on Wednesday, July 30th, two days later. He went up from Bow to Bow Street with a host of friends and was carried off to gaol but on adopting the hunger strike he was released on a 'Cat-and-Mouse' licence the next Saturday and has not yet been taken back. Feeling was running very high at the time in East London and vast meetings and processions were organised in Mr Lansbury's honour as well as to forward Votes for Women and break down the 'Cat-and-Mouse' Act.

On August 10th the Free Speech Defence Committee, a composite body on which sit many Radical and Labour Members of Parliament and Labour leaders, announced a demonstration in Trafalgar Square to protest against the Government's many attempts to suppress the rights of free speech and public meeting and especially against the prosecution of speakers under the Act of Edward III. I was asked to speak with Mr Lansbury and Mr Scurr and Mrs Cohen (who had also been summoned under the Act, though never sent to prison) on condition that I would pledge myself not to go to Downing Street. I replied that I could not agree to this condition and issued a leaflet 'To Lovers of Freedom' saying that after the Free Speech people had done their talking. I should be present in the Square to go with those who cared to come to Downing Street. This I did, and the vast majority of those present went with me as far as we could go. When we were beaten back by the mounted police, eighteen people besides myself were arrested and the windows of a motor bus were broken.

These demonstrations of Militant popular support were a fine answer to those who were saying that public opinion was against the women in their fight for liberty.

On August 15th Parliament was prorogued and there came a season of quiet propaganda work and holidays, but at the end of October we learnt with horror that Mary Richardson and Rachel Peace were being forcibly fed in prison.

On October 13th the East London Federation held a packed meeting in Bow Baths. I got there in disguise. The people held the front door against the police and detectives, but I had not been speaking ten minutes when policemen sprang on to the platform from behind the curtains with truncheons drawn. The people shouted 'Jump, Sylvia, jump!' I jumped as they told me, from the platform into the audience and turned for a moment half dazed with the shock to see policemen with truncheons and those we believe were detectives with loaded sticks, striking the people who were crowded on to the platform and smashing the chairs. Mrs Mary Leigh was knocked insensible, Mrs Ives was held up by the collar and struck with a truncheon so that her arm was broken. Miss Forbes Robertson, sister of the great actor, also had her arm broken and many unknown men and women were seriously hurt. The people in the gallery retaliated by throwing chairs down on to the police. People in the audience then stole up behind me, put somebody's hat and coat on me and led me out that I might speak in Poplar Town Hall next night.

As Miss Emerson was leaving the hall a man we believe was a detective who was annoyed because the people called 'Puss! Puss!' to him, struck her on the side of the head with a lead-weighted instrument. Mr Mansell-Moulhn the noted surgeon stated on examining her that Miss Emerson's skull was fractured and that if the blow had been struck an eighth of an inch further back she would certainly have been killed.

Next night I was recognised by the detectives who crowded the steps of the Poplar Town Hall and a couple of hundred policemen had closed round me before the people could get to me. A man and his wife who rushed towards me were arrested.

I was released after nine days. Though obliged to be carried to speak at Bow Baths and Poplar Town Hall on a stretcher during my week's licence, I was able to be up and doing at the end of the week. A few days after the expiration of my licence I spoke at the Royal Albert Hall and the Hackney Baths and was so well protected by the people that I was able to get away in safety.

On November 5th 1913 a Meeting was held to inaugurate the People's Army which is an organisation that men and women may join to fight for freedom and in order that they may learn to cope with the repressive methods of the Government servants.

On my way to this Meeting I happened to call at Mr Lansbury's house in St Stephen's Road. The house was immediately surrounded by detectives and policemen and there seemed no possibility of escape. But the people of 'Bow' on hearing of the trouble, came flocking out of the Baths where they had assembled. In the confusion that ensued the detectives dragged Miss Daisy Lansbury off in a taxi, and I went free.

When the police authorities realised their mistake, and learnt that I was actually speaking in the Baths, they sent hundreds of men to take me, but though they met the people in the Roman Road as they came from the Meeting I escaped. Miss Emerson was again struck on the head, this time by a uniformed constable, and fell to the ground unconscious. Many other people were badly hurt. The people replied with spirit. Two mounted policemen were unhorsed and many others were disabled.

Twice shortly afterwards I spoke in Canning Town Public Hall and each time went free, the police, though present in large numbers to take me, preferring not to attack. One Sunday afternoon I spoke in Bow Palace and marched openly with the people to Ford Road. When I spoke from the window afterwards a veritable forest of sticks was waved by the crowd. The police had evidently guessed that we were armed, and so treated us with respect.

As last the police won the day. It was at my eighth Meeting, which was held at Shoreditch Town Hall, a district in which the East London Federation had never held a meeting and in which even for this Meeting but little advertising had been done. We had grown over-confident.

As a result of the police raid on Bow Baths on October 13th and the police treatment of the people on Nov. 5th the Poplar Borough Council unjustly refused to let for Suffragette meetings Bow Baths; the Bromley Public Hall and the Poplar Town Hall – the only large public halls in the Poplar Borough.

Whilst I was in prison after my arrest at Shoreditch, a Meeting of Protest against the refusal of the public halls to the Suffragettes was held in Bow Palace on Sunday afternoon, December 14th. After the Meeting it was arranged to go in procession around the district and to hoot outside the houses of hostile Borough Councillors. When the processionists turned out of Bow Rd. into Tomlin's Grove they found that the street lamps were not lighted and that a strong force of police were waiting in the dark before the house of Councillor Le Manquais. Just as the people at the head of the procession reached the house, the policemen closed around them and arrested Miss Emerson, Miss Godfrey and seven men, two of whom were not in the procession, but were going home to tea in the opposite direction. At the same moment twenty mounted police came riding down upon the people from the far end of Tomlin's Grove, and twenty more from the Bow Road. The people were all unarmed. They had no 'mouse' to save, and had expected no trouble. There were cries and shrieks and people rushed panic-stricken into the little front gardens of the houses in the Grove. But wherever the people stopped the police hunted them away. I was told that an old woman who saw the police beating the people in her garden was so much upset that she fell down in a fit and died without regaining consciousness. A boy of 18 was so brutally kicked and trampled on that he had to be carried to the infirmary for treatment. A publican who was passing was knocked down and kicked and one of his ribs was broken. Even the bandsmen were not spared. The police threw their instruments over the garden walls. The big drummer was knocked down and so badly used that he is still on the list for sick insurance benefit. Mr Atkinson, a labourer, was severely handled and was then arrested. In the charge room Inspector Potter was said to have blacked his eye. Mr Atkinson afterwards brought an action for assault against the inspector but though Potter was committed for trial he was not convicted.

57

c

Such happenings show the need that the People's Army should be efficiently drilled and trained. Above all they prove that a voice in controlling the Government should be open to every man and woman and vigilantly used by every one.

Since the New Year opened the people of Canning Town have again made it possible for me both to speak and to come safely away from their Town Hall although wanted by the police.

I have also been able to take part in the Poplar by-election. I lived for the time at our Committee rooms, where we held two Women's Meetings every afternoon, having to turn the audience out at half-time to make room for more people. We also spoke to enthusiastic gatherings from the window every night.

On the eve of the poll we organised a great Votes for Women Procession in which the other Suffrage Societies took part down the dingy East India Dock Road. I marched in the Procession and spoke afterwards to a vast Open Air Meeting at the Dock gates. It was evident that most of the people there were prepared to act the part of bodyguard if necessary. There were many detectives watching by the road, but no more than half a dozen constables were to be seen. It had been widely advertised that I was to be there.

Why was no attempt made to arrest me? Why did not the detectives and policemen come cutting their way through the people with loaded sticks and truncheons. Why? Perhaps because this was the eve of the poll in Poplar, and it is better not to break the electors' heads the night before they vote.

The detectives were heard to say: 'We did not get her this time. There were too many people. There has been too much fighting in the East End.'

What clearer proof of the unpopularity of the 'Cat-and-Mouse' Act can be needed than the fact that the Government fears to enforce it in sight of electors on the eve of polling day?

Early in 1914 the east London Federation of the WSPU changed its name and became the East London Federation of the Suffragettes. We made this change at the request of others. Our policy remains what it has always been. We are still a Militant non-party organisation of working-women.

Some people tell us that it is neither specially important that working-women should agitate for the Vote, nor specially important that they should have it. They forget that comparatively the leisured comfortably situated women are but a little group, and the working-women a multitude.

Some people say that the lives of working-women are too hard and their education too small for them to become a powerful force in winning the Vote, many though they are. Such people have forgotten their history. What sort of women were those women who marched to Versailles?

Those Suffragists who say that it is the duty of the richer and more fortunate women to win the Vote, and that their poorer sisters need not feel themselves called upon to aid in the struggle, appear in using such arguments to forget that it is *the* Vote for which we are fighting. The essential principle of the vote is that each one of us shall have a share of power to help himself or herself and us all. It is in direct opposition to the idea that some few, who are more favoured, shall help and teach and patronise the others. It is surely because we Suffragists believe in the principle that every individual and every class of individuals has a right to a share both in ruling and in serving and because we have learnt by long and bitter experience that every form of government but self-government is tyranny – however kindly its intention – that we are fighting for the Vote and not for the remedying of some of the many particular grievances from which women suffer.

It is necessary for women to fight for the Vote because by means of the Vote, if we combine in sufficient numbers to use it for definite ends, we can win reforms for ourselves by making it plain to Governments that they must either give us the things we want or make way for those that will. Working-women – sweated women, wage slaves, overworked mothers toiling in little homes – these of all created beings, stand in the greatest need of this, the power to help themselves.

One of the principal reasons why it is essential that working-women should rise up in a body and work strenuously for the vote is that when the Franchise Question at last comes up for actual settlement the anti-Suffragists in Parliament will struggle to reduce the number of women voters as far as possible. Any restrictions that they may seek to impose are practically certain to operate most hardly against the poorest women, and the only thing that can safeguard their position is a big and active working-women's Franchise Agitation.

The Reformers of old *worked* to extend the boundaries of human freedom, because they believed the principle to be right, but they *fought and suffered and strove with desperate courage*, because they were spurred on by the knowledge that they or their fellows were suffering and in need. So is it to-day with those who want the Vote.

We have a tremendous task before us. We are only fighting with the courage with which men fight the Government, and men in the mass will only see the suffering and the fighting of the men. Only when we bear infinitely more than men and struggle infinitely harder, will men care enough or understand enough to help women to be politically free. So we must go on striving and try always to see the greatness of our aim.

'A minimum wage for women'

[*The Woman's Dreadnought*, 12 September 1914]

Many people are saying that on the other side of this war we shall come into a new regenerate world; an international commonwealth of happiness and well-being in which the squalor and misery of today will be unknown.

How precious and long desired is that vision, how white are its dear feet upon the mountains of imagination! With fancy's flowers we embroider its glades, and its skies fill with sun and song. Its children are lovelier than the blossoms and more joyous than the birds. Our hearts yearn for such a peace from this world of dreary actuality.

Life does not change like a dream vision, its battlements are *hard and cruel facts*. Yet do not shake your head over the 'new world' vision and turn away from it saying it cannot be. It is too beautiful, too sorely needed to be cast aside, either for lack of care or lack of hope. Neither sit dreaming and fancying that all the forces of evolution make for good.

We are the evolutionary forces, we with our small wills together striving. We, banding together, can hasten our country's upward growing and joining our hands across the seas to countless others, we each of us playing some small upward part, can hasten the great growth international.

Away on the field of war and the scenes of murder, where kindly fathers kill poor mothers' dear young sons in spite of the awful negation of humanity and civilisation in which they are joining, men learn, forced by the hand of stern necessity to play a hero's part. On the field of war, we are told all men of a side are as brothers, sharing alike in sleep and rations: each helping each, and privates and officers alike ready to go to an almost certainty of death, to carry a wounded comrade out of the range of fire.

Stern virtues such as these we who are left at home must practise, if we would make that 'new world' possible after the war. We cannot wait until the war is over, we must begin toiling and building now. We must apply ourselves to the difficult task of rooting up long standing abuses and cope as well with the new emergencies and troubles that arise.

In the first place let us try always to realise that every human being has a right, not merely to a bare existence, the mere food to keep life coursing within the body, but to comfort and joy and the means for upward development.

If, as it may be, even barest necessities grow scarce amongst us during the war, then we must not allow some to go half-starved whilst others live in plenty, but must share here at home as we are told they do away there on the field of war.

In the meantime, while as yet famine does not stare us in the face and may not, let us strive to enforce generally a decent standard of payment for work and for relief.

In Australia where women have the vote a widowed mother is entitled to 5s a week for each child, it costs more than that to maintain it in the Workhouse, that she may keep it with a decent standard of simple comfort, beside her in the home.

Most pitiful is the plight of many British soldier's and sailor's families. One fragile woman from Ranwell Street, Bow, came to us to-day. She has three little children aged four and a half, three years, one year and nine months and is expecting another soon. Her husband is a Reservist and was called up when war began. She had 20s from him and 22s from the Soldier's and Sailor's Families Association. The War Office have sent her £1 19s 6d, i.e. 9s 1d a week for the month of September. 'They said it wasn't as much as I ought to have,' she said, 'but they were getting short of money'. The Soldier's and Sailor's Association had told her to wait until they should come to visit her and she did not know whether she will get any more from them. She was terribly worried, '9s won't keep us,' but she made excuses for the War Office, they were 'busy' she thought. And then she cried, she had heard that 'a lot of Mr Regiment have fallen down.'

The husband of a woman living in Ford Road had the order from his firm 'enlist or go'. He joined the Territorials and went into training at the barracks in Tredegar Road. The firm *promised* him 5s a week whilst he was at the war, but in the meantime he had nothing. There are six little ones whose ages vary from 10 years to 8 months, the baby is wasting, another child has abscesses in her head. The rent is 7s. No money has come from the War Office. The Soldier's and Sailor's Association told the woman to wait until a visitor called upon her.

'When she came to us on Monday there was no food in the house.'

On Wednesday she came again. Still there was no money from the War Office. The visitor from the Soldier's and Sailor's Association had been, but had left without giving her anything, merely saying that she *might* get some money on Saturday.

Surely the British Nation is able, surely it should be willing to grant a fixed payment of £1 a week to soldiers' and sailors' wives who have no more than two children and where there are more than two children to 10s a week for the mother and 5s a week for each child: £1 a week for a mother whose son, who has been her support has gone to the war, 5s a week for the brothers and sisters who have been supported by soldier and sailor brothers.

The men who are out fighting at the bidding of their country's Government are entitled to the knowledge that their families are removed from want. The women whose husbands and sons will probably never return to them, are entitled to this small return for all the anxiety and grief that they must suffer.

One of the most glaring and far reaching evils menacing society has for long been the under-payment of our women. For many years after this war the proportion of women wage-earners is bound to be increased because so many, many men who took their part in the world's work and were the bread winners of families will have lost their lives. If the present gross under-payment of women's labour is allowed to continue the 'new world' after the war will be worse, an infinitely worse one than the world that we know to-day. Let us demand that the standard of women's wages be raised immediately. Let us band ourselves together to insist on a minimum wage for women of 5d an hour, or £1 for a full week's work. It is little enough especially in these days of high prices!

We women can all do our part in getting this minimum enforced. Numbers of us are members of Boards of Guardians, Town Councils, Local Representative Committees for distress and so on and there is hardly a woman's society that is not organising on its own account some kind of employment scheme to cope with the present distress. Through all these avenues we can press for this women's minimum wage of 5d an hour or £1 a week.

Do not be led away by those who tell you that if you pay a fair wage you will be obliged to employ a smaller number and that a larger number will be forced to starve. Those for whom no work can be found the State must be forced to care for, and by paying a miserable pittance to a large number you will be helping to keep down the standard for the Nation. Also you will not be helping as you might to prevent unemployment, for every woman who is paid a decent wage is able to buy clothes and other manufactures and in this way to provide employment for other people.

In all that we do to relieve distress at this juncture, hard though the effort is, as case after case of misery comes upon us we must remember always the 'new world' that we must build and strive to secure that the integrity of our Nation for which men fight, shall be an integrity worthy of preservation for all time.

'Beware the CD Acts!'

[*The Woman's Dreadnought*, 17 October 1914]

Last week we heard that the Leyton Mayor's Local Representative Committee had decided to grant relief from the Prince of Wales' Fund to persons thrown out of employment through the war on the basis of 3s for an adult woman and a maximum of 10s for a family. Now comes news that Lambeth Committee has decided to give 5s for one adult person living alone, 7s 6d for two adults living together, 2s for each child under 14 years, 3s 6d for each adolescent over 14 years.

To these miserable sums is attached the condition that applicants shall undertake whatever suitable work is offered them. The Parliamentary and other power of the men's Trade Unions is probably strong enough to ensure that whatever work is offered to the men shall be paid for at Trade Union rates of wages, but the women unfortunately have no such security.

Threepence an hour is all that they will earn in the Queen's workrooms, and the hours will be limited so that they cannot earn more than a maximum wage of 10s a week. Many women in the Queen's workrooms are earning less than 10s. One writes to me that she is showing other women how to do their work and yet only earns 8s 9d. Some women in some of the workrooms have been kept waiting about for work and have only earned 1s 9d in the week.

The New Constitutional Society are writing to protest that they have been refused a grant from the Queen's Fund for their workrooms because they pay more than 10s a week to skilled workers, although they admit that they pay less than those women previously earned even in the pitiless struggle of commercial life, where women's labour is so habitually exploited.

Such skilled women as those to whom the New Constitutional Society shrunk from paying a weekly wage of 10s have with difficulty extricated themselves from the vast purgatory of grossest sweating. They are pioneering upward towards a better standard of women's pay. But the Queen's Fund takes no account of the status of women's labour; the Queen, with the Liberal Government behind her turns a deaf ear to the voices of those who plead for a living wage for women and the recognition of a trained woman worker's skill.

What is the excuse for this sweated flat rate of 10s a week? That there are 60,000 unemployed women and only £60,000 in the Queen's 'Work for Women Fund'. 'If you pay women £1 a week the fund will only last one week,' they tell us. 'If you pay women 10s a week,' we answer, 'it will only last for two.'

Away with the Queen's Fund, if it is thus to be used as an excuse for sweating! There is plenty of money still in England, and all the women of the country are entitled to a share of it. Why should thousands of working women, in growing numbers, be obliged to cringe and plead and make a display of all the virtues, in order to win a semi-starvation pittance? Why should they be made to bite the dust and suffer untold hardship because War has been declared, whilst some people are going on very much as before?

Mr Austen Chamberlain said, when war was first declared – 'The common interest of all classes is much greater to everyone than the separate individual interests of any one class. We all stand or fall together, to whatever class we belong.' Let us act upon that principle! No one can say that we are doing so whilst the Local Government Board is fixing a scale of 10s a week for two adults to live upon, and whilst nothing whatsoever has been provided for unemployed women but this paltry Queen's Fund of £60,000!

Let us try to think clearly on this question of money. Money is only a means of exchange for food, fuel, clothes, furniture and other necessary or pleasant things. The Government can make as much paper money as it pleases, and so long as there is enough food in the country there is no reason why any should be left to starve. When the scarcity begins, then let us, as Mr Chamberlain said – 'all stand or fall together.'

But how far are we from being prepared to put this principle into practice. The infant lives that have been sacrificed since the war began – because the mothers were kept waiting for the allowance due to them, because the breadwinners on whom they depended were thrown out of work – are a witness to our national unreadiness to play the part of brothers and sisters to our fellows in this international crisis.

People say that sweating is to be deplored, but that women have been sweated for a long time past, and that this is not the time to alter it. Thus they dismiss the problem and push it from their minds. But the difficulties of these women with wages of 10s – and downwards to nothing – still continue and grow as the weeks pass by.

And meanwhile some people are thinking, that as despair settles down on them, some of these women will be driven to earn their living by that awful trade called prostitution – the easiest entered, alas, of all the trades that are!

The Watch Committee of the Plymouth Town Council on October 2nd recommended that to meet the present circumstances the Contagious Diseases Act should be re-enacted. The matter has been deferred, but it will be raised again, and women must remember that the 'special circumstance of the present time,' which makes even possible such an infamous proposal, is the awful economic need, the helpless hopeless poverty in which hundreds of thousands of women live. Remember that the Contagious Diseases Acts, which were placed almost unnoticed on the Statute Book, as a temporary measure, in

1864 and re-enacted in 1866, remained there for 20 years of toil and effort before they were repealed in 1886.

Here is the protest which Josephine Butler, Elizabeth Wolstenholme Elmy, Harriet Martineau, Lydia Becker, Mary Carpenter and Florence Nightingale signed against these Acts in 1869:

These acts are in force in some of our garrison towns, and in large districts around them. Unlike all other laws for the representation of contagious diseases, to which both men and women are liable, these two apply to women only, men being wholly exempt from their penalties. The law is ostensibly framed for a certain class of women, but in order to reach these, all women residing within the district where it is in force are brought under the provisions of the Acts. Any woman can be dragged into Court, and required to prove that she is not a common prostitute. The magistrate can condemn her, if a policeman swears only that he 'has good cause to believe' her to be one. The policeman is not required to produce proof that he has good cause for his 'belief,' and the accused has to rebut, not positive evidence, but the state of mind of her accuser. When condemned, her sentence is as follows:– To have her person outraged by the fortnightly inspection of a surgeon through a period of twelve months; or resisting that, to be imprisoned with or without hard labour first, for a month, next for three months – such imprisonment to be continuously renewed through her whole life, unless she submit periodically to the brutal requirements of this law. Women arrested under false accusations, have been so terrified at the idea of encountering the public trial necessary to prove their innocence, that they have, under the intimidation of the police, signed away their good name and their liberty by making what is called, a 'voluntary submission' to appear every fortnight for twelve months, for surgical examination. Women who, through dread of imprisonment, have been induced to register themselves as common prostitutes, now pursue their traffic under the sanction of Parliament: and the houses where they congregate, so long as the Government surgeons are satisfied with the health of their inmates, enjoy practically as complete a protection as a Church or a School.

The horror of this dreadful system can never be understood, even dimly, by anyone who has not read the detailed account of the tragedies which resulted from it. Josephine Butler's memoirs record cases of perfectly respectable women who were arrested and forced to undergo police examinations. Once examined it was impossible for them to escape from the police net. They had to come back month after month, and some of these women committed suicide, as the only way out of the fearful regimen into which they had been drawn.

The cruelties and the indignities which war places on conquered peoples are terrible indeed, but the infamy from without, which is ever rebelled against, is less destructive than that, more closely riveted, from within, which is passively accepted without protest. Slavery cannot degrade until it is accepted.

Josephine Butler's watchword was: 'Woman is solidaire.' Let us feel that as a living truth. Let us determine that shameful expedients like that of the Plymouth Watch Committee shall never be attempted in our land. Let us determine that behind the daughters of the Nation shall be the National Exchequer and not a paltry charitable fund of sixty or seventy thousand pounds!

'How to meet industrial conscription'

[*The Woman's Dreadnought*, 20 March 1915]

To the women whom they have refused to grant the rights of enfranchised citizens, the Government, through the President of the Board of Trade, has issued an appeal to enlist for War service.

The Women's Societies which the Government has so often flouted are urged to lend their aid in marshalling the volunteers.

Registers of women who are prepared to undertake any kind of paid work, industrial, agricultural, clerical, etc., are to be kept at the Labour Exchanges, and registration forms are being sent out to the women's organisations. Those who register must state their ages and whether they are married, widowed or unmarried; if they have ever done any paid work, and if so, what and when, and in whose employ; if they are free to work whole or part time, or to leave their homes; whether there is any kind of work that they are willing or able to do, and whether they are willing to train for work which they have not previously done.

In view of this appeal, which is being made to women by the Government—appeals by Governments usually tend to become irresistible demands—it is surely time that all the women's organisations, trade union, political, educational and social, should come together to discuss this important matter and formulate their demands to safeguard the position of women of all ranks in the labour army.

The men who signed the Army forms that were sent round to the householders, found themselves called up for service, sometimes much to their surprise. The women who sign their names on the War Service Register will probably find themselves called up too, whether they wish or not. Shall we allow them to go without fair conditions first being assured?

The Government, through Mr Lloyd George and Lord Kitchener, has announced that it is about to take extensive control of industry.

The Government makes it plain that it is determined that the provisions of munitions of war, both for Great Britain and the Allies, shall absorb all our entire national energies, so that all our people may become part of a great war machine engaged either in fighting, supplying the wherewithall to fight, or in providing necessaries of food, clothing, housing and transport for the soldiers or armament makers.

In order to conciliate the British workmen (who, by their votes, have been made the ultimate arbiters of the nation's destiny, though they scarcely realise their power), Mr Lloyd George has held conference with the Great Trade Unions which, as yet, are almost entirely controlled by men. The Government has promised that limits shall be set to the profits of employers, and that good wages and fair conditions of labour shall be ensured.

Various increases in wages have been made, and negotiations are taking place in regard to demands for much larger increases. The Trade Union leaders and Labour Members of Parliament occupy a position of grave and anxious responsibility at this time, for on their handling of the situation the position of millions of workers largely depends.

Perhaps an even vaster responsibility rests on the shoulders of women who are leaders of women at this time. As yet, the working women, the sweated drudges of the world, are but poorly organised, and all the women's suffrage and other political and social organisations must lend their aid at this crisis, in securing the best possible terms for the masses of women workers, on whom the future of our race so largely depends.

It is more urgently imperative than ever that every woman who works for her living should join a Trade Union, in order that she may have a strong organisation to protect her interests, and that she may help to protect the interests of other women.

A national conference of women should be called immediately to formulate demands for the regulation of this industrial enlistment of women. Here are some of the demands which would, undoubtedly, be adopted by such a conference:—

(1) As the Government is already by far and away the largest employer of labour in the country, and may soon be almost the sole employer, it is absolutely imperative that *women who are to be enlisted as recruits in the National War Service shall have the Vote at once.*

(2) That fair wages shall be assured to women. *That where a woman is employed on work hitherto done by men she shall receive the wage hitherto paid to men, in addition to any war bonus or increase in wages which might have been paid for the work now, in the case of men employees. That in no case shall an unskilled woman be employed at a lower wage than the current rate to men unskilled labourers.*

(3) The Government has announced its determination to put an end to industrial disputes, and proposes that, where the parties concerned fail to come to an agreement:—

'The matter shall be referred to an impartial tribunal, nominated by his Majesty's Government, for immediate investigation and report to the Government with a view to a settlement.'

The Women's Conference would undoubtedly demand that *women should have strong representation on this tribunal, and that in all disputes in regard to women's employment, a woman of standing and experience, (the nation has many such to draw upon) should be the chairman of the tribunal, or in case of the appointment of a sole arbiter, a woman should be the arbiter of the dispute.*

(4) That proper safeguards in regard to hours, wages, and conditions be arranged in conjunction with representatives of the women concerned, and that no woman shall be compelled to work under conditions which the representative of the organisation to which she belongs, reports to be unsatisfactory.

This is a moment of very vital importance to women, calling for all our energy and resource, all our earnestness, all our solidarity.

Let us band ourselves together—sinking our differences—to build up a position of dignity and security for our sisters, in order that as free citizens they may give their services to the nation willingly and with enthusiasm.

'Our equal birthright'

[*The Woman's Dreadnought*, 14 August 1915]

Do you believe that if all the wealthy landowners, merchants and manufacturers, all the great financiers the world over, had been told that their incomes would be cut down to a bare subsistence level if war were declared, and so long as war should last, that they would have agreed to war?

Do you believe that they would have agreed to war, if they had known that they would have to starve and stint as you do?

Do you believe that any Kaiser, Czar, or Emperor, could cause war, alone, without the help of the financiers and the people?

Do you know that the great armament firms are international, that they have directors, who are both British and German, and that they have supplied arms to both sides in the war, and that Great Britain is paying a royalty to Krupps of Germany for every fuse we fire?

Do you not think it is dangerous to give the right to supply armaments to any private firm? If a man sells tea, he tries to make you want to drink it, if he sells guns, he tries to make you shoot.

Do you not want to get behind the armament firms that flourish by our fighting, and the merchants and shippers, who in their desire to open markets, consider the people between them and their trading only as pawns in the game?

Do you remember that when the Russian people were fighting for their freedom against an oppression more terrible than anything we know, the financiers of Great Britain lent money to the Czar and his Ministers to crush them down?

Do you remember that when the British dockers were striking, the German dockers sent money to them to help them to hold out?

Do you not want to get behind the financiers, to the workers of the other nations, in order that you may discover together *why* it is that you should fight, and together solve the differences that arise?

Do you remember that on Christmas Day there was a truce between the English and the German soldiers?

How was it that the men who had been murdering each other for months past were able to want this truce and enjoy it together? It was because they were human beings with minds of the same sort, who had lived the same sort of lives, and Christmas had for them all the self same memories. The religious ideal of Christmas, as drawing together all mankind in peace and goodwill as children of one family in the sight of God, and the intimate tender home memories with which it was interwoven in all the soldiers' hearts, accomplished a miracle indeed! It enabled them to cast out fear,—the strongest of our masters—fear of the men of the opposing armies concealed in the opposite trenches, fear of the officers beside them, armed with the frequently exercised power of life and death over those who disobey.

What Christmas did in some portions of the opposing lines, a greater catastrophe than war would also do. If God should send a rain of fire from heaven, or if tremendous floods or an earthquake should arise, immediately the opposing troops would cease their fighting, and as poor bewildered human fugitives, would rush to each other for sympathy and aid.

Deep down beyond all race and class distinctions we are human beings, with the same needs and instincts, and this is revealed to us when we are threatened by great catastrophes arising from non-human things.

We are suffering now, both nationally and internationally, from our imperfect social organisations, and the mistakes and difficulties that come from fear or suspicion of each other. It is because the people of the various countries fear each other that they are prevailed upon to fight. It is because they fear to trust to their equal birthright as human beings that they allow evil social conditions to prevail at home.

Those who are afraid to trust to the possibility of there being enough for everyone, in a state of society in which equal opportunities should be given to all, strive to maintain things as they are.

We must rid ourselves of the idea that there are any *real* class distinctions. The only essential differences that there are between us, as human beings, are to be found amongst the individuals in every social class. The class distinctions that we know at present are due to the system of allowing one individual to benefit by the toil of others, and that of putting money out to interest, under which a sum of money is never spent by its owner, but always remains intact, and enables him to exact an unending toll of the things that other people work to produce. The War loan is a striking example of this.

These things are defended on the ground that production must be organised, but the capitalist is not necessarily an organiser, and we must work towards a state of society in which the person who undertakes the, to him, congenial work of organising, shall not be given a larger share of the general benefits produced, than those who are responsible for other forms of labour.

During the war it has been demonstrated very clearly that production organised by competing individuals, each striving for his own private benefit is inefficient in the extreme.

It is because the inefficiency has been very glaring that the Ministry of Munitions has been instituted. Yet still the Government refuses to take the making of munitions out of private hands and even extends the practice, so that such firms as Bryant and Mays, the match makers, are given facilities for becoming munition makers to the Government, and can get a share of the munition profits; although if munitions had been nationalised, war profits would have been saved. It is universally admitted that shippers, coal owners, and those who deal in wheat, meat and other forms of food, have been making enormous profits out of the war; but the Government refuses to prevent these powerful interests from preying upon the consumers.

There is no doubt that the Government is sacrificing the interests of the people to those of the financiers at the present time. Do you believe that you can trust the Government not to do so, when the terms of peace come to be decided?

Do you consider it is safe at any time to allow the foreign policy of the nation to be hidden from the people?

You will be told that it is useless to try to democratise our British foreign policy, because the foreign policies of the other Powers are autocratic and, therefore, our own regard for the welfare of the peoples of the world could do nothing to prevent wars.

Do not believe that. With certainty believe that there are people in every nation whose faith is built on the brotherhood of mankind and those men and women, though they are unknown to us, are striving even as we strive. Every success of ours makes their fight less difficult. Social reforms initiated in one country spread across the world just as scientific discoveries and the developments in music and painting do.

Before the war, during the war, after the war is done, the old striving for more perfect human development continues and will continue for all time.

As we take our part in the struggle let us determine that we will not want for ourselves more of the world's material goods than the common average for all, but that that common average shall be a high and abundant one for all the people of the world.

'Human suffrage'

[*The Woman's Dreadnought*, 18 December 1915]

Before the War large numbers of women and men were giving all their thought and energy to securing a million votes for the women of the British Isles—a million votes for thirteen million women!

The demand was recommended on account of its 'moderation.' In the light of the great world conflict does it not seem miserably inadequate, timidly weak and mean?

'I believe that a woman should have a vote if she pays rates and taxes.' How that phrase jars and wearies one? Can any tax count beside the toil of hand and brain that a human worker gives in a life time, or in comparison with the bringing into the world of another living, sentient human being, whose thoughts and deeds may add immeasurably to the common stock? When a man goes out to take part in the hideous slaughter of the battlefield the paying of rates and taxes is a forgotten thought to him; the fact that he has paid cannot buy him off, and his being too poor for taxing will not save him from being sent to the front if Conscription comes.

Cast away the trivial ideas of the professional politician. The world conflict, with its dehumanising hate and violence, and the widespread peril and loss that draw poor mothers and wives together, should cause our minds to dwell only on real, vital things.

What is a vote but a voice in the affairs that concern us all? Surely there was never a time in which we could see so clearly as now that the interests of all the people are closely interwoven, and that everyone of us must have a vote in the management of our world.

Cast away the idea that it is expedient to ask for an instalment of justice in accordance with some petty, ill-drafted, fugitive politician's rule, instead of basing our demand on the infinite and eternal fact of our common humanity.

In the hard, hungry days that followed the Napoleonic wars, the brave old reformers did not want the vote for merely academic reasons. They fought for it because they saw in it a means of giving all the people the power to free themselves from gaunt and urgent want, and to protect themselves from cruel exploitation and harsh injustice. They wanted to give every man an equal chance to share in controlling the destinies of the nation.

Those old reformers asked for no half-measures, suggested no paltering compromises, but demanded Universal Suffrage. They were determined to wring from the autocrats in power as much justice as they could, and not to abate their demands until they had got all they asked. Theirs is a spirit that we may well emulate. Our experiences are likely to reproduce theirs in many things.

The War, with its waste and destruction, is intensifying the international strife that is always with us, the struggle of human evolution towards a higher development of social life.

In every nation the forces of reaction are gaining ground because of War conditions. Militarism is becoming more strongly entrenched.

Unorganised individualism is shown to be wasteful, and the extraordinary strain which war is putting upon human energy and material resources, has necessitated, and after the War will continue to necessitate, in every country more extensive control and co-ordination by the central government than has hitherto been known.

State action may be of two kinds. It may mean compulsory regulation of the bulk of the population by a small official class, in the interests of the powerful wealthy few who pull the strings—the vast mass of the people being used as mere pawns in an almost limitless army. Or State action may mean the co-operation of free citizens, each with an equal voice in the decisions which are adopted for the benefit of all.

After the War, in every country the struggle that is always going on between these two ideas, the idea of coercion and the idea of co-operation, will be intensified, and become the supreme issue, both in national and international affairs. In the international field the application of these ideas will be seen, on the one hand by a demand for larger armies and navies, a warfare of tariffs, and a more truculent dealing with the claims of rival nations. On the other hand will be a striving towards international arbitration and disarmament, and the building up of a league of peace to include all nations.

Our attitude towards the franchise issue will be one of the test questions which shall decide whether we are on the side of coercion or on that of co-operation.

At present the franchise qualification in this country is based on property. It is suggested that there should also be a qualification for naval and military service. The forms of service which human beings can render to the nation are infinite. Who shall measure them or decide between them? Every one of us should spend our lives in doing some part of the general service. The only qualification on which we should base our demand for the franchise is that of our common humanity. We should demand a vote for every human being of full age, without regard to property or sex.

The article which we publish from Martina Kramers, of Holland, shows us that the Dutch women have adopted the procedure which the Women's Suffrage Movement has hitherto followed here. When the men had only a narrow and restricted franchise, the Dutch women Suffragists asked that that narrow franchise should be extended to women also. Now that Manhood Suffrage has been extended to the men of Holland, the women at last are pressing for a vote for every woman. Hitherto, they have been sitting on the fence of compromise, and have refrained from declaring themselves for human suffrage. Only now are they making whole-hearted common cause with the forces of democracy.

In every country where the women have begun working for their enfranchisement before the enactment of Manhood Suffrage, the same thing appears to have happened. The women have not thought it expedient to demand human suffrage; they have asked for admission to the existing narrow franchise. *But in each country they have had to wait until the narrow franchise has been swept away.*

They have had the humiliation of seeing their demand for citizenship thrust aside again and again, whilst men have secured concession after concession, until at last, by the granting of Manhood Suffrage, the principle of human right to the franchise has been admitted. Then, in Australia, New Zealand, Finland, Norway, Denmark, Iceland, and thirteen States of America full human suffrage, including men and women, has been secured in a comparatively short time.

In no country, save the little Isle of Man with its handful of inhabitants, *have women succeeded in winning the vote before the property qualification for men had been abolished.*

This fact should not for one moment lead us to think that women should wait for the vote in this country until men have secured Manhood Suffrage. No, indeed! It should spur us on to throw ourselves unreservedly into the struggle for human Suffrage, for every woman and for every man.

Every property qualification must of necessity act more unjustly towards women than towards men, because so much of women's service receives no monetary recompense, because the husbands, and, not the wives, are householders.

It is true that the franchise on the men's present terms would give a majority of votes to women of the working class, because the working class is actually in such an immense majority; but an undue proportion of the women voters of every class would be elderly widows, whose time for developing new ideas, in most cases, has gone by. The young mother with her children growing up around her, who should be voicing the ideals of the coming womanhood, would be disqualified, together with the mass of women factory workers, who need the power of the vote most urgently.

How can we expect that such a restricted form of franchise should arouse that immense volume of popular enthusiasm that assuredly will be needed to sweep votes for women past the old political prejudices, on to the Statute Book?

Women who cling to the narrow demand for the old out-of-date form of franchise will be driven into the camp of the coercionists, and separated from the great democratic movement which, in spite of all attempts at restriction, is growing and consolidating and, perhaps even before the War is over, will arise in full force of overwhelming fervour to demand that the democratic principle shall be applied to every department of our national life.

People say: 'You cannot ask for a vote for every woman, because every man has not got one'; and add: 'You must not ask for a vote for every woman, because the men ought to get more votes, if they want them, for themselves.'

Such arguments are cramping and destructive, they should be cast away from us—lovers of freedom. Fight for freedom for all humanity—they make no distinction of sex.

Surely it is time that the British Suffrage movement should come together, reorganise its programme, and write on its banners: 'Human Suffrage—a vote for every man and woman of full age!'

Part II

Revolutionary communism
1917–24

Pankhurst's socialist–feminist Workers' Suffrage Federation (WSF), formed from the East London Federation of Suffragettes in 1916, began by campaigning for universal suffrage and 'social and economic freedom for the people'. Denounced by her mother, Mrs Emmeline Pankhurst, who was now working for the Government's war effort, and generally unsupported by the people in the East End, Sylvia pursued the pacifist cause and continued to argue for a negotiated peace settlement. But the issue which was to split the Pankhurst women irrevocably and permanently was the 1917 Russian Revolution.

Mrs Pankhurst volunteered to lobby the Russian leader, Kerensky, in person, in order to keep Russia committed to war, and in time became a fervent anti-communist. Sylvia's reaction to the revolution was exhilaration, and beginning on 24 March 1917, she began to publish in *The Woman's Dreadnought*, the paper she had edited since 1914, accounts of the complex political changes taking place in Russia. She embraced the Bolshevik October revolution in her article 'The Lenin Revolution' (reprinted here), and wondered how the tardy workers of Britain could be roused to the same effect. On 28 July 1917, to mark the radicalisation the Revolution had brought, the paper was renamed *The Workers' Dreadnought* (which, to add to the confusion, became plain *Workers' Dreadnought* on 31 January 1920). By early 1918 she was promoting the idea of workers' councils as the revolutionary means of empowering the people and in the same year formed another publishing outlet for communist literature, the People's Russian Information Bureau. Through her publishing endeavours she made available the work of, for example, Lenin, Trotsky, Maxim Gorky, Georg Lukács, Bukharin, Alexandra Kollontai, and Clara Zetkin.

By 1919, Pankhurst was actively working with the 'Hands Off Russia' campaign to stop the Allied blockade of Russia (see 'You Are Called to the War'), and was part of the increasingly revolutionary movement in Great Britain which was spreading through the Scottish shop stewards committees, the Plebs League, sections of the Independent Labour Party (ILP), the British Socialist Party (BSP), the Socialist Labour Party (SLP) and the South Wales Socialist Society (SWSS). But as the article 'Towards a Communist Party' shows, Pankhurst, by February 1920, was against any idea of reformism and was clearly distancing herself and the WSF from those in the BSP and SLP who were much more ambivalent about fielding candidates for Parliament and affiliating to the Labour Party. During the unity negotiations of 1919 and 1920, initiated to try to unite all the separate factions in a single Communist Party of Great Britain (CPGB), and despite Lenin's written appeal to the 'infantile' left-wing groups to drop their opposition to Parliament, Pankhurst's WSF, the SWSS and a number of other groups decided to withdraw from the negotiations and in June 1920 they set themselves up as the Communist Party–British Section of the Third International (CP–BSTI). At this moment, Pankhurst published her manifesto, 'A Constitution for British Soviets' (reprinted here), which concerns the setting up of both workshop and household social soviets, explicitly to enfranchise both workers and mothers, and to provide direct services to meet the needs of women and children. She followed up the rather schematic manifesto with a short story in which such a transformation had taken place and both housework and child-care had been socialised, which she published as 'Co-operative Housekeeping' (reprinted here). Far from abandoning feminism, Pankhurst was the first woman in Britain to see the potential for combining the politics of workers' control and household soviets which would politicise women based in the home and community.

In August 1920, she evaded Special Branch surveillance and made a dangerous clandestine journey to Moscow to attend the Second Congress of the Third International, where she was able to debate with Lenin; her account of her journey, her impressions of Lenin and the revolutionary transformation of Russian society were published in a series of articles in the *Dreadnought*, one of which is reprinted here, and which were later collected in a book, *Soviet Russia As I Saw It* (1921). As a result of these negotiations Sylvia returned to Britain and accepted unity with the CPGB, but against the wishes of the leadership retained her independent voice and the editorship of the *Dreadnought*. Her position was severely weakened in October 1920 when she was arrested for sedition for publishing two anonymous articles inciting the armed forces to mutiny, and sentenced to six months' imprisonment. While she was imprisoned, she wrote a good deal of political poetry, concentrating on the plight of her sisters and on the poverty which had led many of them to commit their 'crimes'; these were published in *Writ on Cold Slate* (1922), two poems from which are republished here.

In her absence, the paper was taken off the list of approved publications of the Communist Party and when, after her release, Pankhurst continued to use the *Dreadnought* to criticise the policies of the CPGB, and the backsliding of Soviet communists, she was expelled from the Party in September 1921. In protest, she wrote in 'Freedom of discussion' on 17 September: 'If we were before the barricades, if we were in the throes of revolution, or even somewhere near it, I could approve a rigidity of discipline which is wholly out of place here and now.' She believed that if 'left' ideas were stifled at the outset, while the Party was still establishing itself, the whole movement would become rigid and stultified. But there was no place for Pankhurst's vision of an open, democratic, feminist communism in the mainstream movement. Though she struggled to publish the *Dreadnought* for another three years, giving space to the ideas of other European left-wing communists, and publishing a number of articles by Alexandra Kollontai on the 'Workers' Opposition' to the soviet government in 1921–22, lack of funds and support finally forced her to close down in 1924. By then she was totally disenchanted with Russian communism which she believed, after the abandonment of the movement towards workers' control and the establishment of the New Economic Policy, had reverted to capitalist principles; her articles 'To Lenin' and 'Capitalism or Communism for Russia?' are brutally critical.

Perhaps she was naive to believe that the Bolsheviks had even come near to establishing a classless, wageless, soviet-run communist system, but at least she continued to remind the international communist movement during this period that its politics ought to be centrally concerned with the transfer of power, not to bureaucratic Party administrators, but to the people themselves, organised into household and workshop councils as 'independent co-operators'.

Pankhurst's struggles inside the communist movement were not esoteric or eccentric, but should be seen in the context of the debates that were being conducted inside and outside the Labour movement about the nature of working-class political organisation and action. Pankhurst elaborated her vision of a democratic communist society which would liberate men and women from classed and gendered oppression, but by 1924, no-one, either inside or outside the communist movement, was listening.

'The Lenin revolution: what it means to democracy'

[*The Workers' Dreadnought*, 17 November 1917]

'Anarchy in Russia', say the newsagents' placards. The capitalist newspapers denounce the latest Russian Revolution in unmeasured terms, and even the working men and women in the street too often echo their angry denunciations. Yet the latest revolt of the Russian Revolution, the revolt with which the name of Lenin is associated, has been brought about in order that the workers of Russia may no longer be disinherited and oppressed. This revolt is the happening which definitely makes the Russian Revolution of the twentieth century the first of its kind. (. . .) We can look with confidence to the votes of the Russian people which, as yet, we cannot feel towards the votes of our own countrymen and women, because the Russian people have lately proved themselves. In the Moscow Municipal elections in the summer 72 per cent of the votes were cast for Socialist candidates. In Petrograd also the Socialists secured the majority of the votes. Compare the recent British Trade Union Congress and Labour Party manifestos with this of the Russian Soviet. Compare the general outlook of such working-class bodies in the two countries! Why are the British organisations so far behind the Russian?

War hardships, greater in Russia than in any other belligerent country, have contributed to make Russia riper for revolution than the others and to increase the need of her people for Socialism; but this is not the sole reason why the Russian workers are politically ahead of ours. In Russia the politics of advanced politicians have long been more definite and scientific, and, above all, more democratic, than the politics of those who are held to be advanced politicians in this country. The British Labour Party has hitherto existed without a programme; the programme which its Executive now proposes for it is so vaguely drawn that Mr Sidney Webb, a member of its Executive, is able to describe it as embodying: 'A Socialism which is no more specific than a definite repudiation of the individualism that characterises all the political parties of the past generation.'

Our Labour Conferences deal chiefly with fugitive partial reforms of the moment, in a spirit rather of opportunism than of adventure and research; and, to a lesser extent, the same thing may be said even of our Socialist Conferences. In the political field we believe we are right in saying that neither a Labour Party, Trade Union nor ILP Conference has discussed, at any rate within recent years, such essential democratic institutions as the Initiative Referendum and Recall, institutions which are all actually in being in the Western States of USA, and which are partially established elsewhere. A Russian Socialist woman said to us: 'People here are actually discussing whether the Referendum is democratic; why, I realised the democratic importance of the Referendum when I was fifteen years of age!' The following evening we heard Mr Bernard Shaw assuming, in addressing a Fabian audience, that our populace is too ignorant to be trusted to use the Referendum, and declaring that if it were established in this country, legislation would be held up altogether. The Lettish Social–Democratic Workers' Party was formed in 1904; at its second Congress in June, 1905, it placed the following political reforms on its programme:—

(1) Government by the people—i.e., the supreme power of the State—to be placed in the hands of a Legislative Assembly consisting of representatives elected by the whole population of Russia.

(2) Adult Suffrage—i.e., the right to an equal, secret and direct vote in all elections, local and national—for all citizens, men and women, who have reached the age of 20, according to the proportional representation system. Biennial elections.

But this was a long time ago; the Russian Socialists are now heading straight for Socialism, and for years past have been busily hammering out the programme and learning confidence in themselves and in it.

The educational value of a programme, which every new recruit to the Party must consider and accept, and every critic must discuss, is very great, and the Russian Socialist parties have not overlooked it. They have insisted that their members shall make up their minds as to what they believe and what they want.

In this country we have in the workers' movement a very large and very cautious body of people which always shrinks from taking any step that appears adventurous or new and which always seems to be looking out of the corner of its eye to find out what the capitalist Press and public is saying and thinking of what it does. There are also, both inside and outside the Labour movement, large masses of people who are vaguely revolutionary in their tendencies and always ready to criticise those in power, but who have never mastered any economic or political theory. Their criticism is purely personal; they believe that if only Mr Asquith, Mr Lloyd George, or Mr Bonar Law can be turned out of office all will be well. Successive Ministries pass and re-pass; they are opposed to all of them but never learn that their quarrel is not with the individual Minister, but with the system which he upholds. Whilst our people are largely divided into one or other of these two categories we shall not make much progress. A great educational work is necessary to open the people's eyes to induce them to study Socialism, and to compare it with the capitalist system, the evils of which they now endure. Without the knowledge that such study will bring them, revolution would only mean a change of master, however successfully it might be accomplished; with that knowledge the people can do without delay all that they will.

The Russian problem is our problem: it is simply whether the people understand Socialism and whether they desire it.

Meanwhile, our eager hopes are for the speedy success of the Bolsheviks of Russia: may they open the door which leads to freedom for the people of all lands!

'Look to the future'

[*The Workers' Dreadnought*, 16 February 1918]

VOTES FOR WOMEN
SEX DISABILITY NOT REMOVED

Women have won the vote; no, let us correct ourselves, *some* women have been given the vote. The new measure only enfranchises from four to six million women out of a total of more than thirteen million.

Less than half the women will get the vote by the new Act. The soldier lad of eighteen years will be a voter, the mother who maintains her children cannot vote till she is thirty years of age, and only then if she or her husband is a householder or latchkey voter, and if neither he nor she has been so unfortunate as to be forced to ask the Poor Law authorities for aid. The adult sons of the household will go to the poll; the adult daughters will be debarred. No, the new Act does not remove the sex disability; it does not establish equal suffrage. And by its University and business franchises the Act still upholds in statute form the old class prejudices; the old checks and balances designed to prevent the will of the majority, who are the workers, from being registered without handicap.

But some people, we learn, are rejoicing with an exceeding joy over the passage of the new Act, and are making impassioned speeches, declaring its coming to be a great victory, which will herald in a 'new world'.

Saddened and oppressed by the great world tragedy, by the multiplying graves of men, and the broken hearts of women, we hold aloof from such rejoicings; they stride with a hollow and unreal sound upon our consciousness. Some of the organisations formed for the work of securing the vote are dissolving, or taking counsel whether to dissolve. The WSF [Workers' Suffrage Federation] has long engaged in many activities which place on its shoulders a heavy burden of toil and responsibility; a burden of necessary work which it would seem almost an act of treachery to lay down now. The franchise is but partly won, but franchise activities have formed a mere fraction of our activities these many years past. This is but a partial prejudiced franchise, which has been extended to women, not graciously, but in a grudging spirit. Yet even had it come in full measure, justly and equally to all men and women, it could not seem to us a great joy-giving boon in these sad days in which Government by politicians has plunged the world into this lengthy War and placed humanity upon the rack! If it is to survive, very robust must be our faith in the possibility of re-creating the dry, crumbling bones of Parliament, and of filling its benches with vigorous uncompromising Socialists, determined to take immediate action to sweep away the all-embracing system of privileges, and corruptions attendant on modern capitalism and to establish Socialism in our time. Is it possible to establish Socialism with the Parliament at Westminster as its foundation? If we would have our policy grow and develop intelligently and usefully with the times, so that we may go forging on ahead in the van of progress, not falling in laggingly at its rear, we must consider very seriously whether our efforts should not be bent on the setting aside of this present Parliamentary system under which the peoples suffer, and the substitution for it of a local, national, and international system, built up on an occupational basis, of which the members shall be but the delegates of those who are carrying on the world's work; and shall be themselves workers, drawn, but for a space, from the bench, the mine, the desk, the kitchen, or the nursery; and sent to voice the needs and desires of others like themselves. (. . .)

'The election'

[*The Workers' Dreadnought*, 14 December 1918]

'No, I'm not going to vote', said a poor woman in a 'bus, 'the British Government would take the blood from your heart'. In those bitter words she summed up her attitude towards the empty political balderdash, which now issues in prolific streams from the mouths of Parliamentary candidates and their supporters, and all but fills the newspapers.

We hope nothing from this election, save that it may serve to spur the workers on to abolish Parliament, the product and instrument of the capitalist system, and to establish in its place Councils of Workers' Delegates, which shall be the executive instruments for creating and maintaining the Socialist community.

The Parliament which is now being elected cannot possibly be fitted to cope with the great and important changes that are impending. The Coalition is the Party of Capitalist reaction, the Liberal Party is but a weaker embodiment of the same thing. As for the Labour Party—if all, and more than all, its candidates were elected, even if, by reason of their numbers, it could capture the reins of Government, it would give us nothing more than a wishy-washy Reformist Government, which, when all the big issues that really matter came to be decided, would be swept along in the wake of capitalist policy. The list of Labour Party candidates presents a curious medley of ex-Liberals, ex-Tories, Jingo Trade Unionists of narrow outlook, middle-class pacifists, with a small sprinkling of Socialists. It would be impossible to secure decisive action from such an assemblage on any really vital question.

Mr Sidney Webb, whose ideas, long discarded by the awakened rank and file in the workshops, still holds the executive in thrall, has foisted upon the Party the tame, middle-class reformism embodied in that document, ridiculous as coming from a workers' party, which is called 'Labour and the New Social Order.' The pettifogging reforms there laid down will change nothing; they will leave the poor still poor, the rich still rich. When every one of those resolutions has been enacted, still we shall have with us men and women dwarfed in every faculty by chronic want: the class that is lectured and patronised, written about and legislated for, and for whom charities are arranged, the parents, whose children it is said to be necessary to 'protect' from their 'ignorance'. The acceptance of Webb's new social order will neither empty the prisons, which are filled by poverty's crimes, nor deprive the rich Theosophists of the opportunity to develop the gentler side of their natures by visiting the slums.

Webb and the majority of the Executive, the Parliamentary candidates, and the prominent personages in the Labour Party, are struggling hard against a philosophy, growing fast amongst the rank and file—a philosophy which it is found convenient to call Bolshevism; but which, of course, is simply Socialism. Says Webb in *The Daily News* of December 10th:—

The essence of Bolshevism is a contempt for Parliamentary institutions; the loss of faith in Democracy as we understand it; reliance on 'direct action' by the wage-earners themselves; the supersession of the House of Commons by 'Workmen's and Soldiers' Councils,' from which all but the manual workers are excluded; and the dictatorship of the Proletariat.' This is the revolutionary epidemic which is now spreading westward over Europe. (. . .)

Webb for a political generation has been called a Socialist. Was he really a Socialist in his youth? If he has ever had a glimmering of the vision of Socialism he must surely realise that, under Socialism, we shall all be the proletariat, that there will be but one class. In the transition stage, when people who employ others and live on incomes they have not earned still remain, surely it is but wise to concentrate the voting strength in the hands of those who are workers. It is right to do this, if only as a symbol that honour is due to the worker, not to those who live as parasites on the wealth produced by others. If in the transition stages the Webbs, as well as the Northcliffes and Rockefellers, should be deprived of votes surely their practice in wielding the pen still gives them more than their share of influence. The tide of Socialism, bringing all power to the workers, is sweeping over Europe and waves of Socialist thought, of working-class longing, are rising to meet it in this country; Webb and those who are holding the reins of power in the Labour Party shrink from it, fearfully trembling. Unconscious lackeys of the capitalist system, instinctively they fear that system's fall. Is there no spirit in their souls to answer to the call of Socialist fraternity? It seems not.

'You are called to the war'

[*The Workers' Dreadnought*, 19 April 1919]

Wake up! wake up! Oh, sleepy British people! The new war is in full blast, and you are called to fight in it; you cannot escape; you must take part!

Out of the old inter-capitalist war between the Allies and the Central Empires, the war, the actual crude, cruel fighting between the workers and the capitalists has emerged. Soldiers who enlisted, or were conscribed for the old war have been quietly kept on to fight in the new war which began without any formal declaration. They have not been asked: 'Do you approve this war; do you understand it?' They have merely been detained and will now fight against their comrades.

Officially the British Government is not at war with Socialism in Europe, though in actual fact British and other Allied soldiers have been fighting it for a long time, and British money and munitions are keeping the soldiers of other governments in the field against it. There has been no official declaration of war, but the House of Commons, on April 9th, expressed its opinion in support of the war on Socialism in general, and on Russian Socialism in particular. This expression of opinion the Home Secretary claims to have been unanimous, and certainly when he challenged Members to express a contrary opinion no voice of dissent was audible enough to reach the columns of Hansard or the press. No Member of Parliament has written to the newspapers to make his protest.

Some Socialists tell us that the floor of the House of Commons is a splendid platform for propaganda; but the trouble is that when they get into the House, their courage seems to evaporate like a child's soap bubble. We have heard of Labour Members of Parliament being ready to do and say all sorts of heroic things to get themselves put out of the House, to arrest the world's attention on some appropriate occasion. That is not much, of course, as compared with running the risk of death in the horrible trenches or with being incarcerated for years in prison; but here was an opportunity, if ever there was one, for Members of Parliament to display all their pluck! Clem Edwards, the notorious anti-Socialist, moved the adjournment of the House, 'to draw attention to a definite matter of urgent public importance, namely, the alleged overtures from the Bolshevik regime in Russia to the Peace Conference in Paris.'

In the debate Brigadier-General Page Croft and Lieut. Col. Guinness suggested that some Members of Parliament support the Bolsheviki. Did any man cry out: 'Yes, we are proud to stand by our fellow workers in their fight for Socialism'? No, on the contrary, the Labour Members broke out into cries of protest against the suggestion that they had any such sympathies. Bottomley rewarded them by an assurance of 'the profoundest and most affectionate respect'. The Home Secretary hammered in the point, saying the debate had called forth 'from every quarter of the House an indignant repudiation that the House contained a single Bolshevik sympathiser.' He described the Soviet Government as 'a mere gang of bloodthirsty ruffians,' and said it would strengthen the hands of the Government to know there is 'no quarter' for any Soviet supporters, 'at any rate in the British House of Commons.'

Even then there was no protest! Where was the lead to the country, and especially to the lads who may mistakenly enlist in the counter-revolutionary armies, which our 'leaders' in Parliament might have given? Of what were the opponents of the resolution afraid? Either they are cravens, or their opposition to the new war is of a very lukewarm character. The real work for the Socialist revolution must be done outside Parliament.

On April 10th, the day after the House of Commons has

thus expressed itself, the first contingent of volunteers set sail for Russia. (. . .)

The British men who are in the army of the Government are fighting against the Workers' Socialist Revolution just as are the men who are fighting in the armies of the capitalist Governments of Germany, France, Italy, America, Poland, Czechoslovakia, and any other governments which are joining in the strife. In all these armies the truth that they are fighting Socialism has dawned on some of the soldiers, and many of them have deserted and joined the Red Armies of the working-class Socialism.

Many who are not actually in the fighting rank have nevertheless ranged themselves against the capitalist governments and on the side of the Soviets. Philips Price, who is editing a Bolshevik newspaper in Russia and many other British people are aiding the Soviets over there. In this country we can also help by working with might and main to establish the British Soviets, by telling the soldiers, sailors, and workers the issues that are at stake in the International Civil War.

That war has now spread far beyond the boundaries of Russia. General Smuts has left Hungary abruptly, finding that Soviet Hungary stood firm for Communism. Shall we presently see the armies of capitalism marching on Hungary? *The Evening News* reported that the Serbs had refused to obey the order of the Big Four to send their troops to attack Hungary, because the Allies has not yet recognised the kingdom of the Serbs, Croats and Slovenes. But the Allies will presently secure a capitalist army from somewhere to carry on the fight. Paderewski is reported to have refused to send Polish troops to fight Communism, unless Dantzig and other territory is conceded to Poland. The Allies will bargain with Paderewski till they have bought his support or substituted a Polish ruler who is more amenable.

Churchill has revealed the fact that Germany is ordered, as one of the peace conditions, to fight Communism, and that the Germans may buy their way into the League of Nations by doing this efficiently. Indeed, the entire policy of the Paris Conference is dominated by the policy its members are pursuing in the war between the capitalists and the workers. Both false and foolish are the stories, so industriously circulated, that the British and American politicians at the Peace Conference are the pacifying influences and that they are working against a peace of annexation and oppression; whilst the French and Italian politicians are the greedy Jingoes, who, by demanding all sorts

89

D

of advantages for themselves, are preventing the peace. The plain fact is that British and American capitalists have got what they set out to gain by the war with the Central Empires and the French and Italians have not. (. . .)

It is stated now that Germany is to pay the Allies between ten and twelve thousand million pounds and that the payments will be spread over fifty years, during which the Allies will occupy Germany, we suppose. Evidently it is thought that fifty years will not be too much for the crushing out of Bolshevism. Moreover, after such a period of occupation, history teaches us to anticipate that the occupying Powers will consider it inexpedient to withdraw. Ireland, Egypt, and India all stand as landmarks calling us to this conclusion.

To this pass has capitalism brought us. Europe, neutral and belligerent alike, is starving: not a household in our country, or any other, but mourns some of its members who lost their lives in the last war; and the world, in order to maintain the capitalist system, stands on the threshold of a time of still more extensive war.

British workers, which side are you on in the International Civil War?

'Towards a communist party'

[*Workers' Dreadnought*, 21 February 1920]

In *The Call* of February 12th Albert Inkpin, secretary to the BSP, gives an account of private unity negotiations to form a Communist Party of the four organisations which at present declare affiliation to the Third or Communist International, inaugurated at Moscow.

Before dealing with the general principles involved, which are of very much greater importance than the mere details of the negotiations I will add a little to Inkpin's account and make also some corrections in it.

The beginning of the negotiations dates a good deal further back than Inkpin puts it; in fact, from the summer of 1918, when members of the WSF [Workers' Socialist Federation, led by Pankhurst], hearing that almost the whole of the BSP Executive would be affected by the raising of the conscription age, approached the BSP in a spirit of comradeship, with a tentative offer of fusion which was very cordially received. The WSF, however, drew back from the negotiations, because in the course of them, E. C. Fairchild stated that he did not think the organisation should decide between Parliament and bourgeois democracy and the Soviets and the proletarian dictatorship, as the goal towards which our propaganda should be aiming. Inkpin and Alexander who took part in the negotiations, did not dissent from Fairchild's statement, and as it was proposed that Fairchild should be co-editor of the proposed joint organ of the new party, it was evident that a revolutionary Socialist body, like the WSF, could not possibly agree to fusion.

At Whitsuntide, 1919, the WSF annual conference instructed its Executive to open negotiations with the BSP, SLP, and South Wales Socialist Society, for the formation of a united Communist Party. The BSP had by this time declared for the Soviets, though it was still waiting to ballot its members on the subject of affiliation to the Third International. Messages had in the meantime come direct from the Third International urging the formation of a Communist Party in Britain and, as Inkpin says, a unity conference was called shortly afterwards.

THE PROPOSED UNITY COMPROMISE

As Inkpin further says, a proposal for unity emerged on the basis of the following planks:-

(1) Affiliation to the Third International.
(2) The Dictatorship of the Proletariat.
(3) The Soviets instead of Parliament.
(4) A Referendum of the new party to be taken three months after its formation to decide whether it should affiliate to the Labour Party.

The WSF contends that it was also decided to take a referendum on the question of Parliamentary action three months after the formation of the new party, a question of great importance in this country, as the letter from W. Gallacher, which follows this article, will plainly indicate to those not already aware of it. As I was at the time acting in a secretarial capacity to the unity conference, I took notes of the conference and wrote to each of the societies embodying these notes. The five points, enumerated above, were set forth in my letter. Nevertheless the BSP and SLP, though they did not dissent from my version of the proceedings at the time, seem to have overlooked the Parliamentary point and did not add it to the ballot of their members, which they took later on.

RANK AND FILE REFUSES LABOUR PARTY AFFILIATION

The BSP ballot paper, as Inkpin points out, grouped the three main planks with the question of a referendum on the Labour Party affiliation, as the condition of forming a united party, and asked its membership to vote 'yes or no.' The result was a majority for unity on that basis.

The SLP asked its membership, as Inkpin says, for two votes; (1) on the question of unity on the basis of the three main planks; (2) on whether a referendum should be taken of the new party on affiliation to the Labour Party. (. . .)

The WSF ballot asked the views of its members on each of the five questions separately, and also inquired whether the members would agree for the sake of unity to the suggested referendum on the Labour Party and Parliamentary action. The result was an overwhelming majority for the three main points, and against Parliamentary action and affiliation to the Labour Party. On the question whether the referendum should be agreed to in order to secure unity of the four parties, the voting was equal.

Inkpin goes on to explain that whilst the unity negotiations were proceeding between the four organisations, the BSP privately make special endeavours to enter into relations with the SLP, but these failed.

Inkpin next refers to a further conference on unity, called by it in January. As a matter of fact there were two January Conferences; one on January 8th, one on January 24th. The SLP did not attend the conference of January 8th, and at the time the result of their ballot was not known; the conference was informed that the SLP had not replied to the invitation.

BSP PROPOSAL

As Inkpin says, he proposed on behalf of the BSP:

that the three bodies accepting the unity proposals should proceed on the lines of the original recommendation, leaving it to the logic of events to bring in the SLP. We suggested the immediate establishment of a Standing Joint Committee of the three bodies, to go into the details of amalgamation — finance, papers, offices, and staffs — prepare a draft platform and constitution for the new party, and summon a great national congress to be held at Easter, of all organisations and branches of organisations, local groups, and societies, that were ready to join in, at which the Communist Party should be definitely launched. This Standing Joint Committee should also be empowered, on behalf of the three bodies, to issue manifestos and pronouncements on all matters of national and international importance, act as the British secretariat of the Third International, and conduct a great campaign in the country leading up to the Easter Congress.

As I pointed out at the time, this proposal would have placed the Standing Joint Committee above the Executive of the existing parties in the matter of national and international policy, giving it the right to issue manifestos in their name *before the parties had arrived at a common agreement on policy, and before they had decided whether to fuse or not!* (. . .)

I stated that in my opinion unity without the SLP would not be the unity of all the Communist parties which we had set out to effect, and that a further effort to obtain the presence of the SLP should be made. Moreover, I expressed as my view and that of the WSF, that the BSP forms the right wing of the Communist parties, and that unless the three other parties came in together, there would be a danger that the right wing policy would predominate.

The resolution to adjourn was carried. At the conference of January 24th, when I was not present, a letter was read from the SLP stating that as a majority of its members had voted against unity, it could take no part in negotiations.

The South Wales Socialist Society then moved that the conference should adjourn until after the forthcoming meeting of the Third International and should then meet to receive the report of the delegates to that conference. Though in neither case had the WSF anticipated that the South Wales Socialist Society's proposals would take the form they did, the WSF again found the SWSS proposal wise, and our delegates seconded it. The proposal was carried.

THIRD INTERNATIONAL DECLINES AGAINST AFFILIATION TO LABOUR PARTY

A very interesting unity conference will now take place, because the Third International meeting, which has just been held, has stated that the affiliation of no Communist party will be accepted which has not completely severed its connection with the social patriotic organisations, amongst which, it declares, is the British Labour Party. Therefore it would seem that if that international meeting can be held to speak for the Third International, the Communists of Britain must either be out of the Labour Party or out of the Third International. This is a matter of great importance to those who are considering the formation of a new Communist party.

THE LABOUR PARTY AFFILIATION, THE PRINCIPLES INVOLVED

But let us now proceed to a fuller examination of this question. Inkpin does not seriously argue it. He seems to regard it as a merit not to hold strong views on this, or perhaps on any question that might hinder unity with the BSP, though the BSP policy is of course in a fluid condition and is in process of emergence, under the pressure of circumstances, from the old ideals of the Second International. Inkpin says:

'Personally, I do, because all past experience has shown the stultification that follows isolation from the main body of the working-class movement. But, as I say, I would take my chance. To me the need for the Communist Party is the supreme question – all others are secondary to this.'

'But would affiliation apply for all time?'

'Of course not. No tactics can be determined now to apply for all time. We are in a revolutionary period, and circumstances might speedily arise to compel the Communist Party to leave the Labour Party. Or it might be expelled. In either case it would be, I think, in circumstances that would witness at the same time the secession of large numbers from the Labour Party, which the Communist Party would absorb.'

It will be observed that comrade Inkpin refers to the Labour Party as 'the main body of the working-class movement.' Another comrade of the BSP, at the Third International, just held, put the BSP position more strongly. He said: 'We regard the Labour Party as the organised working-class.'

We do not take this view of the Labour Party. The Labour Party is very large numerically, though its membership is to a great extent quiescent and apathetic, consisting of men and women who have joined the trade unions because their work-mates are trade unionists and to share the friendly benefits.

But we recognise that the great size of the Labour Party is also due to the fact that it is the creation of a school of thought beyond which the majority of the British working class has not yet emerged, though great changes are at work in the mind of the people which will presently alter this state of affairs.

Social patriotic working class parties of bourgeois outlook, like the British Labour Party, exist, or have existed, in every country; the Noske–Scheidemann Social Democratic Party in Germany, the French Socialist Party, and the Socialist Party of America are typical examples. (. . .)

The social patriotic parties of reform, like the British Labour Party, are everywhere aiding the capitalists to maintain the capitalist system; to prevent it from breaking down under the shock which the Great War has caused it, and the growing influence of the Russian Revolution. The bourgeois social patriotic parties, whether they call themselves Labour or Socialist, are everywhere working against the Communist revolution, and they are more dangerous to it than the aggressive capitalists because the reforms they seek to introduce may keep the capitalist *regime* going for some time to come. When the social patriotic reformists come into power, they fight to stave off the workers' revolution with as strong a determination as that displayed by the capitalists, and more effectively, because they understand the methods and tactics and something of the idealism of the working class.

The British Labour Party, like the social patriotic organisations of other countries, will, in the natural development of society, inevitably come into power. It is for the Communists to build up the forces that will overthrow the social patriots, and in this country we must not delay or falter in that work. We must not dissipate our energy in adding to the strength of the Labour Party; its rise to power is inevitable. We must concentrate on making a Communist movement that will vanquish it. The Labour Party will soon be forming a Government; the revolutionary opposition must make ready to attack it.

The BSP sees the division of parties into communist and social patriotic factions which is taking place throughout Europe, but it still wishes to cling to the Labour Party. Why? Does it hope to capture the Labour Party and secure in it a majority to support the Third International? Such a majority has been secured in the Italian Socialist Party, which seems, on a superficial view, to be one Socialist party in Europe which need not split. But the Italian Party will also split. The Third Internationalists captured a great majority of the Bologna Conference, but the majority of the Parliamentary Party is opposed to the majority of the Socialist Party itself, and will undoubtedly secede, taking with it a certain faction.

THE LABOUR PARTY FORTIFIED AGAINST PROGRESS

But the British Labour Party is a much more difficult body to capture than the Italian Party. It is said that the Labour Party is not, strictly speaking, a political party at all, because it is mainly composed of affiliated trade unions; but that fact makes it much more difficult to effect changes in the British Labour Party than in the French, German, Italian, or any other Socialist Party. In such parties both the election of the Executive and officials, and the resolutions governing the policy of the party, are voted upon at the party conferences by delegates from the branches acting under branch instructions. Party Executives and officials are seldom changed; apathetic members, unaware of the changing situation, vote to keep people and things as they are and reactionary officials, retained for old services, nullify any forward move adopted by conferences. Nevertheless new ideas may gradually surge upward, and come to the top at some time or other. But in the British Labour Party there are special brakes to prevent even the slow changes possible in the Continental Socialist parties. Officials appointed for life or for long terms of years, immovable fixtures, bar the way to progress. In many unions a proportion of the delegates to annual conferences is appointed by the national executive. The branches neither appoint delegates to Labour Party congresses, nor vote on resolutions. Divisional conferences and national Executives, national and local officials, prevent the opinion of the rank and file from making itself felt. In all Europe there is no social patriotic organisation so carefully guarded for social patriotism as the British Labour Party.

The British Labour Party is moreover less Socialist than any of the other adherents to the Second International. It was the last to join the Second International because only lately had it advanced even thus far. Its dominant figures were loth to take any step even so small a step as joining the Second International, which might appear to divide them from the capitalist Liberal and Tory parties. The man whose policy represents the centre and majority policy of the Labour Party is Arthur Henderson, the friend of Kerensky. (. . .)

THE COMMUNIST PARTY MUST NOT COMPROMISE

But that is not the mission of the new Communist Party, which must enunciate the Communist programme that is yet to stand when the Soviets are erected and the proletariat dictatorship is in force. The Communist Party must keep its doctrine pure, and its independence of Reformism inviolate; its mission is to lead the way, without stopping or turning, by the direct road to the Communist Revolution.

LABOUR CANDIDATES

Those who believe that a Communist Party can remain in the Labour Party and take part in Parliamentary contests, should realise the position of the unfortunate Communists who elect to become candidates under such auspices. They must first present themselves for selection by the local Labour Parties; after which they may be vetoed by the Party Executive. Since the Labour Party is still thoroughly reformist, but few local Labour Parties are prepared to adopt candidates with any Communist leanings, if any Communists succeed in getting adopted as candidates they must run as 'Labour' candidates only; no other title is allowed; they will be held responsible for the Labour Party's reformist programme; they will be expected to have speaking for them reformist speakers; their election addresses will be subject to the approval of the local Labour Party. Should any Communists suffer all this and secure election to Parliament, having duly taken the oath of allegiance to the Crown, they will become members of the Parliamentary Labour Party and subject to its discipline, which is strict.

The Parliamentary Labour Party decides on most questions; what line the Party shall take, who shall voice its views, and how its members shall vote. The Speaker of the House of Commons is notified by the various Party representatives which of the Party members are to speak in the debates. The Speaker arranges with the Party representatives the order in which the speakers shall be called upon. Until all the persons thus arranged for have been called on the Speaker will allow no other Member to catch his eye. Only if the debate has virtually broken down will the unchosen Communist get an opportunity to speak! And if he does, the other Members of Parliament can silence him by leaving the Chamber, for the debate can only continue whilst 40 Members remain.

Inkpin says that he advocates affiliation to the Labour Party, because he experienced the stultification that resulted when the BSP stood outside the Labour Party. But is Inkpin quite sure that this was the real cause of the stultification? Was it not, perhaps, that the BSP policy and programme were not far enough removed from those of the Labour Party, to create any strong current of feeling in the opposite direction? We ask this, reflecting that many of the men who then led the BSP, and most notably, H. M. Hyndman, are today Social Patriots of a most extreme order, their Reformists being too weak, and their bourgeois Imperialism too strong, even for the Labour Party!

But again, comrade Inkpin, does it not occur to you that the times are changing? Do you not see that the Revolutionary Communism that today is stirring the blood of the workers' advance-guard in every country, and has won through to power in Russia, seemed, in the days when the BSP stood outside the Labour Party, too impossibly remote to gain adherents, except amongst the dauntless daring few, the very dauntless, very daring few?

The War and the Russian Revolution have helped to bring Communism nearer. The increasing consciousness of the Workers, which was developing even before those world-shaking events, is preparing the way for the Communist Party which will one day assume control. But even today, the convinced Communists, those who will work actively to build the Communist Party, and to bring the Communist Revolution, are, in Britain, very few in number.

A SOUND PARTY MORE IMPORTANT THAN A BIG ONE

Do not worry about a big Communist Party yet; it is far better to build a sound one. Do not argue, comrade Inkpin, that the BSP membership is larger than that of some other parties. Do not let us pretend to be big, comrade Inkpin; we are all very small in size; and if some are smaller still, it really does not matter. The great point is, just now, that we should be advancing the propaganda of Communism. When the workers are ready to accept Communism, we shall see a big Communist Party. Until that time comes, the Communist Parties that are really Communist Parties, will certainly be small.

In the meantime, we must persevere with Communist propaganda, and never hesitate lest we should make it too extreme. Let it be clear-cut and absolutely Communist; the more extreme our doctrine is, the more surely it will prepare the workers for Communism.

Comrade Inkpin is right in thinking that we should do propaganda in the Labour Party; yes, and in the Trade Unions Congress, and in the other affiliated bodies. Of course we do, and of course we must, but we can do it without affiliating to the Labour Party. In every industrial organisation, there are some Communists. We must see to it that their number grows, and that they all link up with the Communist Party, and push its programme and policy, they must fight for the acceptance of the programme and tactics of Communism in the Labour Party, in the trade union congress, in the trade union branches, in the workshops — everywhere. To influence the workers who are today in the Labour Party, it is not necessary for the Communist Party to ally itself with the Labour Party; that they are susceptible to outside influence has been proved time and again — by Lloyd George, as well as by the workers' advanceguard — but the future is with us.

HOW WE CAN INFLUENCE THOSE WHO ARE IN THE LABOUR PARTY

Comrade Inkpin speaks of the Labour Party as 'the main body of the working class movement.' It no longer represents the revolutionary workers. More and more they are congregating outside its ranks! Gallacher's letter shows us the position in Scotland, and the same tendency is at work in England and Wales.

In Italy, which is several stages ahead of us in revolutionary progress (as our Correspondent, in his article, 'Soviets in Italy' shows), the Socialist majority has already recognised that the revolutionary movement must be based on the workshop, and they are preparing the

Soviet organisation on that basis; there are differences of detail within the Italian Party, but it is generally recognised that the working class must be reached by a direct appeal within the workshops. An enormous work lies before us there. Until we have done the propaganda necessary amongst the rank and file workers, we shall neither influence, nor expel the officials at the head of the Labour Party and the trade unions.

I shall return to the subject of the new Communist Party next week.

'A constitution for British soviets. Points for a communist programme'

[*Workers' Dreadnought*, 19 June 1920]

The capitalist system must be completely overthrown and replaced by the common ownership and workers' control of the land, the industries of all kinds and all means of production and distribution.

Parliament must be abolished and replaced by a system of Soviets formed by delegates from the industries, the homes, the regiments and the ships.

All Soviet delegates may be changed at anytime. They must be instructed by and report to those whom they represent. No person may take part in any Soviet, or may vote for or be elected as a Soviet delegate who lives, or attempts to live on accumulated wealth, by private trading, or the labour of others whom he or she employs for private gain.

HOUSEHOLD SOVIETS

In order that mothers and those who are organisers of the family life of the community may be adequately represented, and may take their due part in the management of society, a system of household Soviets shall be built up.

URBAN AREAS

Every urban district shall be divided into Household Soviet areas, each of which shall include, as nearly as possible, 250 people.

The women members of these families who are over 20 years of age, and who are mothers and housekeepers shall form the Household Soviet for the area. (. . .)

The Household Soviet shall meet weekly. It may be called together in the interim for urgent business by the delegates.

The Household Soviet shall make rules for its own guidance, and instruct its delegates upon the following matters:—

* Furnishings, repairs and decorations required for the houses within its area.
* The settlement of additional families or individuals in vacant or partially occupied premises in its area.
* The prevention of overcrowding in its area.
* Supplies of food and clothing for the inhabitants of its area.
* Efficiency of the water supply, lighting, fuel, cleaning and sanitation, removal of refuse, window cleaning, etc.
* Bathing and laundry facilities.
* Co-operative housekeeping.
* Children's nurseries.
* Provision for nursing for the sick.
* Midwifery and care of pregnant and nursing mothers and all questions affecting mothers, infants, and family matters generally.
* All public or political questions affecting the women who form the Household Soviet of the Area.
* The Household Soviet shall elect a delegate to the Household Soviet of the district. (. . .)

HOUSEHOLD SOVIETS OF TOWNS

District or Sub-District Household Soviets which form part of towns with a population of over 50,000, shall send to the Household Soviet of that town one delegate for every twenty Soviet Areas. Thus to the Manchester and Salford Soviet the various sub-districts would send altogether 207 delegates.

The Household Soviets of towns shall appoint delegates to the Town Soviets. (. . .)

[There follows the organisation necessary to create Household Soviets in rural areas.]

INDUSTRIAL SOVIETS

The workers in each industry shall prepare and adopt a scheme for the administration of the industry, both locally and nationally, by the workers in the industry, and this scheme shall be submitted for ratification by the National Council of Soviets.

In each industry the following general lines shall be followed:—

In each workshop shall be formed a Workers' Committee, or Soviet composed of all the workers in the shop, of both sexes, and of all grades. A committee of delegates from each workshop, and as far as may be necessary, from each craft and technical branch, shall be formed in the factory. Foremen and managers shall be appointed by vote of the workers in the factory, and on the advice of the District, Town, Regional, or National Council for the industry.

District Soviets, and, where necessary, Sub-District Soviets, shall be formed for the industry, and the workers in each factory shall send delegates to the District or Sub-District Soviet.

Regional Soviets and National Soviets shall also be formed for each industry.

The District Soviet for each industry shall be represented on the general Soviet of the district, the various industrial Regional Soviets will be represented on the general Regional Soviet and the National Councils of the industries will be represented on the National Council of Soviets.

National Regional and District Economic Councils, composed of delegates from the various industries and from the general Soviets will be formed in order to co-ordinate the various industrial functions and to overlook questions of distribution and supply. The workers in the distributive trades, into which will be absorbed both the present co-operative employees and the employees of private firms, will, however, undertake the main work of distribution. These workers will have their Soviets like the workers in other industries.

PUBLIC HEALTH SOVIETS

All persons connected with the care of the sick, surgeons, medical practitioners, nurses, and so on, will form their own industrial Soviets;

Soviets of public health shall be formed consisting of one half delegates of the medical and surgical workers, one-half delegates from the general local Soviet. Public Health Councils will be formed for districts and groups of districts, towns, with a population of over 50,000, regions and counties, and also a National Council.

EDUCATIONAL SOVIETS

Soviets for the schools, colleges, universities, and other educational institutions will be created. Each educational institution will have its Teachers' Soviet and its Pupils' Soviet. Each school for children under sixteen years of age will also hold meetings of parents and teachers, and will elect a council composed of teachers' and parents' representatives, with one representative of the District Soviet and one representative of the District Educational Soviet.

In schools for children between sixteen and eighteen years of age the pupils may send a representative to the School Council, and in schools and colleges for pupils between eighteen and twenty the pupils shall appoint one-fourth of the Council, the parents, shall appoint one-fourth and the teachers half; an appropriate number of expert representatives shall be appointed by the District Educational Soviet. (. . .)

[Soviets for the Army, Sailors and Seamen, and Agricultural Workers are similarly described.]

THE SOVIETS

The Soviets, which are the central organs of social administration, the instrument of the proletarian dictatorship against capitalism, are built up from District or Sub-District Soviets of delegates from the Industries, the Home or Household Soviets, the Army and Naval Soviets, and so on.

The District Soviets shall be formed of one delegate for every Industrial Soviet in the area, and from any Soviet of the Army, Navy, or Mercantile Marine that may be situated there, and an additional delegate for every 500 workers in the industry, one delegate for every 300 members of the Household Soviets, a delegate from the Educational Soviet for the district and one delegate from the District Teachers' Soviet, with an additional delegate for every 300 members of the Teachers' Soviet; also a delegate from the Public Health Soviet and one for every 300 members of the Medical and Surgical Workers' Soviet. The business of the Soviet is to be the co-ordinating link with all other committees, to create any new committees that may be required, and to put into effect the general political policy of the workers. (. . .)

NATIONAL COUNCIL OF SOVIETS

A National Council of Soviets shall be formed. Two-thirds of it shall consist of delegates from the Regional and County Soviets in the proportion of one delegate for every 100,000 of the population, and one-third shall consist of delegates from the National Council of Household Soviets, the National Economic Council, the National Soviets of the main groups of industries, the National Agricultural Council and the National Council of Household Soviets, Public Health and Education. (A similar Council shall be formed for Scotland if so desired.) The National Council of Soviets shall meet every three months and sit as long as may be necessary.

The National Council of Soviets shall elect an executive committee of 300 persons which shall carry out the directions of the National Council of Soviets and appoint the presidents of the National Councils of Household, Industrial Public Health, Education, Army, Navy, and so on.

It shall also elect the secretaries of such additional national departments as may be necessary—for instance, foreign affairs. An executive committee shall be appointed by the National Executive Committee to work with such secretaries.

The presidents and secretaries of the National Departments shall together form a committee of Peoples' Commissaries. Their president shall be chosen by the National Executive Committee.

'Co-operative housekeeping'

[*Workers' Dreadnought*, 28 August 1920]

I haven't described our Co-operative home to you. It is built round a square garden and there is another garden round it. There is also a garden on the roof. The dining-room and kitchen are on the top floor. The school nursery, crêche, and children's garden is at the end of the block of buildings. There are a tennis court, croquet lawn, a hall for meetings, concerts, dances, and so on, a sewing room, workshops for all sorts of crafts, a library and gymnasium, and two big summer houses in the garden, one of which is for the older children. (. . .)

I had only just got upstairs again when there was a knock on our door and some one called 'Cleaners?' 'Not here,' I said, and I heard them go on to the next door. Then I peeped out and saw some young men and women in blue overalls. They had all sorts of machines I had never seen before with them, including a thing I recognised from pictures I had seen as a vacuum cleaner. I felt sorry I had missed the chance of seeing it work. But presently, one of the young women came back and said she thought my flat had been missed out by mistake. I just opened the door and let them come in with the vacuum cleaner and all the rest of their tackle, so that I could see how the cleaner worked.

Ethel, careless little minx, had made some nasty black marks on the new carpet, through not cleaning her muddy shoes when she came in I had wiped up the mess as best I could, but the marks still showed, and I thought I should have to wash the corner of the carpet with soap and water. When the cleaner had passed over the place, the marks had quite disappeared. It seemed quite a miracle to me then.

I was just beginning to wash up—I hate washing up—I loathe housework—when one of the young women in blue said: 'Look! we do it like this!'

Before I could interpose, she began packing the plates into a rack in a cupboard over the sink—I had wondered what that cupboard was for. When she had put them all in, she turned a tap that sent streams of hot water over them. She could make it soapy or plain. When they were clean, she turned on another tap that sent a gust of hot air over them until they were dry. 'You can leave them in these until you want to use them again,' she said, 'but I should do as little as possible of that up here if I were you—it's much nicer having meals in the common rooms.'

I had put some of the children's pinafores to soak. 'Oh don't do that. We get those done in the laundry; if you don't mind, we'll take them down in the tub as they are. We'll let you have it back later.' 'Frank, will you please carry that tub into the trolley for me; it has to go down to the laundry?' 'I see you know how to use the electric cooker. Mary has done the pans for you. If you want to do them for yourself at any time, just use the automatic pan cleanser as soon as you've finished with them; turn that on for a few seconds, so, then that, that, and that, so, so, and so—you'll find it only takes a few seconds—but really, I shouldn't bother with cooking up here, if I were you.'

The place was now all spick and span: it would have taken me the greater part of the morning to do the cleaning, and now in a few minutes it was finished, and far better than I could ever have done it. I stood there feeling a fool and uncomfortable, as though I were having the work done for me under false pretences.

After the cleaners had gone, I decided I would do my shopping and take Rene and Laura with me, but they were nowhere to be seen in the garden, and I called and searched till a nurse came out of what I found to be the baby's garden. She told me that two fresh pupils had come unannounced to the nursery school, and that these were probably the children I was looking for. 'You'll find they've made themselves quite at home with us!'

I went with her and discovered Rene and Laura. Rene was doing musical exercises with some other children, who were following each other round and round on a circle painted in white on the floor. Rene was pointing her toes and dancing along like a little peacock! Laura, I could see through a doorway in another room; she was wearing another pretty, new overall, with an apron over it, and was helping to wait on some little girls and boys who were sitting at a table, having buns and milk.

I called to my children. Rene looked over her shoulder and tossed her head at me laughing. 'I can't mother, I'm too busy.' Laura didn't even hear me. I went for Laura first, took the dish of buns out of her hands, and began to undo the apron. She screamed and cried.

One of the teachers came to me. 'Won't you let your little girl stay?' 'No, I will not!' I called Rene again, while I wrenched off Laura's overall; she was resisting with all her might. Rene took no notice of me until one of the teachers told her to go to me. I dragged my children away. They were both crying as hard as they could, and the worst of it was, they wouldn't stop when I got them home.

When Ethel came in from school, her first question was: 'May I go to dinner with the other children?' I told her, 'No.' She pouted and grumbled that she didn't want 'a nasty old dinner all by ourselves.' She took the part of Rene and Laura, who were still sulking and crying. 'Why can't you let them go to the nursery school, where they'd enjoy themselves and learn something? I think it's too bad of you, mother!'

Presently, Ethel burst out: 'Our school is quite different since we went away—all been done up; you wouldn't know it; and the lessons are much nicer; all the teachers are new; I'm going to learn the piano, and French, and all sorts of things. Everything's better than it used to be!'

When she was in the doorway, ready to go, she went on again: 'I don't care what you say, mother, I'm *going* to have tea with the other children; I'm *going* to see what everything's like. I'm *not* going to live all to ourselves. I've been hearing all about it from the other girls in playtime, and I think it's lovely, whatever you say, so there! You told me they were horrid people, but they are not—and why don't you try it yourself, mother? The other girls' mothers like it.'

She banged the door, and then opened it for a moment, smiling, and shaking her head at me. 'Now mind, I'm not coming in to tea!' I was so much astonished, I just sat and looked at her; then I called: 'Ethel, Ethel!' but she'd gone scampering downstairs.

Another hour's crying and nonsense from Rene and Laura was too much for me, and I thought, after all, it was only sending them to school a few years earlier, and they'd soon get tired of it, anyway. So I washed their faces and brushed their hair, and let them run into the nursery school with a message: 'Mother says we can come now.'

After that, I felt very uncomfortable—every one else was working, and I had nothing to do. The children didn't like coming home to meals, they kept running off to have their's with the other children; the cleaners came in every morning. I was still getting an allowance as a working housekeeper, but I felt I was getting it under false pretences, and I wondered whether it wouldn't be stopped on that ground.

One day, when a member of the House Committee came to ask why I didn't put out my basket of things for the mendery. I said that I'd done all my mending, but I'd help to mend someone else's things in the mendery, if they'd have me to work there. She said yes, they'd be glad to have me; but perhaps I'd like to see some of the other neighbouring workshops too; she offered to take me that afternoon, if I'd like to go, and I agreed.

When we got to the mendery, I felt ashamed of what I'd been calling mending, for the menders there were making the things look as good as new. Much of the work was done by machinery. I saw that it was a new trade that I'd have to learn. It was the same in the kitchen and the laundry; it was all run by experts, and I realised that I had not learnt to do anything properly. I told my guide how I felt. 'Every one feels like that at first,' she said, 'but you'll soon learn.'

After we had seen the domestic workshops serving our house and others near it, we went to see the boot and clothing factories, a book bindery and finally a pottery. The pottery fascinated me, and when we came to the china-painting room, I said: 'If only I could learn that! I've been wanting to work at something like that all my life.' 'But why not?' said my guide. 'You can begin learning the trade to-morrow.' And so I did. I got myself engaged the same afternoon.

That evening, I threw all my reserves away. I went with my children to supper in the Household Common Room, played tennis with some of the other inmates, and finished up, with a dance on the roof.

Since then, I have tried to be a Communist and to help the Communists in every way that I can. I am so fortunate in my work; I do enjoy it! I like the Communist life in every way, and I'm anxious to see it made more complete. I hope it will soon spread all over the world.

There are the children! Let us go to meet them.

'Soviet Russia as I saw it in 1920: the Congress in the Kremlin'

[*Workers' Dreadnought*, 16 April 1921]

Almost immediately after my arrival at the Djelavoi Dvor, a message came: 'Lenin has sent for you to come at once to the Kremlin.'

The Commandant wrote out a little pink *probusk*. The motor car took me over the cobbles to the walls of the Kremlin. The Red Guards, five or six of them, checked the car to examine my *probusk*, and three times afterwards I was obliged to display it before I reached my destination. Once, later on, when I walked to the Kremlin to keep an appointment with Lenin, I was stopped for twenty minutes at the gate, because I had only the pass issued by the Conference, which was by that time out of date. Unable to understand the reason why I was being held up, I ran past the guards with their rifles and fixed bayonets, through the open archway to the telephone on the other side. 'You might have been shot,' a comrade told me later. 'What would be the use of shooting me; I could not do any harm?' 'It was a woman who shot Lenin!'

Passing the Czar's big bell, which lay on the ground with a piece chipped out of it, the road led to the private apartments of the Czar and the Throne Room where the Congress was held. Looking at the great entrance, one sees a mighty staircase. Today it was all hung with long red flags blazoned with the sickle and corn-sheaf, and at the end, a painting of 'Labour,' huge and naked, breaking the chains that bind the earth, hideous and ill-proportioned, but having a certain effective vigour. The walls of the corridors and ante-chambers were lined with photographs, posters and literature. The Russian Communists are indeed great propagandists!

LENIN

In the innermost of the private apartments of the Czar's, Lenin, with smiling face, came quickly forward from a group of men waiting to get a word with him.

He seems more vividly vital and energetic, more wholly alive than other people.

At first sight one feels as though one has always known him, and one is amazed and delighted by a sense of pleasant familiarity in watching him. It is not that one has seen so many of his photographs, for the photographs are not like him; they represent an altogether heavier, darker and more ponderous man, instead of this magnetic and mobile being.

Rather short, rather broadly built, he is quick and nimble in every action, just as he is in thought and speech. He does not wear a picturesque Russian blouse, but ordinary European clothes that sit loosely upon him. His brown hair is closely shaved, his beard lightish brown, his lips are red, and his rather bright complexion looks sandy, because it is tanned and freckled by the hot sun. The skin of the face and head seem drawn rather tightly. There seems to be no waste material to spare. Every inch of his face is expressive. He is essentially Russian with a Tartar strain. His bearing is frank and modest. He appears wholly unconscious of himself, and he met us all as a simple comrade. His brown eyes often twinkle with kindly amusement, but change suddenly to a cold, hard stare, as though he would pierce one's innermost thoughts. He disconcerts his interviewers by suddenly shutting one eye and fixing the other sharply, almost fiercely, upon them.

I had been sent for to take part in the Commission on English affairs, which had been set up by the Third International.

We sat at a round table in the Czar's bedroom. Lenin was on my right hand, and on my left, Wynkoop of Holland, who was translating the German speeches into English. Lenin has a complete knowledge of English: he more than once humorously pulled up Wynkoop for misinterpreting the speakers.

BUKHARIN, RADEK, ZINOVIEV, TROTSKY

Bukharin, Editor of the *Pravda*, and one of the leaders of the Left in the Russian Communist Party, regarded the excited debaters from other countries with laughing blue eyes. Young and vigorous, he had the expression of one to whom life is full of enjoyment. In brown holland blouse and sleeves rolled up to the elbows, he looked like a painter who has just laid down his brushes. During Committee meetings he is continually drawing caricatures of the delegates, but no important point in the discussion escapes him. Today he drew Wynkoop as a solemn, pompous owl.

Radek, who was going to the Polish front in a few days, was also smiling and cheerful, with a detached, dreamy air. One is constantly impressed by the absence of strain or excitement amongst the Russians. These men, standing against a world of enemies, appear to face the situation with perfect calm and much humour.

Zinoviev is of another type: the controversy seemed to bore him. He was a little impatient with the opposition, and criticised, with a tinge of contempt which he doubtless regarded as salutary for the Communist Parties which had not yet learnt how to appeal successfully to the masses. One of the American delegates said of Zinoviev that he always talks to one as though he were taking a bath.

During an interview he seems generally bent on hurrying away to another appointment. An indefatigable pamphleteer, he was probably, even then, composing another Thesis; but he was ready to enter vigorously into the discussion and to speak at considerable length when his turn came.

His voice is not musical, but he is evidently a very popular orator.

At the great meeting in Moscow's biggest theatre, which was the final demonstration of the Congress, Zinoviev and Trotsky were the principal speakers. Trotsky received by far the greater reception. Coming from the Polish front, with the fall of Warsaw to the Red Army daily anticipated, he was naturally the hero of the occasion. He spoke without effort, without any shouting, breathless excitement, but with perfect control and ease. Outwardly well-groomed, he had evidently an excellent mental equipment. He proceeded slowly and leisurely up and down the platform, with an ever varied flow of tone and gesture. The still audience listened eagerly, but he spoke so long that at length he tired them, in spite of their great interest and admiration.

Zinoviev, on the other hand, held the people to the last and finished amid a brisk round of cheers.

At the Commission on private affairs in the Czar's bed-room, Zinoviev sat a little apart from the table. He leaned back comfortably on a soft lounge. Beside him was Levi, of the German KPD. The French, the Austrians and others were also represented on the Commission. The Italians, characteristically, were unrepresented because they could not agree on which of their number should represent them. They were nevertheless present in force and took part in the discussion, Bordiga even presenting a Thesis for discussion against Parliamentary action.

Obviously Lenin enjoys an argument, even though the subject may not seem to him of first class importance, and though the adversaries may be unskilled. At present he was in a bantering mood, and dealt playfully with the British delegates. The majority of them were objectors to certain passages in a Thesis now under discussion, written by Lenin himself, on the tasks of the Communist Party.

LENIN AND THE BRITISH LABOUR PARTY

The passages in dispute dealt with the British Communist Parties and declared that they should affiliate to the British Labour Party and make use of Parliamentary action. Lenin evidently does not regard either of these questions as fundamental. Indeed, he considers that they are not questions of principle at all, but of tactics, which may be employed advantageously in some phases of the changing situation and discarded with advantage in others. Neither question, in his opinion, is important enough to cause a split in the Communist ranks. I am even inclined to suspect that he has not been uninfluenced by the belief that the course he has chosen is that which will appeal to the majority of Communists, and will therefore cement the largest number of them in united action. As to the question of affiliation to the Labour Party (a question that may presently arise in similar form for decision by the Communist Parties of Canada and the United States), Lenin says: 'Millions of backward members are enrolled in the Labour Party, therefore Communists should be present to do propaganda amongst them, provided Communist freedom of action and propaganda is not thereby limited.' When, afterwards, in the Kremlin, I argued with Lenin privately that the disadvantages of affiliation outweighed those of dis-affiliation, he dismissed the subject as unimportant, saying that the Labour Party would probably refuse to accept the Communist Party's affiliation, and that, in any case, the decision could be altered next year.

LENIN AND PARLIAMENTARISM

So too with Parliamentarism; he dismissed it as unimportant, saying that if the decision to employ Parliamentary action is a mistake, it can be altered at next year's Congress.

When, however, it is argued that Communists should not go into reformist Labour Parties or bourgeois Parliaments because they may be affected by the environment and lose the purity of their Communist faith and fervour, Lenin replies that after the proletarian conquest of power, the temptation to weaken in principle will be much greater. He argues that those who cannot withstand all tests before the Revolution, will certainly not do so later.

He is for attacking every such difficulty, not for avoiding it: he is for dragging Communist controversy out into the market-place, not closeting it amongst selected circles of enthusiasts.

He does not fear that Communism will be postponed or submerged by the advent to power of reformists. Convinced that reforms cannot cure or substantially palliate the capitalist system, he is impatient for the rise to power of the Reformists in order that their importance may be demonstrated. When I talked with him in the Kremlin, he urged that British Communists should say to the leaders of the Labour Party: 'Please Mr. Henderson, take the power. You, to-day, represent the opinions of the majority of British workers; we know that, as yet we do not; therefore we cannot at present take the power. But you, who represent the opinions of the masses, you should take the power.'

In those days, news had come that Councils of Action had been set up to stop Britain declaring war on Soviet Russia in support of Poland.

Lenin declared that we should inform Henderson that he must no longer scruple to seize power by Revolution, since he and his Party had already committed themselves to that by setting up a Council of Action charged with the work of bringing about a general strike in the event of further war measures by Britain against Russia. Such a strike, as Henderson, Clynes and their colleagues had frequently themselves declared, would be a revolutionary act. The Labour Party was now committed to it.

Lenin said that the creation of the Councils of Action were due to a wave of revolutionary sentiment in the British masses, which had forced their Labour leaders to take some sort of action. That the declarations of the Council of Action failed to satisfy Communists, and that the Council was inactive, merely meant that the wave of mass feeling had not yet gone very far and had largely subsided.

The feeling of the masses rises and falls, he argued, in irregular tides; it does not remain at high-water mark.

'We in Russia,' he said, 'seized the power at the moment the masses had risen. When they receded from us, we were obliged to hold on till the next wave of feeling brought them back to us.'

Lenin argued, that in order to explode the futility of reformism and to bring Communism to pass, the Labour Party must have a trial in office. Therefore British Communists should affiliate their Party to the Labour Party and come to arrangements with it for the formation of a joint Parliamentary block and the mutual sharing out of constituencies. In addition to the Thesis under debate, Lenin had prepared and had translated ready for the Conference, a book called *The Infantile Sickness of 'Leftism' in Communism* This book was intended to confound and convert those of us who disagree with its author, and who assert that the Labour Party will in any case come to power, and the British Communist Party cannot dissociate itself too early and too clearly from the Labour Party's reformist policy, and must by no means enter into alliances or arrangements with it. We also assert that Communists can best wean the masses from faith in bourgeois Parliamentarism by refusal to participate in it.

LENIN AND TRADE UNIONISM

The passages in Lenin's Thesis on Trade and Industrial Unionism, and Zinoviev's Thesis on Unionism were also the subject of hot debate.

Lenin and the other Russians of his school, regard the Unions primarily as agglomerations of workers providing opportunities for Communists to win the masses for Communism. The dissentients, who belong to the highly industrialised Western bourgeois democracies, are unable to detach themselves from the view that an industrial organisation is an organisation for fighting the capitalist employer. Moreover, they are most of them influenced by the view that, if the industrial organisations the workers are developing for themselves under Capitalism do not actually become the organisations which will administer industry under Communism, they are at least a training ground for preparing the workers in the shops to administer Communist industries on Soviet lines. (. . .)

Whatever the merits of the rival contentions might be, the Theses of Lenin and Zinoviev, and indeed all the Theses and resolutions coming from the Russian Communist leaders, because of their great achievements, were certain to be adopted at this first anniversary of the founding of the Third International.

The Russians, although the sixty delegates of their Party had between them but five votes, like the British, could steam-roller anything they chose through the Congress.

We, who were in opposition on certain matters, nevertheless argued our case in spite of the hopelessness of the task, and Lenin argued against us, as though our defeat had not been a foregone conclusion.

The Congress meeting in the Czar's Throne Room the following evening, allowed me to extend to twenty-five minutes, the allotted five minutes in which I had to accomplish the stupendous task of replying to a Thesis and book of Lenin and innumerable speeches.

The Congress had lasted a month. As the speeches were delivered in various languages and translated, delegates streamed restlessly in and out to an adjoining room, where tables were loaded with slices of bread and butter and sardines, caviare, preserved meats and cheese, and saucers filled with sweets wrapped in coloured papers. Glasses of hot tea were always on hand there. Angelica Balabanova often had to complain that very few auditors were present to hear her translation. Giving but a cursory sketch of rambling speeches, empty of real matter, Balabanova always rendered well and fully the words of those who had anything to say, though she was ill and very tired.

Artists sat amongst the delegates, making drawings of them or roamed about looking for models. Balabanova protested, as she always does against such portraiture.

On the defeat of the English amendments and the unanimous adoption of Lenin's Thesis, with which, in the main, I am in complete agreement, the Congress ended. The delegates sprang up singing 'The International', the Editor of the Italian Socialist paper *Avanti!* led the singing of the 'Carmanol.' John Reed and others caught Lenin, and though he resisted, hoisted him upon their shoulders. He looked like a happy father amongst his sons.

Writ on Cold Slate (1922)

[Volume of poetry written during Pankhurst's imprisonment for sedition in 1920–21]

WRIT ON COLD SLATE

Whilst many a poet to his love hath writ,
boasting that thus he gave immortal life,
my faithful lines upon inconstant slate,
destined to swift extinction reach not thee.

In other ages dungeons might be strange,
with ancient mouldiness their airs infect,
but kindly warders would the tablets bring,
so captives might their precious thoughts inscribing,
the treasures of the fruitful mind preserve,
and culling thus its flowers, postpone decay.

Only this age that loudly boasts Reform,
hath set its seal of vengeance 'gainst the mind,
decreeing nought in prison shall be writ,
save on cold slate, and swiftly washed away.

FOR HALF A YEAR

Like to Persephone upon the brink,
a moment pause I from the dock to gaze,
before descending by those narrow steps
unto a world of shades for half a year;
amid the dusky Court a mist there swims
of ruddy faces blending into smiles,
and one stands forth, dead white, with staring eyes.

Exalted on the Bench that harsh old man,
clad in the purple of his Mayoral state,
mouthing impatiently with hands a-twitch,
the while I speak, by right of law allowed.

Oft interrupting, now he breaketh forth,
his parchment cheeks distort, his eyes spit hate,
libel on libel hurls, that hired Press scribes
may circulate for gulling simple folk,
masking what lights may glimmer forth to show
their present exploitation and his sins,
by talk of loot, loot, loot, and pillage cruel,
and silly ogre stories, patent lies,
'gainst Soviet Russia, whence I'm late returned.

His soul sits in a cellar hoarding gold;
o'er mighty realms his power extending rules;
knowing no bounds in his ambitious dreams,
which still to what he has, add more he would.

His paper tokens pass the world around,
compel in Africa the Negro's toil,
make magic fingers of far Japs to ply,
their art mis-prized for its so meagre cost,
because on little rice they can exist.

For him, in India, poor ryots toil,
their immemorial Communism crushed,
robbed of their produce and by famine scourged,
dying like flies whilst he exports their grain.

For him, in Britain too, the miner delves;
weavers and spinners follow ceaseless toil,
their wage by far competitors depressed,
children and parents in those Eastern mills,
worse fed than beasts and nothing better housed.

Here, in Wealth's citadel, old wretched dens,
for him each week provide most monstrous dues,
a blighting charge upon their tenant hordes.

For him are children stunted, infants die;
poor mother drudges leave their wailing babes;
herself the exploited maiden cheaply sells
to snatch youth's pleasures, else debarred from her;
for bare indeed the pittance he accords,
to such as she who are so swift replaced.

Upon his call to war, go millions forth
prepared to die if he will give them bread.

This is the very hub and central spring
of that I fight, that hoary power of wealth;
he's its defender, its first magistrate;
I who attack it, being tried by him,
to mine antagonist must plead my Cause.

He hath the power, and he will vengeance take;
that was decided ere the case was called;
for me remains one duty, one resource;
to cry a challenge in this Mansion House,
this pompous citadel of wealthy pride,
and make its dock a very sounding board
for the indictment of his festering sins,
that shall go ringing forth throughout the world,
and with it carry all my wit can tell
of that most glorious future, long desired,
when Communism like the morning dawns.

When in the black and jolting van I pass,
to narrow cell of dingy walls and drear
and little window high, with small barred panes;
when's clanged the heavy door and double-locked,
and brief day to an early evening fades,
crouching with stiff cold limbs on lowly bed,
the bruised spirit longing to be free,
and deep-shocked senses trembling from the stroke,
riseth that white face in the darkness here.

'Freedom of discussion'

[*Workers' Dreadnought*, 17 September 1921]

Movements, like human beings, grow and develop from stage to stage and pass through many crazes and illnesses. The Communist Party of Great Britain is at present passing through a sort of political measles called discipline which makes it fear the free expression and circulation of opinion within the Party.

Since its formation the Communist Party of Great Britain has fretted itself at the existence of the *Workers' Dreadnought*, an independent Communist voice, free to express its mind unhampered by Party discipline.

At the inaugural Party Conference, as I am informed by the Executive, it was even debated whether members of the Party might be permitted to read the *Dreadnought* since it is not controlled by the Executive of the Party. The position of the *Scottish Worker*, *Solidarity*, the *Plebs*, the *Socialist*, and the *Spur* were also discussed. (. . .) The letter issued by the Executive to branches of the Party recommended the *Plebs*, *Solidarity*, and the *Worker* for circulation by the Party, but stated that the question of circulating the *Dreadnought* must be left in abeyance. Many branches took this to mean that the *Dreadnought* must not be circulated, and some of the Party's organisers carried on a campaign against the *Dreadnought* in this sense, making it a question of loyalty to the Party not to take it. (. . .)

Soon after my release from half a year's imprisonment I met a sub-committee of the Communist Party Executive, which consisted of Comrades W. Paul, F. Peat, F. Willis and T. Clark. This sub-committee put it to me that 'as a disciplined member of the Party' I should hand the *Workers' Dreadnought* over to the Executive, to stop it, or continue it, and, should it continue the paper, to put it to any use or policy it chose, and to place it under the editorship of any person whom it might select; I was not to be consulted, or even informed, till the decision should be made. Thus, with a spice of brutality, the disciplinarians set forth their terms to one who had for eight years maintained a pioneer paper with constant struggle and in face of much persecution.

I replied that I could not agree to such a proposition, but would consider carefully, and in a comradely spirit, any proposal that the Party might make to me regarding the paper. I said that I believed in the usefulness of an independent Communist paper which would stimulate discussion in the movement on theory and practice; but just released from prison, the united Party having been formed whilst I was inside, I was anxious to look around me, and hear all points of views. I invited the sub-committee to lay before me any suggestions they had to make. The members of the sub-committee, however, failed to respond in the same spirit; they merely repeated their former demand for an absolute and blindfold renunciation of the paper. (. . .)

The comrades intended to enforce discipline in its most stultifying aspect. Comrade McManus, as Chairman, informed me that they would not permit any member of the Party to write or publish a book or a pamphlet without the sanction of the Executive. Those who may differ from the Executive on any point of principle, policy or tactics, or even those whose method of dealing with agreed theory is not approved or appreciated by the Executive, are therefore to be gagged.

I told the comrades that if we were before the barricades, if we were in the throes of the revolution, or even somewhere near it, I could approve a rigidity of discipline which is wholly out of place here and now.

I told them that whereas we are face to face with an opportunist and reformist Labour Party, and since in the midst of capitalism, there is the ever-present tendency and temptation towards compromise with the existing order, it is essential for a Communist Party to be definite in excluding Right tendencies. A Communist Party can only preserve its communist character by using its discipline to prevent Right opportunism and laxity from entering the Party; it must insist that acceptance of Communist principles and avoidance of reformism be made a condition of membership; that is obvious. On the other hand, the Communist Party cannot afford to stifle discussion in the Party; above all, it must not stifle the discussion of Left Wing ideas; otherwise it will cramp and stultify itself, and will destroy its own possibility of advancement.

I stated that in my opinion every member of the Party should be allowed to write and publish his or her views, and that only in cases where these views prove to be not Communist should the question of a member's fitness to belong to the Party be brought into question.

I told the Executive, and it is my strongly held opinion, that in the weak, young, little-evolved Communist movement of this country discussion is a paramount need, and to stifle it is disastrous. Therefore when I was asked whether I would obey the discipline of the Executive I was obliged to say that it was impossible for me to give a general answer to such a question, if discipline could be strained to prevent the expression of opinion, and that I could only decide whether I should obey when a concrete case should arise.

As before, my reply to the demand to surrender the *Workers'* *Dreadnought* was, that I was willing to discuss any proposal made by the Executive, but I was still of opinion that the *Dreadnought* could best serve Communism as an independent organ, giving expression to Left Wing ideas, which include opposition to Parliamentarism and Labour Party affiliation, but which have many other aspects, now clearly showing themselves to be the minority view in the Third International, and which represent the most advanced and thorough-going Communism. I said I believed one of the most useful offices I could perform for the movement was to edit the *Dreadnought*. I was confirmed in this view by recent happenings in the International. The decision to exclude from the Third International the industrialist, anti-Trade Union, anti-Parliamentary and highly revolutionary Communist Labour Party of Germany, which played so important a part in the Ruhr Valley rising, is leading to a division in the Third International, and the publication of a new international organ which it is important to study. The growth of the Workers Opposition in Soviet Russia, which was dealt with in an article by Alexandra Kollontai, published in last week's *Dreadnought*; the growing cleavage between Right and Left in the Russian Communist Party; the tendency to slip to the Right, which is regrettably manifesting itself in Soviet Russia, (. . .) all show the importance of independent discussion. The drift to the Right in Soviet Russia, which has permitted the re-introduction of many features of capitalism, such as school fees, rent, and charges for light, fuel, trains, trams, and so on, is due, doubtless, to the pressure of encircling capitalism and the backwardness of the Western democracies. Nevertheless, there are strong differences of opinion amongst Russian Communists and throughout the Communist International as to how far such retrogression can be tolerated. Such questions are not discussed in the *Communist*; it is a Party organ under the control of the Right Wing of the British Communist Party, and of the Executive in Moscow, which is at present dominated by the Right Wing policy. It presents merely the official view.

The *Workers' Dreadnought* is the only paper in this country which is alive to the controversies going on in the International Communist movement; it is the only paper through which the rank and file of the movement can even guess that there are such controversies. Such controversies are a sign of healthy development, through them the movement grows onward towards higher aims and broader horizons; by studying them, by taking part in them, the membership will develop in knowledge and political capacity.

I stated my case. The executive replied that it would not tolerate the existence of any Communist organ independent of itself. I informed the Executive, as is the case, that the great financial difficulties under which the *Dreadnought* is labouring have made us decide reluctantly and with great regret that this issue must be the last. (. . .)

Comrade McManus rounded off the discussion; the Party had no alternative but to expel me, he contended.

But this farcical parody of discipline is a passing error; it will disappear as the Party is faced with more serious issues, and as its power to take effective action on things that matter develops. If my expulsion assist the Party in passing more speedily through this phase of childishness it will have served a useful purpose. (. . .)

Let there be no mistake; I am not expelled for any tendency to compromise with capitalism; I am expelled for desiring freedom of propaganda for the Left Wing Communists, who oppose all compromise and seek to hasten faster and more directly onward to Communism.

The great problem of the Communist Revolution is to secure economic equality, the abolition of the wages system, and the ending of class distinctions. Russia has achieved the Revolution, but not the Communist life which should be its sequal. The porter, silent and ill-clad, still awaits the tip; still there are some who go shabby on foot with broken boots, whilst others, smartly dressed, are whizzing by in motor cars. Still there are wages of many grades, still there are graduated food rations. The 'responsible worker must have an adequate supply of food, or his work will suffer', therefore if there is a shortage of food the 'responsible workers' must have a higher ration than the rest of the people; that is the argument. But how is the argument to be strained so as to explain why the wife and family of the 'responsible worker' should have higher food rations than other people, should have higher rations than their neighbours, even in those cases when the 'responsible worker' is not living at home with them? These are the old injustices, the old criminal errors of capitalism persisting under the reign of the Soviets.

How grievous (if it be true, as we greatly hope not) is the news that school fees have been introduced into Soviet Russia! What could be the reason of such a retrograde step? Is it because there are not yet enough school places for all the children, and the fees are a means of ensuring that the children of the higher paid people shall have the preference? Is it the old vicious system of penalising the child whose parents are poor?

We look to Communism as the state of society in which, whilst work shall be a duty incumbent on all, the means of life, study and pleasure shall be freed, without stint, to everyone, to use at will. If a shortage compel rationing in any direction, it should be equal. The principle of paying according to skill, speed, or the length of training required for the work, is wholly bad. If it be true that necessity compels differentiation, then it is the most regrettable of necessities.

The dictatorship of the proletariat, at which some foolish persons desire to play (within their Parties before the Revolution), is a stern necessity of the transition period when capitalism is being overthrown and is striving to re-establish itself again. Such dictatorship is anta-gonistic to the Communist idea: it will pass away when genuine Communism is reached.

To those who are not familiar with the details of the position, it is necessary, in conclusion, to make clear that the *Workers' Dreadnought* was founded by me, and from the early days of its existence remained under my personal control, in the first instance in order that any risks of prosecution attaching to it might fall on me alone.

When the WSF, of which the *Workers' Dreadnought* was the organ, was merged in the Communist Party, it was made clear that I should remain responsible for the *Dreadnought*, and the Party at its Cardiff Conference passed a resolution affirming that that was the case. When the present united Communist Party of Great Britain was formed I definitely stated that the *Workers' Dreadnought* would remain outside, and give an independent support to the Communist Party. There is no question either of my having subverted a party organ, or of desiring to maintain a Party organ uncontrolled by the Party.

The position is that the *Dreadnought* is an independent organ; and that the Executive of the Communist Party of Great Britain has decided that it will not permit me, as one of its members, to publish an independent paper.

I do not regret my expulsion; that it has occurred shows the feeble and unsatisfactory condition of the Party: its placing of small things before great: its muddled thinking.

I desire freedom to work for Communism with the best that is in me. The Party could not chain me: I, who have been amongst the first, as the record of the papers published, both in this country and abroad, will prove, to support the present Communist Revolution and to work for the Third International, shall continue my efforts as before.

'To Lenin, as representing the Russian Communist Party and the Russian Soviet Government'

[*Workers' Dreadnought*, 4 November 1922]

We address you as representative of the Russian Soviet Government and the Russian Communist Party. With deep regret we have observed you hauling down the flag of Communism and abandoning the cause of the emancipation of the workers. With profound sorrow we have watched the development of your policy of making peace with Capitalism and reaction.

Why have you done this?

It seems that you have lost faith in the possibility of securing the emancipation of the workers and the establishment of world Communism in our time. You have preferred to retain office under Capitalism than to stand by Communism and fall with it if need be.

Yet if a great call, a high call, and a disinterested call to Communism might go out to the people at this time, from some source that could inspire them with trust, it seems that, in the terrible circumstances of the present hour, it must bear tremendous fruit. A period of great misery has fallen upon the peoples; they are suffering great bitterness in the bondage of this ruthless system of Capitalism, which is decaying from the awful and overwhelming growth of its own iniquities.

The exchanges are rising on the one hand, falling on the other, with a startling velocity, which is reflected in the miseries of the people. In the lands of high exchange values falls the blight of unemployment and lowered wages; in the lands of low exchanges is the merciless increase of prices, which forces the toilers to work, faster and ever faster, whilst starvation and want drain them, like cruel leeches, of the very life force they are expending, with desperate recklessness, upon their ill-requited toil.

The financial manipulators rule the world; they are the real Governments; and these puppet Governments, which take the stage for a time, must do their bidding or disappear from the scene.

In Italy we see once more the collapse of the old politics; but it is an evil and vile reaction which, in the shape of Fascism, has taken advantage of the general disgust with the sham fights and the futile tinkering and marking time of the Capitalist politicians. The Fascisti have acted. Because whilst others have so long been content only to talk through the welter of popular distress, the Fascisti, though with wickedness, have acted, multitudes have either followed them, or at least have refrained from actively opposing them. Because the talkers have only talked, no force has opposed the violence of the Fascisti.

The Fascisti have provided a means of existence, even though it is gained by the murder and terrorism of their class brothers and sisters, to masses of destitute demobilised soldiers. The talkers have done not even that; they have spoken of general well-being, but have produced nothing. Reformism can produce nothing of permanent value; it cannot change the essential features of Capitalism which are grinding the agonised masses between the upper and nether millstones.

These days of great misfortune are revealing, with piercing and ruthless clarity, the utter powerlessness of those who would reform the iniquitous system and would heal the grievous wounds which it inflicts. 'Work or maintenance for the unemployed', cries the reformist. In so far-as the claim is conceded, the local burden of the concession is immediately placed on the shoulders of the working-class householders and their families and lodgers. In so far as unemployment maintenance is made, what is described as a national charge, it is transmitted, in the great complexities of the Capitalist system, into higher prices and reduced remuneration to the wage-earning community, which, having nothing to sell save its labour, has no means of recouping itself for its losses in the labour market and reduced purchasing power, since it cannot pass on its burden to be borne by someone else.

So it is with all the reforms projected by the reformer, in so far as they ever pass beyond the stage of discussion, for the populations of the world are in the grip of the great Capitalists, and there is no possibility of improvement till that stranglehold has been destroyed.

Even the most ignorant and unsophisticated are to-day instinctively aware of this; they realise that the reformist and his panaceas cannot help them; they observe, on the contrary, that every action of that costly monstrosity, the Capitalist Government, is attended by a devastating increase of parasitic and opulent administrators, the burden of whose maintenance, since they cannot pass it on to others, always falls on the classes least able to bear it. Realising their hopeless position under Capitalism, the people sink into spiritless apathy, concentrating on the effort to maintain an individual existence. In fear of a catastrophic future, they long vainly for a return to the grey humdrum of the pre-war struggle, which was less fierce than this of to-day.

Urgent is the need for the strong call to Communism, the clear explanation of the Communist life: its sane and wholesome mutual service: its large and all-embracing fraternity: its escape from this nightmare of poverty and power.

What have you done, O one-time trumpet of revolution? In your impatience of the slow awakening of far multitudes, you have turned your face from the world's lowly and enslaved. You have dabbled in the jmuggleries of Capitalist diplomacy; you have bartered and bargained with the destinies of the Russian proletariat; and broadcasted the message of your own desertion of Communism, wrapped up in tortuous and misleading casuistry, to the Communist movement throughout the world. By your subtle and specious arguments, and by the glamour of the Russian Revolution, through which you were regarded, you have diverted from the quest of Communism many who had been aroused by the call of Soviet Russia. Therefore we find those who lately set out bearing the standard of Communism, now working to place in power a Party which openly declares its opposition to Communism.

Therefore, instead of placing the knowledge of Communism before the peoples, we find the parties of the Third International urging the masses to continue fighting for a hotchpotch of futile and impossible reforms.

'The truth about the Fascisti'

[*Workers' Dreadnought*, 4 November 1922]

The *Daily Herald*, the Labour Party organ with unexampled treachery to the cause of the workers, and to all that makes for progress, has attempted to whitewash the White Terror of the Fascisti, which holds Italy in its grip today.

Mr Hamilton Fyfe, the editor of the *Daily Herald*, who ought to be sent to the right for his gross errors, literary as well as political, observes: 'Whether the Italian Fascisti are enemies to the point of view of the workers in this country is not very clear.' He further declares: 'It is impossible not to feel a certain amount of admiration for this man who has organised what he calls a bloodless revolution.' Then he proceeds to argue that the Fascisti came into being to oppose the violence of the Communists.

Mr Hamilton Fyfe is not alone in his suggestion that though the Fascisti have made use of violence they are rather splendid people, and that their final triumph has been a bloodless one. Bloodless it has been, in so far as its victims have succumbed to superior force, as an unarmed man obeys the order of 'Hands up!' when he finds himself covered with several powerful revolvers.

What is the truth concerning the Fascisti and the Italian Proletarian movement which they were created to fight? At the close of the War the Socialist Party was the dominant force amongst these Italian workers. The movement was strong and virile. In each town it had its People's House, combining lecture halls, library, theatre, dance halls, cafe, restaurant and hotel. The co-operative societies were powerful and closely linked with the Socialist Party, as were the Trade Unions which also provided technical instructions in a large variety of trades.

The extensive character of the movement, with its fine buildings and splendid equipment, was far beyond comparison with anything we have in this country. The widely-read Socialist Party organ, *Avanti*, had a fine printing plant in Milan and in Turin, where several weekly and monthly organs and first-class colour printing were produced. (. . .)

The Italian workers were profoundly impressed by the Russian Revolution. The *Avanti* gave an enthusiastic support to the Russian Revolution and the Soviets, and to the Bolsheviki in the early days of their power, and the *Avanti* was moulding the opinion of the workers who read it so widely. On the walls of the industrial cities, Turin and Milan, one saw chalked up the slogans of the proletarian revolution, with 'viva' the revolution and Lenin, who was regarded as its leader. (. . .)

At the annual Conference of the Italian Socialist Party, in Red Bologna, in the autumn of 1919, the old Reformist leaders, Turati, Treves, and Modigliani, were left with only a handful of followers, and the centre party of Serrati and the *Avanti* received an enormous majority over the Right, whilst the anti-Parliamentarians had a substantial following.

The Serrati faction declared for revolution on Russian lines, for the Soviets, and for the abolition of Parliament; but this faction was determined to use Parliament in the meantime, and they refused to split the Party, by excluding the Reformists, who were opposed to making preparations for the clash of actual force with Capitalism, which the revolutionaries declared inevitable, and which, as events proved, was soon to come to pass.

The question of whether the moment had come for direct preparation for the coming struggle, and the setting up of the Soviets, was hotly argued; but, at this juncture, Lenin, on behalf of the Russian Communists, wrote urging the Italians to go, not to the Soviets, but to the elections, and declared that the Italian revolution should be delayed on the score of the unreadiness of the proletarian revolution in France and Britain.

Shortly afterwards Lenin proceeded to attack the Serrati faction for not expelling the Reformists; but the Serrati faction desired to retain the Reformists just because they feared to split the votes of their supporters and to jeopardise their Parliamentary success by expelling these popular Parliamentary figures. The followers of Lenin's policy presently obtained the upper hand, and Serrati was placed in a minority; but the Parliamentary policy remained dominant, and, as events have proved, the movement did not develop the capacity to meet the forces of Capitalist violence which were soon to face them.

In 1920 the employers in the metal industries attempted to lock out their workers; the workers, organised in their shop committee movement, proclaimed the Soviets in the workshops and occupied the factories.

The employing classes believed that the proletarian revolution had come, and that resistance was unavailing. There is abundant evidence of that today. Many and many a businessman has since confessed that he then saw no other alternative, and not a small number were even willing to try the experiment as an escape from the post-war anxieties that have befallen the trading community in the trade depression holding Europe in its grip.

At every stage the Soviet movement had been obstructed by the opposition of the leaders of the Trade Union Movement and by the older Socialist leaders. The metal workers had arisen spontaneously; they had placed barbed wire round the factories, and machine-guns on the roofs, and other workers were rising to join them. Engineers, seamen and others were giving proof of their solidarity; rural workers were rising in squads of twenty, fifty, or 100,000, to seize the landed properties.

The Anarchists approved and supported the movement; but the Anarchists, with their newly started daily, the *Umanita Nova*, were without the organisation to cope with the situation; it was not they, but the Socialists, who had the ear and the confidence of the great masses. And what did the Socialist Party, in which there were still the Reformists, Turati, Modigliani and Treves, as well as Serrati and Bombacci, the Maximalists and Bordiga, who had been given a seat on the executive as representing the Parliamentary abstentionists?

The great Socialist Party held aloof from the struggle and turned it over to the Trade Union leaders of the Italian Confederation of Labour. (. . .)

HOW THE WORKERS WERE BETRAYED

And what did the Trade Union leaders to whom the Socialist Party had left the revolution? They led the workers into an absurd bargain, by which a Commission (on the Sankey plan, which was used here to sidetrack the miners) was formed of twelve members nominated by the General Confederation of Labour and twelve members of the Employers' Federation, and with two experts on either side, to formulate proposals for joint control by the employers and the Trade Union. Some slight wage increases were granted on a sliding scale to rise and fall with the cost of living. The control boards afterwards established as a result of this Commission proved worse than useless. The workers soon refused to work them. Thus the movement, which could not be crushed, was betrayed into defeat.

When the crisis was over; when the workers had thus been led to surrender their conquests for a mere nothing, Capitalism heaved a sigh of relief and determined to run no risks. The organisation of the Fascisti, the brigand White Guards with the black shirts, began. Mussolini, the renegade ex-Socialist who deserted the Party to join the Jingoes in the war, was supplied with funds by the great industrial employers of Italy. These funds were used to organise a force of the more ignorant and reckless of the destitute ex-soldiers and the reactionary young men of wealthier classes to destroy the Socialist movement of Italy by brute force. The premises of the Socialist, Co-operative, and Trade Union movements were invaded and wrecked, and meetings of the working-class organisations were broken up by the Fascisti with armed force. Socialists, Communists, Trade Unionists and Co-operators were killed and injured. Municipalities with Socialist majorities were attacked, the council chambers looted, the members wounded or killed, and forced to resign. Newspapers of all shades of opinion opposed to Fascism were systematically terrorised and their printing machinery was destroyed.

Capitalism provided the funds for the Fascisti; Giolitti, the Prime Minister, encouraged its growth. Bonomi, who succeeded Giolitti, went further: he even permitted officers and soldiers of The Regular Army to join the Fascisti. Then the Fascisti began to run candidates for Parliament, and on a small number of these being elected, they took their firearms into the chamber to terrorise the assembly. The Fascisti hold 20 seats in the Italian Parliament: in numbers a negligible minority, but as Mussolini says, they are determined that Fascism shall be the State. They desire power, and they will have it. Therefore, they mobilised to seize the power. The Facta Government took steps to resist the Fascisti advance; it declared martial law and stopped the railway traffic, placing the engines under military guard.

The King now came forward to aid the Fascisti. Was it in terror that he might be deposed, like the numerous officials of all sorts who have been violently ejected, because they displeased the Black Shirts? Or was it in sympathy for the forces of reaction? Be the reason what it may, the King refused to sign the decree of the Government declaring martial law against the Fascisti: the Facta Government resigned, and the King called Mussolini to form a Government. Thus Mussolini has won the first round, amid the plaudits of reaction everywhere. The Fascisti have made a bloodless revolution, says the *Daily Herald*: they have acted 'with tact', says a *Daily Telegraph* correspondent. The tale of the latest Fascisti terrorism has yet to be told; but the Press telegrams published in the Capitalist daily Press record already that the Fascisti, on their triumphal entry into Rome, invaded the newspaper offices, destroyed the machinery, even of Capitalist papers opposed to them, and terrorised the editors with firearms.

'What is behind the label? A plea for clearness'

[*Workers' Dreadnought*, 3 November 1923]

Men and women call themselves Socialists, Communists, Anarchists, Individualists, thinking they thus explain their views to themselves and others. Yet question them, but a little; you will discover how few of them have any clear conception of what they mean by their labels. Thus it is that many fail to recognise a brother of their faith, unless he bear a label, discourse he never so fully and clearly upon his beliefs and ideals.

When we are considering the as yet intangible things of the future, the life of our hopes beyond our present experiences, precise thinking is difficult; prolonged research and meditation are necessary to arrive at any clearness of aim. Therefore behind the labels we find abundant confusion. The advocate of such an extreme form of State interference with the liberty of the individual as compulsory birth-control is found to label himself Individualist. Zealous upholders of Capitalism also label themselves Individualists, though Capitalism could not be maintained an hour without the power of the State forces, which protect private property, and prevent those who have not enough to satisfy their needs from despoiling those who have something to spare.

Self-styled Anarchists are found who have not thought out a single fundamental of a society without law, and who support variously nationalisation of the land, the single tax, and other State organised panaceas, Trade Unions with their centralised mechanism and oppressive officialdom, and petty trading and production for profit, which, like the larger Capitalism, necessitates law and its forces to protect the property-holder from being dispossessed.

So-called Socialists are found whose idea of Socialism consists in various reforms of the Capitalist system: Parliamentary legislation to secure such things as more liberal charity towards the poor or closer supervision over them, higher taxation or taxation on a new basis, municipal trading, State Capitalism, State subsidies and other encouragements to great Capitalism, or, on the other hand, war on great Capitalism, and State encouragement of small Capitalism, and other confused and conflicting expedients.

Self-styled Communists are found whose aims differ little if any from those of the most confused and vague of the reformists.

'What is Socialism, what is Communism, what is Anarchy?' ask a multitude of would-be converts, weary of the cruelty and waste of Capitalism and eagerly desiring an alternative. For answer they receive only confused denunciations of existing things; no hopeful vision of the new life which the labelled ones are supposed to advocate is vouchsafed them. They turn away empty and discouraged.

Programmes become cramping and conservative influences if men and women worship them as holy writ, and refuse their thoughts permission to go on before an accepted formula. Yet without discovering for ourselves what our aims really are, without defining them so that they may be understood by others, how shall we work for them, how shall we sow the seed that shall create a movement to achieve them?

Our aim is Communism. Communism is not an affair of party. It is a theory of life and social organisation. It is a life in which property is held in common; in which the community produces, by conscious aim, sufficient to supply the needs of all its members; in which there is no trading, money, wages, or any direct reward for services rendered.

The Individualist emphasises his dislike for coercion by the collectivity, his desire that the individual shall be free. We also dislike coercion and desire freedom; we aim at the abolition of Parliamentary rule; but we emphasise the interdependence of the members of the community; we emphasise the need that the common storehouse and the common service shall provide an insurance against want for every individual.

We aim at the common storehouse, not the individual hoard. We desire that the common storehouse shall bulge with plenty, and whilst the common storehouse is plenished we insist that none shall want.

We would free men and women from the stultifying need of making their own individual production pay; the peasant toiling uncounted hours with inadequate tools, the fear of incapacity and want always dogging his thoughts; the little business man counting his losses and profit with anxious mind; the wage-slave selling his labour cheaply and without security; the artist debarred from the effort to improve his skill and quest for his ideals by the insistence of the economic spur.

We aim at the common service; we desire that all should serve the community, that no longer should there be divers classes of persons; the hewers of wood and the drawers of water; the intellectuals, the leisured classes, who are merely parasites. The Individualist cries: 'Freedom.' We answer: 'Thou shalt not exploit.' 'Thou shalt not be a parasite.'

Yet we would have nothing of dictatorship: we believe that a public opinion can be treated which will produce a general willingness to serve the community. The exception to that general willingness will become, we believe, altogether a rarity; we would not have the occasional oddity who will not join the general effort disciplined by law; the disapprobation, even the pity of his fellows will insure his rarity.

The thought: 'I will not produce because I can secure a better living as a non-producer,' whether it be the thought of an employer, or of an unemployed worker, is a typical product of Capitalism. A society in which that thought predominates is inevitably one of poverty and exploitation. The thought: 'I will not produce if I can avoid it' falls like a blight upon society to-day. It is the inevitable product of the capitalist system.

Let us produce in abundance; let us secure plenty for all; let us find pleasure in producing; these thoughts must pervade the community if it is to be able to provide, in lavish measure, plenty for all—in material comfort, in art, in learning, in leisure. At such a community we aim. We emphasise the need for the Workshop Councils.

The Individualist fears that even the autonomous Workshop Councils may lead to the circumscribing of personal liberty. We however desire the Workshop Councils in order to insure personal liberty.

In the Communist Society at which we aim all will share the productive work of the community and all will take a part in organising that work.

How can it be done?

In these days of great populations and varied needs and desires people are not willing to return to the stage at which every individual or family made its own house, clothing, tools, utensils, and cultivated its own patch of soil and provided all its own tools. A return to productive work, a discarding of artificial and useless toil, we desire and expect to see, but work in which many workers co-operate we expect and desire to retain.

The building of engines and ships and all sorts of machinery, the construction of cables, weaving and spinning by machinery, and numberless other things are dependent on the co-ordinated work of large numbers of people. It is probable that developments in the use of electricity and other present and future inventions, will tend to render less economically necessary than used to be the case, both the vast workshop and the vast city. Moreover the influence of profit-making being eliminated, the unhealthy and uncongenial massing together of people will be checked. Nevertheless for at least a very long time, the large scale production wrought by many inter-related workers, will remain a necessary condition of maintaining both plenty and leisure for all.

If large numbers of people are working together and if the varied needs of large populations are to be supplied, the work will come either to be directed from above or from below. Unless each individual in the work shop is an independent co-operator, taking a conscious share in the organisation of the collective work, then all the workers in the shop must be under the direction of a manager; and that manager must either be appointed by those whom he directs or by some outside authority.

The same principle applies throughout the entire field of production, distribution, and transport; unless the workshops co-ordinate themselves, unless they themselves arrange their relationship with their sources of supply and the recipients of their products, then that co-ordination must be affected by an outside authority with power to enforce its authority.

In order to promote the liberty and initiative of the individual, as well as for the welfare of the collectivity, therefore, we emphasize the need for the autonomous workshop councils, co-ordinated along the lines of production, distribution and transport.

'Women members of Parliament'

[*Workers' Dreadnought*, 15 December 1923]

The return of eight women to Parliament marks an advance in public opinion. People have realised at last that women are persons with all the human attributes, not merely some of them and that women have an equal right with men to take part in making the social conditions under which they live.

This country has not been first in admitting women to political equality with men: other countries preceded us in admitting women to the legislature, and we have not yet reached political equality in the franchise here, although the women of this country led the way in agitating for political and legal equality.

It is interesting to observe that the legal barriers to women's participation in Parliament and its elections were not removed until the movement to abolish Parliament altogether had received the strong encouragement of witnessing the overthrow of Parliamentary Government in Russia and the setting up of Soviets.

Those events in Russia evoked a response throughout the world not only amongst the minority who welcomed the idea of Soviet Communism, but also amongst the upholders of reaction. The latter were by no means oblivious to the growth of Sovietism when they decided to popularise the old Parliamentary machine by giving to some women both votes and the right to be elected.

Election to Parliament is always much more a question of the strength of the party machine than of the qualities of the candidate. An archangel would be defeated at the polls if he lacked a strong party backing. The majority of the electors vote without having heard or seen the candidate, who actually plays but a minor part in the election. Nevertheless, there was undoubtedly some prejudice to be overcome by the first women candidates; which acted as a makeweight against them, outbalancing what would otherwise have been the normal strength of the party behind them.

This election is the first in which the electors have voted for the successful women candidates to any appreciable extent on the merits of those candidates. Lady Astor, Mrs Wintringham, and Mrs Phillipson entered Parliament merely as deputies of their husbands. This fact, from a democratic standpoint, was particularly objectionable in the case of Lord Astor since he was thus given a voice in ruling the people through both Houses of Parliament.

The women who entered Parliament in place of their husbands introduced no original policies, nor do we anticipate that their successors will do so. They were nominated candidates and have been elected to represent certain parties, and, in the main, their parliamentary doings must follow that of their men colleagues in the party, otherwise the party will cast them out.

Most of these hardships, and the more serious of them, cannot be remedied within the system. Most of them, too, cannot even be mitigated without tampering with economic conditions; and there, at once, the general party policy will certainly obtrude itself, and the party woman will be called to heel by the whips like a party man if she stray too far from the party plan.

Nevertheless, on questions of the special hardships of women and on questions specially related to sex the women members of the various parties may sometimes show themselves a trifle before or a trifle behind the general standard of their party by adhering in some respects to what has come to be generally regarded as the accepted programme of feminism. It is so regarded because it was adopted by certain women of the middle and upper classes, who were, for their day, more or less advanced though narrow and prejudiced in many respects, but who were of forceful energetic personality and built up a movement reflecting their conception of what should be the legal status of their sex and primarily of their class. That programme is, in many respects, retrograde and, and in all respects, incompatible with Socialism.

One should not expect to find new policies on any subject springing up from Parliament; the atmosphere there is arid, the life stultifying to thought. At best — at very best — the Members of Parliament carry on the politics they adopted before they entered there, or catch up some vibrations or movements going on outside. Parliament is a decaying institution: it will pass away with the capitalist system: it will be replaced by the industrial soviets, when production, distribution and transport pass out of the hands of the capitalist, to become the joint concern of the whole people, each branch of industry being administered by those who are engaged in it.

Women can no more put virtue into the decaying parliamentary institution than can men: it is past reform and must disappear.

Once the special legal disabilities of women in politics were in large measure, though not wholly, removed, it became inevitable that there should be little difference between the woman in politics and the man in politics. That is as it should be.

The women professional politician is neither more nor less desirable than the man professional politician: the less the world has of either the better it is for it. The time to look forward to is that in which there will no longer be a body of persons whose business it is to rule or to listen to speeches of the rulers and their puppets and to while away hour upon hour waiting to record their votes in division lobbies to the call of the party whips.

The Soviets, under Communism, will meet for the administration of the services of the community, not to carry on the party warfare which is inevitable to present-day society, because it is based on competition and torn by the struggles of warring classes. To the women, as to the men, the hope of the future lies not through Parliamentary reform, but free Communism and the soviets.

'Capitalism or Communism for Russia?'

[*Workers' Dreadnought*, 31 May 1924]

The appeal which we publish on our front page from the Workers' Group of Russia, reveals the struggle still continuing there between the opposing ideals of capitalism and communism. Capitalism is still in the ascendant. In Russia, the cue of its protagonists is no longer to sing the praises of private enterprise and the right of every man to do as he likes with his own. They pose now as the prophets of centralised efficiency, trustification, State control, and the discipline of the proletariat in the interests of increased production.

The Communist advocates of the New Economic Policy (NEP) of intensified capitalism explain their lapse from principle by the plea that Russia must be developed by capitalism before she will be fitted for Communism. They hope to keep the teeth and claws of capitalism to reasonable proportions.

The non-Communist manipulators of the NEP are working in an element which habit has made appear to them the only natural and possible state of affairs. They are growing in power and numbers and will passionately adhere to their own post-revolutionary acquisitions. To the dominant class it is always easier to maintain things as they are and proceed by the old methods than to forge new ones.

The result is that the Russian workers remain wage slaves, and very poor ones, working, not from free will, but under compulsion of economic need, and kept in their subordinate position by a State coercion which is more pronounced than in the countries where the workers have not recently shown their capacity to rebel with effect.

In spite of the NEP and the advocates of State capitalisation and trustification, however, the urge towards free and complete Communism is not dead in Russia as is evidenced by the existence of the Workers' Group and other Left Wing bodies.

The Left Wing bodies, both consciously and doubtless also unconsciously to a certain extent, are forces working towards the disintegration of capitalism and all its methods. They are working towards the creation of a new system in which instead of society being maintained under the control of a centralised directorate imposing its will by economic compulsion and backed by force of arms, social needs will be met by self-motivating units co-operating for mutual ends.

Those who, professing the Communist faith, yet fail to recognise this part which the Left Wing bodies are destined to play in the evolutionary process are apt to regard with regret the very existence of a Left Wing movement. In Russia such superficial observers complain that Left-Wing activities will arouse discontent with present conditions, and so, perhaps, hinder the growth of production and cause various troubles by upsetting the disciplined acceptance by the workers of the directing authorities.

In the same manner the educationalists who have sought to awaken the pupils' own initiative and to institute self government and pupils' organisation of the curriculum in the schools, have been met with objections that order has been replaced by chaos and that the ratio of knowledge acquired by the pupils has been grievously reduced.

The educational pioneers have persevered in spite of discouragement and have been able to produce schools in which the pupils are able to maintain a more fruitful and harmonious order than that which the old schools imposed from above. They have been able to demonstrate by results that the knowledge which they have stimulated their pupils to acquire for themselves becomes a permanent possession and part of the personality.

So it will be with the ideals of those who are working for the complete emancipation of the race from economic subjection and the authoritarianism that accompanies it.

Many Communists outside Russia object to the searchlight of fact being turned upon Soviet Russia by their fellow Communists. They desire to have it appear that everything is perfect there. They imagine it to be bad propaganda to admit frankly the failures and shortcomings in the land of revolution and to criticise the methods and expedients resorted to by those who have secured the power. Their objections are short sighted, for after all, what we desire to vindicate and to achieve is Communism itself and not the policy or position of any party.

If we pretend that the present regime in Russia is Communism, is actually the sort of life towards which we are striving, those who observe its shortcomings will naturally tell us that our ideal is a very faulty one.

Part III

Women and citizenship, 1930–35

After the closure in 1924 of the *Workers' Dreadnought*, the Communist newspaper which Pankhurst had edited since 1917, Pankhurst withdrew from full-time political campaigning, moved out of the East End which had been her political home for ten years, and opened a workers' tea-room in Woodford, near Epping Forest. The venture was shared by Silvio Corio, an Italian anarchist who had lived in London for many years and who had worked on the *Dreadnought* since 1917. He became her long-term partner and father to her only child, a son, who was born in 1927 when Pankhurst was forty-five.

She now embarked on a remarkably productive period of writing; in the five years up to 1930, her publishing interests were extremely eclectic and included a book on the politics of India, a pamphlet on Interlanguage, a world language, and a translation of a Romanian epic poet, Mihail Eminescu. But by the end of the 1920s her writing became much more firmly focused, as she returned to women's politics as her subject. Her first major book on women since *The Suffragette* (1911) was *Save the Mothers* (1930), a social report on the appalling condition of women during pregnancy, labour and the post-natal period and the gross inadequacy of the maternity services in Great Britain. It was a sign that all Pankhurst's hopes for revolutionary change had long disappeared that she should write a 'plea' to the reform-minded middle-class to ameliorate the conditions of working-class mothers, but she did so on the basis of women's citizenship and the denial to women of their proper political inheritance. The text is discussed in detail in the Introduction.

The anger in 'Women's Citizenship' (reprinted here) came from her recognition of the yawning gap between the vision of the pre-war

139

women's movement and the present lack of achievements. Where are the equal opportunities for education and training? Where are the new houses, nurseries, schools, and health services that would so benefit the majority of women and their families? Why do the women of today not fight for what is theirs by right? With another World War menacing, Pankhurst saw time slipping away.

Save the Mothers

*A plea for measures to prevent
the annual loss of about 3000
child-bearing mothers and 20,000
infant lives in England and Wales
and a similar grievous wastage in
other countries* (1930)

[FROM CHAPTER 1: THE PRESENT WASTAGE]

The heavy loss of mothers in childbirth today commands the attention of the entire civilised world. In England and Wales alone more than 39,000 mothers lives were sacrificed in the birth process during the last ten years.

Whilst the death-rate from all other causes in all civilised countries has shown a great and constant reduction, the maternal death-rate alone has remained practically stationary since the beginning of the century.

To this statement one exception must be made; the rate of still-births, so far as statistics are obtainable, is also apparently stationary; whilst the death-rate of infants under one month of age, and especially under one week, has by no means shared in the great reduction of the infant death-rate during the subsequent eleven months of life, which has occurred almost universally during the last twenty years.

The causes of still-births and of infant deaths in the first days and weeks of life are, in the main, the same causes which lead to the maternal deaths and maternal invalidity. Birth injuries are a major cause of still-birth and neo-natal death.

In England and Wales, out of an average of 750,000 births, some 3,000 mothers die annually, approximately one mother losing her life for every 250 babies born. There is an average of three still-births for every hundred live births. In 1928 there were 660,267 births and 2,920 mothers died in childbirth, a mortality rate of 4.42 per 1,000 births, the highest recorded since the revised classification in 1911. (. . .)

Statistics reveal that the English and Welsh counties and county boroughs where maternal mortality is highest are the textile towns of Lancashire and Yorkshire, where mothers bear the dual burden of factory and household toil; the Welsh mining areas, where housing and sanitation are deplorable and domestic work peculiarly heavy, and the scattered mountainous districts where medical assistance is difficult to obtain at short notice. The textile towns, where maternal mortality is grievously high, are still grave offenders, also, in relation to infant mortality. Wigan in 1923–27, showing an infant mortality of 108 per 1,000 births, is seventh on the black list for maternal mortality. Burnley and Oldham, with an infant death-rate of 107 and 105 per 1,000 births, are sixth and third in the maternal death-rate. (. . .)

Septic infection in all countries heads the list [of principal causes of death] causing a toll of more than 1,100 deaths; wholly preventable by proper precautions against infection; yet, through neglect of these, it remains the principal cause of maternal mortality in all countries. Other dangers to the mother are the toxæmias of pregnancy, including albuminuria, with its common and terrible manifestation, eclampsia, or puerperal convulsions, which should be treated by pre-natal care and dieting; haemorrhages before or after delivery, often the cause of fatality and requiring immediate aid; disproportion between the head of the child and the mother's pelvis, mal-presentations (the child lying crossways or otherwise badly placed for delivery), uterine inertia, and many other conditions leading to prolonged and difficult labour, calling for great skill on the part of whoever is aiding the mother in what has become a mortal struggle to give birth. Injuries and shock from difficult labour are a frequent cause of death. All these ills are declared by the experts to be largely preventable.

The origin of puerperal sepsis is the subject of much discussion. Auto- or self-infection by the sufferer's own organism has been spoken of as a possible source, but is generally dismissed as applying if, at all, only to a very small minority of cases. It is generally agreed that infection is most commonly carried to the mother during or after labour, by the hands of an attendant, by the mother's own fingers, by the use of imperfectly sterilised instruments or dressings. The origin of infection has been attributed to ulcers and sores on the body of the infected mother herself, her husband or someone who has waited upon her, or other patients in the same hospital ward, and to contact with persons suffering at the time from an unhealthy condition of the throat and nose from whatever cause. Infection spreads rapidly from patient to patient. It may travel with the doctor and midwife from house to house. In maternity institutions any failure to isolate infected patients and disinfect wards, any laxity in permitting attendants to pass from infected patients to others, is punished immediately by devastating results.

Where labour is difficult and prolonged and the mother is exhausted by her travail, where her general physique is poor, she is vulnerable to sepsis, and to all the ills which may follow childbirth. Lack of care, or of judgment in the accoucheur, undue haste, unwise or unskilful operative interference may lead to her death.

The overwhelming importance of the nutrition available to the pregnant woman in relation to her powers of resistance to infection is suggested by the experiments into the anti-infective properties of Vitamin A amongst maternity patients of the Jessop Hospital Sheffield in 1929, carried out by Mellanby and Green. During the two years 1927–28 there had been a mortality amongst certain septic cases of 92 per cent, twenty-two mothers out of twenty-four having died. In 1929 five infected cases were treated with Vitamin A and all recovered, though each of these patients had been precariously ill when the treatment began.

It should be obvious that for pregnant mothers a sufficient and suitable diet should be treated as an essential. (. . .)

The following budget of an expectant mother living in East London, and having three children under twelve years, indicates the poor diet available for her, and her inability to provide either for herself or her children the vitamins and calories prescribed by the scientific dietician. The husband's wage is 44s., and 1s. 4d. is stopped for Unemployment Insurance and National Health. [see over page]

The poor little balance of 1s. is too small indeed for all that remains unmentioned—including the husband's and children's pocket-money. Five pounds a year, at the rate of 2s a week, is a meagre reserve indeed to provide clothing for the whole family and repairs and replacements of utensils and furnishings; for illness, amusements and emergencies. Obviously it is insufficient; many urgent necessities can only be provided by cutting down the food allowance indicated in the budget on the latter days of the week. This the habitual proceeding in poor

	s.	d.	
Rent	12	0	
Insurances . . .	1	0	
Coal, 1 cwt.	2	4	Some people pay 1s. per week into Coal Club all year round and have in bigger quantities as they want it.
Gas, approx. . . .	1	6	
Bread, 8d. per day . .	4	0	(Bread for six days)
2lbs. margarine . . .	1	0	
Milk 2 pts. per day . .		10½	
2 tins cond. milk . .		7	
Soap and soda . . .		7	
Flour		5½	
4 lbs. sugar		10	
1 lb. tea	2	0	
Dinners	10	6	Average cost 1s. 3d. per day except Sundays, which would be 2s. 6d. or 3s.
Cheese, 1 lb. . . .	1	0	
Preserved meats . . .	1	0	For packing man's lunches.
Tallyman or Club . .	1	0	For clothing, boots, curtains, etc.
Loan Club	1	0	From which money can be borrowed for confinement, illness or emergencies paid out at Christmas.
£2	1	8	

homes, the mother being the first to go short. The budget makes no provision for fruit, though by getting fish when it is cheap, instead of meat, some pence for fruit may be spared. It should be observed that a woman regarded as shiftless may sometimes be one who spends a relatively large proportion of the family income on food and a smaller proportion on clothing than her neighbour, who, with the same income, presents a more prosperous appearance, but who in some cases is more ill-nourished and suffers accordingly.

The National Baby Week Council, in co-operation with the *Daily News*, recently offered prizes to County Boroughs, Boroughs and Urban Districts, showing the greatest percentage reduction in the rate of infant mortality in the first four weeks of life. Inquiries were made of the Medical Officers of Health in the nineteen competing areas to ascertain the influences thought to have led to the reductions obtained. Seven areas ascribed improvement to better midwifery, seventeen to better institutional accommodation, seventeen to attendance at ante-natal clinics, eighteen out of nineteen to the provision of the Local Authority of milk and meals for necessitous expectant mothers.

[FROM CHAPTER 2: THE MOTHER'S CASE]

The working-class mother comes to her travail worn with toil. Week by week she has become increasingly unfit for the daily round. Her growing burden weighs heavily upon her, almost unsupportable. Her back aches, her legs swell, her feet burn. Often she is overcome by vomiting and almost frantic with headache; yet there is no rest for her. The needs of the family call her constantly to her tasks, and if, in prostration, she is compelled to neglect them, innumerable resultant discomforts surge up around her, and work accumulates hugely for another day. The children must be sent to school clean and tidy; the washing for them makes a big drain on her energies. When they are all in bed she is darning the great holes in their stockings and patching their clothes. At night she is too tired and discomforted to sleep. She is oppressed by a suffocating sensation of pressure; she has cramp in a limb, her feet and ankles burn, her teeth ache. The cheap flock mattress has gathered into lumps, the slack springs of the old bed sag and creak under her weight. Fearing to waken her husband, she creeps away to a chair. When in the early morning sleep steals over her the children begin to rouse. The youngest already shouts to be taken to her arms. The husband will soon be rising to go to his work.

Even where poverty is not acute, the many claims on the income of a small wage-earner necessitate continual sacrifice of desires and needs. The mother habitually denies herself at every turn to provide the requirements of husband and children. In the stress of morning work she commonly gains the habit of eating no breakfast. Her other meals are interrupted by the necessity of feeding the younger children and waiting on the whole family. The habit of self-neglect is scarcely broken in each successive pregnancy. The clamorous needs of the children about her often obscure the claims of the unborn, in spite of her rueful thought for it. Her own needs are unconsidered. Moreover, her appetite is poor, her digestion awry; she has acquired the habit of snatching a slice of bread and a cup of tea after the meal is done. The food she has cooked for the others is nauseant to her. To prepare something special for herself, which might be a little more costly, would seem to her an impossible selfishness. In times of stress it is always she who goes hungry, to leave more food for the breadwinner and the children, taking herself only what meagre scraps may be left. 'Mate' he calls her, and truly a mate she is, steadfast as steel, in the enormous multitude of homes.

What more terrible spectacle than the woman who needs to feed for two yet lacks the food for one! Back through the years there flashes on me the vision of a cold grey morning in smoke-ridden Manchester: I in the Oxford Road on my way to school, a woman in a shawl, gauntly emaciated, yet big with child. She stretches a fleshless arm to take from the butcher's board a long bone, utterly meatless. Two well-groomed gentlemen, one with a tall hat, pass me and break into a run, seizing her a few paces from the shop. She turns to them a haggard and tragic face. The butcher runs out, a crowd gathers, a policeman appears.

My knees are trembling, my heart beating to suffocation, the sound of torrential waters roars in my ears. I lean against the wall, feeling in a storm of pity and indignation a poignant regret at being only a helpless little girl. The sad procession, with the policeman's helmet showing above the heads of the people moves slowly on.

In East London, many years later, I entered a butcher's shop in the Old Ford Road, bent on distributing suffrage literature to the crowd there. From the darkness outside a woman at the unglazed window, the glare of the gas lamps falling upon her, snatched some scraps of meat. The butcher leapt with a shout, thrust his great girth through the aperture and grasped her wrist. Then, seeing her pregnant, suddenly he released her. 'You can take it; that's all right—to you.' She slipped away, but again he shouted: 'Here! some of you! Tell her to wait a minute!' To a clamour of friendly voices the people turned her about and hustled her forward. He rushed to his block, hacked off a great lump of beef and cast it to her: 'That'll be better for you!' Tearfully grasping the gift of his rough kindness, again she vanished into the shadows.

'Hard work is the finest thing in the world for a pregnant woman!' runs the complacent old saw, the falsity of which only the woman compelled to practise its harsh precept knows. A young Borough

Councillor, who tentatively inquired from her colleagues whether the Medical Officer at the Ante-natal Clinic ought not to have power to supply 'home helps' before the confinement was confidently assured that such a provision would be absurd. A few days later she visited a friend whose wife, a University student, was expecting a second child in three weeks time. The woman was already confined to bed and absolutely incapacitated from working by excessively swollen legs. This was a revelation!

On the fourth floor of a block of barrack dwellings is a woman with a face of unutterable suffering. Her eyes are dull, her limp hair falls neglected. She is dressed in shabby, ungainly clothes. Once she was like those bright, active little girls who climb on her knees, boisterous and unheeding. They too, in their early womanhood, may be faded and worn as she—repellent thought!

In a few days' time she will bring forth another life. She is tortured by a varicose ulcer; her leg terribly swollen, she cannot bear to put her foot to the ground. But there is work to do. She rests her knee upon the seat of a chair, dragging herself on this cumbrous crutch about the room, dressing the children, making the bed and washing up the crockery used at the last meal; and with a slow, painful effort stooping to pick up the odds and ends the little girls have littered about the floor.

At last, unable to endure her pain, she lies on the bed for a brief space, but just as the agony of that leg which should have rest begins to ease, she must be up, for the children are asking for their tea. Stifling the impatient protest, which for a moment rises to her lips, she crushes the noisiest little youngster in her arms, kissing and praising her in a burst of self-reproachful love. But her leg is tortured; she doubles it under her, pressing all her weight upon it in the attempt to deaden sensation, while she spreads the margarine on the bread.

These two cheerless rooms are a 'model dwelling' built by the London County Council. The water tap at the sink, shared by several families, is outside on the landing. A drawer for the coal is in the living-room. Above it the cupboard provided for food has a door of perforated zinc, through which the coal-dust flies in and settles on the food. Everything in the room is of the poorest and oldest, save the sewing-machine, by which for years she has mainly supported her household.

She is alone with the children. Her husband, seldom in work, has a 'job outside London' now and sends an occasional dole.

Relief from heavy housework in the later stages of pregnancy would be a boon of inestimable worth to poor mothers; few indeed can obtain it, and many bring about miscarriages and displacements by lifting and reaching. It is the mother herself who prepares the lying-in room; unsparing in her care and anxiety to make the best appearance possible, if her spirit be not already broken. She gives the whole house a special clean down, in view of the strangers who will come in to take control of it when she is incapacitated. Frequently it happens that climbing to dust the top shelf, or hang clean curtains, unwieldy with her burden, she falls from the chair she had perched upon a table or a box to reach thus high. (A step-ladder is a non-essential and therefore absent from poor dwellings.)

During the agony of her labour and the weakness which follows, the mother is torn by anxiety, for the welfare of her children, disturbed by the worries of a small, poor home, overcrowded and lacking innumerable essentials of comfort and privacy, devoid of peace. Often during the painful struggle of the birth crisis, some little child, terrified by the withdrawal of the all-protecting mother care, and the advent of a strange woman, hungry and tired, has hidden itself in poignant misery under her bed of pain, to be found there sleeping at last, when tardy anxiety was aroused on its behalf. A group of little ones, denied admittance to the home during the long hours of travail, sits huddled together on the doorstep in the cold winter evening, far past bed-time, listening in anxious sorrow to the faint, recurrent sound of a mother's groans. Sometimes the toddler youngest in age has contracted a chill, with protracted or even fatal results.

What I know of many little family histories leads me to the belief that statistics showing the proportion of cases in which the onset of fatal illness in children took place during the mother's confinement would probably reveal a heavy incidence during that period.

As soon as the mother is able to stagger to her legs, and long before she has regained her normal state, she may have to take upon herself the exhausing duties of sick nurse to a child who fell ill during her confinement, in addition to nourishing and caring for the new-born baby and performing single-handed all the exacting labours of a home neglected during her brief period of surrender. Whether she be attended by a midwife, who visits once, or at most twice daily for the ten days following the confinement; or whether it is a doctor and a handy-woman who deliver her, such attention as she receives can rarely be considered nursing and is far indeed from the comfort of the well-do-do woman, with her doctor and trained monthly maternity nurse, holding the CMB certificate. Even during the ten days of the midwife's attendance, the working mother is too often not free from housework. Little children cry about her bed, whimpering to be taken into consoling arms. Toddlers fall, and are hurt, she reaches down to draw them up to her. Elder children come with basins and ingredients, that she may mix the pudding; with bowls of water and soap, that she may wash the napkins of the newly-born, or the knickers of the child of last year's birth. Presently there is a scream; a little girl has scalded her arm, or another child's foot, in pouring from the kettle she boiled that mother might wash the clothes. Even if some neighbour or relative can come in to help with the heavier housework, many tasks inevitably fall to the lot of the lying-in mother and her little ones. If they are able to drag themselves out of bed, mothers often get up during the ten days to do work that is pressing. Many a mother has told me that after doing so she has washed her feet that the midwife might not know.

The result of this premature toil is prolapse of the womb, varicose ulcers and other ills, mothers who wear a ring to mitigate a displacement and visit the out-patients' departments of hospitals to get it changed, or, shrinking from the presence of students and the hours of waiting which must be faced, prefer to pay what they can ill afford to a private practitioner to get it done; mothers in still worse case, whose condition calls for attention, but who drift on without it, mothers who are lying in the Gynæcological wards, their lives a martyrdom.

'Pardon me for writing to you,' a mother pleaded, 'but I am in such pain I don't know what I am doing. Well, to begin with, my husband went away on August 6th to the Great War, 1914–18, and my baby was born on August 13th. That is three years ago, and having six children I got about too soon, and had to take to my bed for eight weeks, and I have had my leg bad ever since. I have been in bed four weeks, three weeks, and two weeks; but the doctor said that if I don't rest till it is quite well I shall be an invalid all my life—think of me, only thirty-eight years old, not being able to look after my little ones. You know I make everything they wear and knit their socks and vests; I am not a lazy woman. I thought if you could get me away, so I could sit down and rest my leg, I would get better and be a help to everybody, for I am only in the way like I am, a misery to myself and my husband; he has been home for a year now. If it were not for him I think I should go mad. . . . Oh, do your very best for me so that I can get better—a very miserable mother!'

'Women's citizenship'

(n.d., approx. 1934)
[from file 131, Pankhurst Papers, International
Institute of Social History, Amsterdam]

This is the twenty-first anniversary of the day Emily Wilding Davison gave her life on the Derby race course to make Britain pause and think of the women's great fight for citizenship. Literally, thousands of women went to prison for that cause; many died, many were injured and maimed, lost their employment, sacrificed ease and prosperity.

Are we satisfied with the results? Have we achieved what we desired from women' citizenship for the nation and for the world? No! I for one, am not satisfied — I want much more! In the decade before the war, the women's movement led the country; no other movement had such faith and fire. British women led the women of the world; by our lead they were also enfranchised.

Much has been gained since then: women have flocked into professions and businesses, distinguished themselves in many fields; they have entered Parliament, achieved Cabinet rank. Their family, social and political status has been immensely raised.

Yet the torrential Women's Movement has dwindled to a mere streak. The average woman, who, by the hundred thousand, was enthused twenty years ago with the sense of a social mission, is today concerned merely with her own or her husband's financial prospects, with dress and a round of visits and amusements with no great vistas.

Amongst crowds of young women, the emancipation of today displays itself mainly in cigarettes and shorts, and there is even a reaction from the ideal of intellectual and emancipated womanhood to be seen in painted lips and nails, and the return of the trailing skirts which impede progress, and other absurdities of dress and deportment, which betoken the slave woman's sex appeal rather than the free woman's intelligent companionship. The heedless beauties immersed in the social world, flitting from a party at Ascot to the midnight ball, whilst the international firmament is dank with the menace of a world conflict and the cry of despair rises from the mothers of the unemployed, recall Nero fiddling while Rome burned, and Marie Antoinette, in her blindness, enquiring of the starving populace; 'Why don't they eat cake?' The social butterflies of today recall their prototypes of eighteenth-century France in an epoch trembling to its fall.

Even the women who have passed through Parliament have failed to realise the magnitude of their charge. They have secured some little noticed, though good humanitarian legislation, but mostly have trotted obediently to the Party's Whip. They have sponsored no epoch-making causes.

Yet we predicted women's citizenship would open a new era of world happiness and social wisdom; would raise society to a higher plane of friendship and efficiency, do nothing less than end war once and for ever; sweep away poverty and the slums; transform education and ethics; place everything affecting the home and family on a surer and lovelier basis; cherish maternity, infancy and old age. We declared the creative spirit of motherhood transcends the smaller, more ephemeral differences of nationality and of class. Between that tremendous hope and the state of the world today, how terrible the gulf!

It may be that the greatest social advance we expected from women's citizenship was frustrated by the fact that we won the vote, not in peace time, but in the last exhausted year of the Great War. Instead of the great social advance anticipated, we have unemployment of a magnitude never known in history, economic stagnation and chaos checking all social reforms and progress.

It was in the surge of the great movement of twenty years ago that voluntary organisations of women set going the Infant Welfare Clinics before the Government contributed a penny. Initiated by British women, these clinics have spread almost throughout the world, affecting a revolution in infant nurture, which has reformed the practice of the medical and nursing profession in this regard, and produced a great reduction in infant mortality. Yet the foundation has not been built upon; the death rate of mothers, which has seen no reduction during the century, still rises. Despite the verdict of the

Ministry of Health, after a three years' inquiry into maternal deaths, that more than half the mothers who died could have been saved had they received adequate care, the promised National Maternity Service moulders in the Parliamentary pigeon holes. Here and everywhere it awaits the solution of mother wit.

The slums are still with us. The fall in the natural death rate is slowing down, the fall in the birth rate accelerating. Our population is on the verge of declining as the French. I write it sadly, not as one who thinks of the loss of man-power for an army, but because I see in it a grey lack of fulfilment for millions of human lives. Rooms in someone's house with children barred, or to buy a house which will make a drain on the small income, leaving no place for children, are the only alternatives facing countless young couples today(. . .)

Education has made no great strides here this century. See the gloomy and inefficient school buildings, the cheerless play-grounds of our public elementary schools, without a leaf or a blade of grass, a toy or a scrap of gymnastic apparatus; the teachers struggling with excessive numbers and two or more classes in a room. Go to the hosts of little private schools, where parents send their children, hoping to do better for them, and see there children of all ages and stages crowded into one room, taught by a single teacher.

Yet I know, and you know that, under modern conditions, we, collectively, can produce an abundance of all the material things in life. Only our lack of collective ability to cooperate and our poverty in zeal for the general welfare are responsible for the present stagnation and death.

Women are immeasurably better equipped for achievement than they were when they suffered martyrdom and imprisonment, and their hard-spared cash poured up to the militant platforms. Only the actresses and a few novelists earned substantially then. Now, there is a veritable host of professional and business women, but their aims are mainly narrowed to personal needs. Even the dismissal of the married women teachers and others employed by the public authorities, retrograde and cruel as the step has been, and utterly futile as an expedient for dealing with the huge economic stagnation and unemployment today, has met no effective protest, from the professional women, whose imperative duty it was to prevent the victimisation of their sisters.

Alas, we must sorrowfully admit that the great days of the women's militant social protest have not been followed by great days of social construction. A few stand out as beacons; Montessori and her scientific philosophy of the self development of the child has set a permanent seal upon educational standards; Mrs Chesterton's Cecil Houses have done more for homeless womanhood than all the local authorities have conceived of; Lilian Baylis, of Sadler's Wells and the Old Vic, as a valorous pioneer in popular art. *The Call* which is gathering strength for a great daily newspaper, owned and controlled by a million women shareholders, in the women's interest, holds promise of vitalising support for all such efforts and many more, and a breath of something new in the ethics of our time.

We need the fire which lit the pre-war militant movement. If women would combine, there is nothing they would not do. They could promote ambitious ventures; the long hoped for re-housing of the people, carried out with the vigour and intensity such as was put into the making of death-dealing material during the war, garden suburbs, electric homes, co-operative homes to meet the needs of the millions, with collective nursery schools, laundry, cleaning and repair services, people's theatres, schools on the newest lines, the urgently needed maternity and health services, are objectives not too difficult of attainment. They could promote great things by their own efforts, force their demands for the health and happiness of the people on local and national authorities, compel the nations to abolish armaments and maintain peace.

The Votes for Women Movement was a wide liberating and civilising movement. Behind it was the thought that women are human beings as well as mothers, and that personal liberty, citizenship, education, professional skill, opportunity to be, to do and to serve, must be open to them. It was also a Movement to substitute reason for force, to exalt justice above mere power, to bring to the nation and to the world the protective and creative love and care which is at the root of motherhood.

We need a rebirth of the Women's Movement today. The saving power of motherhood was never more needed. The world in its travail welters in economic chaos, trembling under the menace of a war which would destroy all civilised life in a devastating rain of poison gas and disease-producing bacteria. No day has ever been so critical, no call so great! I believe our womanhood will again be stimulated to great ends, looking more deeply than heretofore into the whirlpool of social chaos.

153

F

Part IV

Remaking socialist–feminism 1931–35

In the early thirties, Pankhurst wrote her best-known book, *The Suffragette Movement* (1931) which is discussed in detail in the Introduction. It was the first of three autobiographical histories, in which Pankhurst takes the reader through her childhood and family life in Manchester and London, her years as an art student and her life in the militant suffrage movement. It is a powerful construction and celebration of a socialist–feminist political history which was already being written out of the official version of the pre-war women's movement.

Following on the success of this volume (George Bernard Shaw was to compare Pankhurst to St Joan after reading it), she followed it up rapidly with *The Home Front* (1932), a rather stylistically incoherent account of her experiences in the East End of London during the First World War. Rather than a continuous narrative, Pankhurst presents the reader with a series of short autonomous sections juxtaposed one after the other, as if to underline her inability, as a socialist, feminist and pacifist, to represent coherently what she saw as the enormous obscenity of the war, and the degree of injustice and suffering that it brought to the destitute people of the East End. She provides many individual case studies and describes the rudimentary social services her East London Federation of Suffragettes set up to ameliorate the worst suffering, including cost-price restaurants, milk centres and baby clinics, a nursery and a toy factory to provide women with employment.

The third volume of her autobiographical history, In the Red Twilight, remains as a draft in several hand written notebooks among her papers at Amsterdam. It takes her history through her revolutionary years as a communist, from the time she set up the People's Russian Information Bureau, and began to play a leading part in the 'Hands Off Russia' campaign to stop the Allied blockade, to her hazardous clandestine journeys across Europe to make contact with revolutionaries such as Clara Zetkin in Germany, and Lenin in Moscow.

However, for reasons that are not explained, she abandoned the project and began to write a biography of her mother, which was published in 1935, as *The Life of Emmeline Pankhurst*. The 'plot' was the same as for *The Suffragette Movement*: militant suffragism was a product of the evangelical–socialist movement at the turn of the century (represented in the text by Keir Hardie), but was perverted by its leaders, principally Christabel Pankhurst, but supported by Mrs Pankhurst, when they began to ignore its inheritance, became autocratic leaders, and finally repudiated and betrayed its principles during the First World War. However, compared to the representation in *The Suffragette Movement*, Mrs Pankhurst appears in the biography as tragically weak rather than malevolent, lost and confused rather than dictatorial, with the effect that Sylvia provides little convincing evidence for the basis of her mother's enormous popularity within the movement, or her stature as one of the most respected champions of women of her generation.

The Life of Emmeline
Pankhurst (1935)

Since the 1870s, when she took her husband's part in his discussions
with her father, Emmeline Pankhurst had counted herself a Socialist.
The Doctor[1] and she had been early members of the Fabian Society.
They would have joined the Social Democratic Federation, but the
personality of H. M. Hyndman and his anti-feminist attitude repelled
them. They met Keir Hardie at the International Socialist Congress
of 1888, rejoiced at his return to Parliament for West Ham in 1892,
and his brave stand for the unemployed. When, in 1894, the
Independent Labour Party he had formed the previous year engaged
in its first Parliamentary contest at Attercliffe, they went down to
help. Of all the people she knew in politics, of all the men who came
into Emmeline Pankhurst's life, the one, after her husband, who
meant most to her was undoubtedly Keir Hardie.

Dr Pankhurst's adhesion to the ILP aroused excitement in Manchester.
The Party was being assailed with great bitterness. The Doctor was
boycotted by old clients. He did not flinch; nay, increased his platform
activity; and at the first annual conference of the ILP accepted
membership of its executive. Mrs Pankhurst told the *Manchester
Labour Prophet*, a little local Labour organ, that since she joined the
Socialists she had not received the customary invitations to the Town
Hall. On July 20th, 1894, she was adopted as an ILP candidate for
the Manchester School Board; though not returned, she was forced to
make a serious beginning on the platform.

The winter of 1894 was marked by a crisis of unemployment. In

---

1 Dr Richard Pankhurst, Emmeline Pankhurst's husband. He was a doctor of law,
practising in Manchester

those days there was no insurance, no public relief of any sort for the so-called 'able-bodied poor,' save admission to the workhouse, which the bulk of the unemployed would not accept; had they done so, only an insignificant fraction of them could have been housed. Under the stirring lead of Dr and Mrs Pankhurst, a Committee for the Relief of the Unemployed was formed. Two thousand people were fed daily in Stevenson's Square, large numbers also in Ancoats, Gorton and Openshaw. Mrs Pankhurst drove out each morning collecting gifts of food from the stallholders in Shudehill Market and the city merchants, then took her place on a lorry handing out soup and bread. She formed a women's sub-committee to cope with the urgent need of the mothers and children. These efforts were used as the basis for the demand that Parliament should make itself responsible for the unemployed, and empower local authorities to acquire such land, machinery and materials as might be needed to provide them with work at Trade Union rates. In the height of the agitation, Mrs Pankhurst was elected to the Chorlton Board of Guardians, heading the poll in Openshaw, where distress was greatest.

When the unemployed, led by her husband, marched to the Chorlton Poor Law offices, she was there, on the Board, to compel the admittance of a deputation. Its claims were scornfully rejected in a heated scene, but under her protests, by turns passionate and persuasive, and the deafening roar of the indignant crowd outside, the Guardians hastily reversed their decision, and dispatched a deputation of their own to the City Council, urging it to find immediate work for the unemployed, and to take joint action with the Guardians in establishing arrangements to prevent the recurrence of such crises. Her success in securing this unprecedented action gave her an ascendancy on the Board which she never lost.

In September 1895, she read a paper at the North Western Poor Law Conference on 'the powers and duties of Poor Law Guardians in times of exceptional distress,' contending that Statutes of Elizabeth and George III had empowered Boards of Guardians to employ workless people in all kinds of industry and to acquire land and material to this end. These powers had never been withdrawn by Parliament, but had been put out of use by the restrictive action of the Poor Law Commissioners and their successors, the Local Government Board. In that conference of case-hardened administrators and experts, it was the first time such proposals had been heard; yet the agitation which had raged through the previous winter lent point and weight to them, and her presence, unexpectedly gentle and persuasive, induced a respectful hearing. Sir Walter Foster, MP, observed that he had never listened to a more able and lucid explanation of the problem, or one more calculated to assist in its solution. Sir John Hibbert expressed agreement with the demand for wider powers for Boards of Guardians.

The stir created by the paper enhanced her influence on the Chorlton Board. The clerk, David Bloomfield, gave her every assistance in his power. Reform of harsh and hoary abuses was overdue. The old men and women who had come into the workhouse to end their days sat feebly huddled on backless forms; they had nowhere to keep their letters and little keepsakes, the women lacked even a single pocket in their clothes. The children were without nightwear. Little girls of seven and eight years, clad, winter and summer, in thin cotton frocks with low necks and short sleeves, their miserable little legs devoid of nether garments, were set to scrub draughty stone corridors, as were pregnant women until the very day of their confinement. Corruption and waste were rife. The diet was mainly of bread, served out daily by weight, in one solid ration, as in a prison. The majority of the inmates left a large portion of it; immense quantities went to the swilltub. The hospital and insane asylum were ill-managed and understaffed. A single young probationer was nightly stationed alone in charge of three pavilions.

Emmeline Pankhurst demanded reform with sorrowful wrath and persuasive plea, offering a practical solution for every difficulty. A group of supporters gradually formed around her. Lockers for their belongings, wooden arm-chairs were provided for the old people. Dress and diet were reformed. The bread was cut and spread with margarine, made into puddings, substituted by other foods, each inmate having as much as he or she could eat. The hospital was reorganised. Best of all, in her eyes, was the decision, secured by her early in 1895, to remove the children to cottage homes in the country. She was on the building sub-committee, and expended a wealth of energy and zeal that the homes should be well built, both comfortable and pleasant to the eye. To achieve all this, she had tremendous contests with the reactionary rate-savers on the Board; the chief of whom was a boot merchant named Mainwaring, who was seen to write on the blotting-paper before him a self-caution for the expected contest: 'Keep your temper!'

She delivered long reports to her Openshaw constituents, and now spoke also at big Socialist meetings in Manchester and elsewhere. Her speeches were simple and untechnical, mainly devoted to municipal Socialism. The miseries of destitution daily forced themselves upon her as Guardian; as Socialist comrade she heard them from the working-class mother's own angle, and learnt the bitter humiliations and inadequacies of both public and private charity.

Stronger than ever was her desire to get her husband into Parliament because of her daily contact with social conditions desperately calling for change. In the General Election of 1895, he accepted the invitation of the ILP to contest the Gorton Division, of which Openshaw was a part. She was elated; her work there would aid in winning the seat, and in Parliament he would have Keir Hardie and this hopeful young Party around him! Sir William Mather, the retiring Liberal Member for Gorton, urged his supporters to vote for Dr Pankhurst, as a man who, above all Party considerations, would be a notable asset to the House of Commons. The President of the local Liberal Association withdrew in his favour; but the Liberal Association, unable to strike a bargain by securing the withdrawal of an ILP candidate in a neighbouring constituency, sent out its fiat against the Doctor. In vain Mrs Pankhurst, with tears in her voice, appealed at street corners: 'You put me at the top of the poll; will you not vote for the man who has taught me all I know?' In vain she dashed up to Liverpool to plead with T. P. O'Connor for the Irish vote; he answered: 'We have nothing but admiration for your husband, but we cannot support the people he is mixed up with!' 'When Keir Hardie stood up in the House of Commons for the people with a faithful, earnest, manly appeal, he stood alone. — Are you not going to send other men to support him?' Dr Pankhurst asked. The voters answered: Hatch 5,865, Pankhurst 4,261; the expenses were: Hatch £1,375, Pankhurst £342.

Next day, Mrs Pankhurst, bravely overcoming disappointment, hired a trap and drove off alone to the Colne Valley to help the ILP candidate there. Returning through Gorton after another defeat, she was recognised and stoned by a crowd of roughs, who had celebrated the Tory victory in free beer.

The ILP maintained a vigorous outdoor propaganda; to check it, the Parks Committee, whose Chairman had been opposed by an ILP candidate, John Harker, prohibited the ILP meetings in Boggart Hole

Clough, an uncultivated open space. The meetings continued despite the prohibition; Harker was fined. Dr Pankhurst, defending him, gave notice of appeal. Mrs Pankhurst and others kept up the meetings and were proceeded against in their turn. The men were fined, and refusing to pay, were soon in jail; the case against her was dismissed, though she clearly stated her intention to repeat her offence as long as she were permitted to be at large. Sunday after Sunday she took the chair at the Clough meetings now of enormous size, her pink straw bonnet a tiny rallying point in the great concourse, grouped on the slopes of that natural amphitheatre. All her old diffidence disappeared, her mellow, effortless tones carrying far beyond the shouts of excited men. She challenged the Court to imprison her, but her case was continually adjourned. Others were proceeded against; they could not be imprisoned because she was not.

The Town Clerk, the Chairman of the Parks Committee and the Lord Mayor himself had gone to see the meetings; they were compelled to appear, obliged to deny the words of their own Counsel, Keir Hardie and the best-known speakers of the ILP got themselves arrested. Great crowds assembled outside the Court to cheer the defence. The City Council passed a new by-law prohibiting all meetings in the Manchester parks except by special authorization of the Parks Committee, making it clear that no ILP meetings would be sanctioned. The Home Secretary compelled the Council to revise the by-law, and give him an undertaking that no reasonable application would be refused. It was a tremendous victory for Mrs Pankhurst, the heroine of the struggle.

* * *

[FROM CHAPTER V]

The Labour Party Emmeline Pankhurst had so ardently desired in the 1890s had come. The Trade Union Congress of 1899 had accepted Keir Hardie's scheme to run Labour candidates under the auspices of a Labour Representation Committee of affiliated Trade Unions and Socialist organisations, of which the largest and most effective was his own ILP. The Socialists thus gained the mass backing they had lacked. The Taff Vale judgement of 1901, which was a terrible reverse to the Unions, swung almost the whole Trade Union movement into line for political action. ILP enthusiasm ran high.

Mrs Pankhurst shared in the rejoicing. As we have seen, she had formed her political opinions in an atmosphere of reform and liberation. Her impressionable nature was now to be influenced by a narrowly exclusive feminist school, which saw the world of Labour in terms of 'beef-steaks and butter for working men; tea and bread for working women,' refusing to admit that the welfare of the working woman, either as mother or wage-earner, was in any degree involved in raising the status of the working class as a whole. The hitherto dormant political interest of her eldest daughter was suddenly aroused by contact with the North of England Society for Women's Suffrage. When the ILP propagandists came as usual to stay at Nelson Street, Christabel heckled them fiercely. Old friends, like the Bruce Glasiers, were dismayed by her insistence on what they considered a mere barren issue of bourgeois politics. They had broken out of political Liberalism burning with the hope of a Socialist Commonwealth. They did not, like the active feminists, feel the disfranchisement of women as a searing brand of inferiority. Some of the opportunists were actually opposed to votes for women, declaring they would vote Tory, being more reactionary than men. Philip Snowden, later a strong supporter, was then an anti. Mrs Pankhurst was thrown into a ferment; was it for this that she had devoted nine years of service and sacrifice to the ILP? She bitterly seconded Christabel's reproaches to her that she had allowed the cause of women to be effaced. From that time forward she often told me: 'Christabel is not like other women; not like you and me; she will never be led away by her affections!'

As was characteristic of her, once she had re-entered the franchise struggle, it became for her the only cause in the world. Moreover, this, and this only, was the critical moment to push it forward. Another Reform Act was due. If manhood suffrage went through without women, it would be impossible to get the franchise question reopened for a long period: and the difficulty of getting the vote would be enormously increased. The Labour Party, now becoming a reality, must make the freedom of women 'A Party Question'.

She resolved to form a new organization to be called the 'Women's Social and Political Union', taking as its slogan not 'Women's Suffrage', as of yore, but the more vivid battle-cry, 'Votes for Women!' It is curious to recall that the telling phrase was so tardily coined. On October 10th, 1903, she invited a few obscure women members of the ILP to her home, and with them formed the new Union.

Then Keir Hardie appeared; he cordially welcomed the new movement and approved its tactics; a single-clause Bill to abolish the sex disability, leaving other franchise reforms to be dealt with subsequently; a new organisation of women to push forward their own cause. Under his urge, the ILP agreed to support Dr Pankhurst's original Bill admitting women to the Parliamentary vote on the same terms as men.

The difficulty facing those who desired to make Votes for Women popular with Labour people was the complicated and backward state of the electoral law. The poor man could qualify only as a householder; or perhaps as a lodger, if he occupied unfurnished rooms, the rateable value of which was not less than £10 a year. The man of property could vote, without restriction, wherever he could prove a qualification as householder, freeholder, copy holder, £10 occupier, University graduate, and under other heads beside. If the vote were to be extended to women on the same terms, the working-class mother would not be able to qualify, for her husband, not she, would exercise the single vote open to them as householders. The ill-paid workwoman who was a lodger had seldom sticks to furnish a room even if it were rated high enough to carry a vote. On the other hand, the wives, daughters and mothers of the rich would easily provide themselves with the required qualification. To murmurs that Votes for Women on the existing terms would increase the power of wealth, Keir Hardie replied by inviting the ILP branches to take a census of the women already voting in Local Government elections. Forty branches undertook the arduous task; they recorded that out of 59,920 women voters canvassed, 82.45 per cent. were of the working class. Here, it was claimed, was the evidence needed to silence opponents, who denounced what they termed the Ladies Bill. The ILP annual Conference in Cardiff, at Easter 1904, showed its friendship to the cause of women by electing Mrs Pankhurst to the NAC[2] and instructing it to sponsor the Women's Enfranchisement Bill. Keir Hardie immediately arranged for the measure to be formally introduced by the Labour Members of Parliament.

That autumn I went to London with a National Scholarship to the Royal College of Art, and took up lodgings at 45 Park Walk, Chelsea.

2 The National Administrative Council, the executive body of the Independent Labour Party

In February 1905, my mother came to stay with me for the opening of the new Parliamentary session. Our mission was to induce some Member of Parliament to sponsor Votes for Women on one of the Friday afternoons set apart for the Second Reading of private Members' Bills, places for which were drawn by ballot. We were alone in this quest; not even the officials of the old National Union[3] were there. Keir Hardie, from the first, had promised us his place, but not another Member acceded to our pleading. Daily from the assembling to the rising of the House, often past midnight, we were there. Keir Hardie drew no place; the first twelve were pledged to other measures, but Bamford Slack, the holder of the thirteenth, agreed to take the Bill.

A thrill of life ran through the whole Suffrage movement, which had sunk into an almost moribund coma of hopelessness. That fact must always be given due emphasis when the history of the movement is reviewed.

The Bill had been set down for May 12th, the best place to be had, but only as Second Order of the day; the opponents could prevent it coming on at all by prolonging discussion on the First Order, a small utility proposition to compel road vehicles to carry a light behind as well as before. Keir Hardie had pulled every string he could to get it withdrawn. Mrs Pankhurst was almost frenzied at the unimaginative folly of men who could hold this 'trumpery little measure' against the claimant need of womanhood in bonds.

On the fateful 12th, the Lobbies of Parliament were thronged with women, Suffragists from near and far, Lancashire textile workers, more than 400 from the Co-operative Women's Guild, confident of success and mustered quite unofficially by an Australian, Nellie Alma Martel, who had run for the Commonwealth Parliament. Spurred to new eagerness by this responsive crowd, Mrs Pankhurst saw through the 'peep-hole', by which visitors may look into the House, uproarious legislators rolling in laughter at the absurdities by which the debate was being prolonged.

The Bill was talked out, of course. The placid representatives of the old National Union at once withdrew, but Mrs Pankhurst would not mildly accept frustration; a meeting of protest must be held at the door of Parliament. She thrust forward Mrs Elmy, senior in age and longest

---

3 The National Union of Women's Suffrage Societies, formed in 1897 and led by Millicent Garrett Fawcett

worker in the cause; but the police rudely jostled her and all of us down the steps. We gathered at the statue of Richard I, beside the House of Lords. The police inspector intervened. Where could we meet then; where could poor women voice their indignation? Mrs Pankhurst demanded, with tremulant voice and blazing eyes, passionately feminine, proudly commanding. The police inspector hesitated, argued, led us to Broad Sanctuary by the Abbey Gates. Keir Hardie stepped into the ranks, taking the hand of old Mrs Elmy. The little unnoticed meeting vainly demanded Government intervention to save the talked-out Bill. Yet a new note had been struck; the Militant Suffrage movement had begun.

* * *

I was back again at College. Annie Kenney joined me at Park Cottage with two pounds, advanced by Mrs Pankhurst, 'to rouse London'. We organised for the opening of Parliament, on February 16th, 1906, a procession of women and a meeting in the Caxton Hall. Keir Hardie found a donor to pay the cost. Alfieri, of the then new *Daily Mirror*, W. T. Stead, and others, kept the movement in the news; already the *Daily Mail* had christened us 'Suffragettes'.

On the day of the meeting, 400 poor women from East London marched to the Caxton Hall. Already it was thronged; Suffragists, nobodies, somebodies, were there to see those extraordinary Suffragettes. Emmeline Pankhurst stood before them, appealing, compelling, wearing the dignity of a mother who has known great sorrow; her habitual elegance of dress and manner told with them as women. With scarcely a gesture, phrases of simple eloquence sprang to her lips, her eye flashed lightnings. Her wonderful voice, poignant and mournful, and shot with passion, rose with a new thrill. Deeply she stirred them; many silently pledged their faith to her for life. News came that the King's Speech was read, that it promised to democratise the men's franchise by abolishing plural voting; but to women offered nothing. She swept them out, and on with her to the Commons. The rain was pouring in torrents; that was the least of it; they were following her into the militant movement, and knew not whither the step might lead. For the first time in memory the great doors of the Strangers' Entrance to Parliament were closed during the session of the House. The Commons police were on guard to prevent the admittance of any woman. The militant and her following stood at the door defiant; Parliament buzzed with interest. At last the Speaker agreed to permit relays of twelve women within the Lobby. Hour after hour, in the rain, they waited their turn to interview legislators who promised nothing! The experience stoked the spark of militant impatience she had lit.

Within the citadel, Keir Hardie, replying to the King's Speech, as leader of the new Labour Party, demanded the removal of the 'scandal and disgrace' of treating women no better than the criminal and insane. Had the Party been ready to second him vigorously in that demand, there might have been a different history to write, for the Liberals were then keenly susceptible to the competition of the rising Labour movement. In this, as in much else, however, his colleagues failed to support him. They had fought the election on a programme of immediate demands, for which their constituents expected them to fight. Votes for Women had scarcely figured in that programme. (. . .)

There was many an acrid and painful discussion in Hardie's rooms in the old Elizabethan house at 14 Nevill's Court, off Fleet Street, wherein he sat, dark-browed and silent, and Mrs Pankhurst wept and stormed. He was doing all he knew for the cause she loved, but it was not in him to argue or protest. She believed that to force through Votes for Women would buttress his power and that of the Labour movement. She was convinced he could do it if he were determined, and had the strong personal desire that he should do it out of his friendship for her. This strain made the contest more sharply poignant. She was torn between her affection for Hardie and the Socialist movement, her passionate zeal for the women's cause, and the growing influence of Christabel, who desired to cut the WSPU entirely clear of the Labour Movement; already she believed Votes for Women would be given by the Tories, because, to 'dish' the Liberals, they had given Household Suffrage to men in 1867.

The Labour Party decided that any places for Bills drawn by its members should be put at the disposal of the Party, to be allocated by majority vote. Keir Hardie nevertheless promised us that if he should draw a place himself, it would go to our Bill, whatever the majority might have to say. He was unsuccessful, but five places were drawn by other members of the Party. All foresaw that four of them must go to the repeal of the Taff Vale decision, the right of the unemployed to work, the feeding of destitute school children, and Old Age Pensions, for these were measures foremost in the Party programme. One place remained in doubt. Mrs Pankhurst demanded it should be given to Votes for Women, but the Party decided for a checkweighing Bill to protect the earnings of workmen. She could not forgive the blow. That the Labour Party won triumphant success in this first session only embittered her disappointment.

The Suffragette Movement (1931)

[FROM BOOK IX, CHAPTER 1: 'CAT AND MOUSE' ACT IN PRACTICE]

(It is 1913 and the Government has passed the Prisoners Temporary Discharge for Ill-health Act, which allows hunger-strikes to be let out of prison on license to recover for a few days. Suffragettes faced the prospect of almost indefinite imprisonment.)

I felt sick and cold when I got to Holloway, bruised from the struggle. In spite of me, I resented the dreary confinement of the cell, yet, beneath all, I was happy and confident; already my hope was beginning to be realised. I did not undress at all during my imprisonment, but remained, as it were, momentarily awaiting release. Yet I composed myself to write, lying on the bed and hiding my work. As before, I had a bag of paper and pencils round my waist under the skirt. There were resolutions and leaflets to draft, new plans to devise. 'I get all my good ideas in Holloway,' I gained the habit of saying during the next year, for there were long vistas of solitary hours in which to think, and the brain was ever alert. I was writing at that period unpaid weekly articles for the *Clarion*, the *Merthyr Pioneer* and the *Glasgow Forward*, as well as some paid articles for American publications, and many letters to the Press. As before, food was constantly in the cell: tea and bread and butter, chops and steaks, jellies and fruit. These offered no temptation; but for water, had I allowed myself to dwell on the thought of it, I should have craved intensely. Indeed there is nothing which tastes so sweet as the first draught of water after the thirst strike is over. It has a peculiar, delicate flavour, only noticed then, for accustomed to other and stronger tastes, the palate grows dulled to it.

I used to say in those days that the Biblical manna must have been hail. In the thirst strike there is always a horrible taste in the mouth, which grows more parched as the days pass, with the tongue dry and hot and thickly coated. The saliva becomes thick and yellow; a bitter tasting phlegm rises constantly, so nasty that one retches violently, but is denied the relief of sickness. The urine, growing thicker, darker, more scanty, is passed with difficulty. There is no action of the bowels during the imprisonment. Each day one's bones seem more prominent, the flesh falling away, the skin shrivelled, the hands and feet a dull purple with bright red streaks. One is always cold, and if one accepts the hot water bottle the wardress offers, it seems to burn, not to warm, the one place it touches, and to leave even that place cold as before when moved away. Pain settles in the small of the back and in the chest; occasionally a sharp stinging pain in the right breast. Griping pains seize one suddenly in the stomach and abdomen. The pulse becomes swift and irregular. There are palpitations and pain in the region of the heart. If one rises from bed, one grows faint and giddy, and there comes at last a constant ringing in the ears, when one is lying flat, which changes, if one stands up, to a deafening roar, with a sensation of pressure in the ears, as one breathes. The consciousness of pulses in the head, throbbing in unison with the beating of the heart, distresses and disturbs. If one refuses to lie still and take things quietly, all the symptoms are intensified, and become a nightmare-like torture of pain and misery. The nights, from the first, are sleepless and painful. When the wardress opens the cell door at half-past five in the morning, one is still awake. After that one may fall into a hazy, half-sleeping, half-waking state, which may last perhaps an hour or two, perhaps for the greater part of the day.

This is what the prisoner feels; the medical version of the experience was:

The tissues are depleted of moisture, the muscles waste, the bowels and kidneys cease to act normally. The poisons are unable to pass out of the body, and are retained and absorbed. When absorption occurs, the patient feels shivery. She has headaches, nausea, and more or less fever. More than one of the prisoners has come out jaundiced, and in a toxic condition. In one person toxicity may affect the nervous system; in another the digestive or respiratory tracts.

Illness grew on me rapidly; I had not recovered from the forcible feeding of February and March, and I was worn out when I entered the prison on Tuesday. By Friday I determined to remain quiescent no longer, for I was to speak at the Bromley Public Hall on the following Monday, and must bestir myself to get out. I commenced to walk about my cell; faintness overpowered me. I fell or stumbled to my knees, drowned in darkness and pain and rushing noises. By Saturday, to stand for a few moments made me fall fainting to the ground. I did it repeatedly, the sooner to be free. I had fainted when they came to bring me the order of release on Sunday evening.

The members had begged me, if ever I should be under the 'Cat and Mouse' Act, to come down to them in the East End, in order that they might protect me; they would not let me be taken back to prison without a struggle as the others had been, they assured me. On the night of my arrest Zelie Emerson had pressed into my hand an address: 'Mr and Mrs Payne, 28 Ford Road, Bow.' Thither I was now driven in a taxi with two wardresses. As the cab slowed down perforce among the marketing throngs in the Roman Road, friends recognised me, and rushed into the roadway, cheering and waving their hands. Mrs Payne was waiting for me on the doorstep. It was a typical little East End house in a typical little street, the front door opening directly from the pavement, with not an inch of ground to withdraw its windows from the passers-by. I was welcomed by the kindest of kind people, shoemaking home-workers, who carried me in with the utmost tenderness. They had put their double bed for me in the little front parlour on the ground floor next the street, and had tied up the door knocker. For three days they stopped their work that I might not be disturbed by the noise of their tools. Yet there was no quiet. The detectives, notified of my release, had arrived before me. A hostile crowd collected. A woman flung one of the clogs she wore at the wash-tub at a detective's head. The 'Cats', as a hundred angry voices called them, retired to the nearby public-houses; there were several of these havens within a stone's throw, as there usually are in the East End. Yet even though the detectives were out of sight, people were constantly stopping before the house to discuss the movement and my imprisonment. Children gathered, with prattling treble. If anyone called at the house, or a vehicle stopped before it, detectives at once came hastening forth; a storm of hostile voices rose. Here, indeed, was no peace. My hosts carried me upstairs to their own bedroom, at the back of the house, hastily preprepared; a small room, longer, but scarcely wider, than a prison cell—my home when out of prison for many months to come. (. . .)

In that little room I slept, wrote, interviewed the Press and personalities of all sorts, and presently edited a weekly paper. Its walls were covered with a cheap, drab paper, with an etching of a ship in full sail, and two old-fashioned colour prints of a little girl at her morning and evening prayers. From the window by my bed I could see the steeple of St Stephen's Church and the belfry of its school, a jumble of red-tiled roofs, darkened with smoke and age, the dull brick of the walls and the new whitewash of some of the backyards in the next street. There were certain odd hints and memories of the vanished country, still remaining from the time ere London slumdom had crept up to Bow, which was once far out of town. It is said that the slum houses were built with rubbish tips for foundation; that well may be, for vermin seems to infest their very bricks and mortar. Mrs Payne told me that as a young bride she hung her bed with pink curtains, but plunged those curtains into a bucket of water the night of her marriage on account of the bugs she was horrified to find crawling over them. When I lit my candle on sleepless nights, I would see a dozen or more of them on the wall, though disinfectants were always burnt in the room during my absence.

Our colours were nailed to the wall behind my bed, and a flag of purple, white and green was displayed from an opposite dwelling, where pots of scarlet geraniums hung on the whitewashed wall of the yard below, and a beautiful girl with smooth, dark hair and a white bodice would come out to delight my eyes in helping her mother at the wash-tub. The next yard was a fish curers'. An old lady with a chenille net on her grey hair would be passing in and out of the smoke-house, preparing the sawdust fires. A man with his shirt sleeves rolled up would be splitting herrings; and another hooking them on to rods balanced on boards and packing-cases, till the yard was filled, and gleamed with them like a coat of mail. Close by, tall sunflowers were growing, and garments of many colours hung out to dry. Next door to us they bred pigeons and cocks and hens, which cooed and crowed and clucked in the early hours. Two doors away a woman supported a paralysed husband and a number of young children by making shirts at 8d a dozen. Opposite, on the other side of Ford Street, was a poor widow with a family of little ones. The detectives endeavoured to hire a room from her, that they might watch for me unobserved. 'It will be a small fortune to you while it lasts!' they told her. Bravely she refused with disdain: 'Money wouldn't do me any good if I was to hurt that young woman!' The same proposal was made and rejected at every house in Ford Road. (. . .)

I was to speak again at the Bromley Public Hall. My licence had expired. A long, close-fitting dark coat with a high collar, a hat pulled down over the eyes, as women wore them then, and a touch of rouge on the cheeks were enough to transform my appearance, for I never could bear my throat or eyes constrained, my face was still blanched from the hunger strike, and cosmetics were most alien to me. Almost suffocated by the beating of my heart, I passed through the lines of detectives waiting to seize me, and up the stairs with the people streaming into the hall. The seats were full, the gangways thronged. A detective snatched at me as I hurried to the platform. His action betrayed his presence; men and women hurled themselves upon him; he was hustled out and down into the street. A crowd of stalwarts shut and guarded the main door. I had torn off the dark coat and hat; the air was rent with cheers. Whilst I was waiting to speak, a paper was passed to me—a note from Zelie Emerson that she had found me a hiding-place in the hall. I shook my head. She knew that I was determined to go out amongst the people as before. I saw her face flush, and her lips tremble. She went out, pouting and frowning, with tears on her face. A shadow seemed to fall on me. 'Poor girl, she is not fit for this!' I thought with compunction. In speaking, all else was forgotten. To me it was a great struggle, not for the vote alone; for the uplifting of these masses, the enlarging of their horizons. I spoke to them as I felt. 'They say that life is sweet and liberty is precious; there is no liberty for us so long as the majority of our people lead wretched lives. Unless we can free them from the chains of poverty, life, to us, is not worth preserving, and I, for one, would rather leave this world.'

I jumped down amongst the people, hatless, in light dress, easily discernible amongst the dark-clad people. Pressing together, we passed out and slowly descended the stairs. The police were massed outside the only entrance, dozens of detectives with heavy sticks, and a hundred or more of uniformed men, ready to pounce as our mass inevitably narrowed at the doorway. Suddenly they were deluged by a tremendous torrent of water. Zelie Emerson, with her quick ingenuity, had arranged for our stalwarts guarding the doors to turn the fire hose upon the 'Cats'! Helter-skelter they went! A group of us ran out to the right as the stream followed the scurrying policemen leftward.

Down the dark road we ran. 'Where are we going? Where are we going?' I asked as we ran. My companions waited each for the others to answer, for none of them knew. It had been intended that we should take shelter in a member's house near by, but she was not with us, and no one knew the address.

We rushed down an alley. It was blind. We heard footsteps hurrying in the rear. Like trapped wild things, we thrust ourselves against every door: one of them gave. We found ourselves in a dark, disused stable. We shut the door and huddled against it, holding our breath; then discovered there were bolts, shot them, and retired to the darkest recess to hide lest the door should be forced. Footsteps and voices approached. We saw through an upper grating the light of a bull's eye lantern playing about the window. The police! They tried the doors. The old bolts creaked, but they held. The minions of the Law passed on.

* * *

Behind all this the secretly perpetrated militancy of the WSPU continued; every day brought its tale of buildings burnt, windows smashed, pillar-boxes fired. Two men threw mouse-traps at the Members of Parliament from the Strangers' Gallery of the House of Commons, and one of them struck fear into their hearts by firing a toy pistol into the air. The hunger strikers were dragged in and out of prison. Kitty Marion got a release licence of two days only, Lilian Lenton of one day. A. M. Thompson, in the *Clarion*, wrote:

> The women are winning again. What they lost by window smashing has been restored to them and multiplied a hundredfold by the Government's 'Cat and Mouse' Act. That, by God, we can't stand!

An unparalleled scene in Trafalgar Square on Sunday, July 27th concluded that hectic week. Again the Men's Federation had obtained police permission for the plinth on our behalf, and though it was advertised that I should speak, and it was common knowledge that I should again lead the crowd to Downing Street, the permit was not withdrawn. Norah Smyth came down to my hiding-place to bring me a wig. Mrs Evans dressed me up in an aggressively American shepherd's plaid coat and skirt, stuffed with newspaper across the chest, and a transparent veil, which assisted in disguising without hiding the face. There was a great procession from the East End, and the largest crowd

I had yet seen in the Square, overflowing on to the surrounding streets, and the steps and terrace of the National Gallery beyond. Nevinson wrote:

The Square was crammed as I have never seen it since the Unemployed riots of the 'eighties, or since Bradlaugh's demand to take his seat as an elected Member. . . . There was no mistake about the feeling of the crowd. Even the Government papers have not questioned it. I doubt if any Trafalgar Square crowd of that size has been so unanimous and so deeply moved.

Mrs Evans and a party of us motored to the Square and mounted the plinth together. My knees trembled so much from weakness and suspense that I could scarcely walk. I seated myself on the pedestal of one of the Landseer lions. Stout Superintendent Wells was behind me; I heard him ask: 'Has Miss Pankhurst come?' A detective answered 'No'.

When my turn came I rushed to the edge of the plinth and tore off my wig, while friends closed round me, fiercely suspicious of any outsider who dared approach. Throughout the vast throng was a waving of hands and a roar of cheering. The people were with me, it seemed, to a man and to a woman. With a storm of acclaim the resolution was adopted to carry our 'Women's Declarations of Independence' to Downing Street. (I had a great roll of them one of the stewards had handed me as I spoke.) When I leapt from the plinth the people caught me and took me with them. We had swept from the Square and across the road into Parliament Street, the whole great concourse moving after us, before the police could bring up their massed forces waiting in the side streets. Detectives were everywhere in the crowd, but the people always knew them, despite their civilian dress, and hustled them away. There was a strange, deep, growling sound in the crowd about me I had never heard before: the sound of angry men. At the top of Whitehall, mounted policemen met us; we rushed between. The people protecting me gathered in a thick bunch with their arms about each other, thrusting the horses aside.

'Coppers behind us! Coppers behind us!' hoarse voices shouted. We had gone too fast; the police had broken into the crowd and were dragging at us from behind. A company of policemen came running to meet us up Whitehall. They closed with us, striking at men and women. A thin, bald-headed man, in poor clothes, was knocked down beside me. He rolled on the ground. I cried out, but we were swept on—over him, I feared. 'Keep back! Keep back!' the people in front were shouting. There was someone else on the ground. We tried in vain to stop, and called to those behind us; impelled from the rear, they could not pause. I saw something dark on the ground, felt something soft. It was a woman, I thought. I was borne forward by the arms and shoulders. I raised up my feet that I might not step on what was beneath me—it was all I could do.

A taxi-cab stood in the road before us. Friends about me opened the door, begged me to drive away and elude the police. I answered: 'No, I am going with you to Downing Street!' The cab door was slammed, and on we went. Reinforcements from Scotland Yard, a great company, came dashing upon us, beating their way through the people protecting me, striking and knocking them down, arresting some. Finally I was seized, and as I was dragged past the end of Downing Street, I saw it was guarded by a double cordon of police with a mass of mounted men behind. We were feared, it seemed. I called to the crowd to go there. At Cannon Row police station the charge room was crowded by policemen and their prisoners; eleven men and thirteen women under arrest. Irritated that I had not succeeded in doing more, I snatched up a tumbler and broke a window, in the vain hope of getting in touch with the people outside.

Soon I was back in Holloway, and at first so horrified by the return there that I felt I could have knocked my head against the wall. I had determined this time to strike against sleep, as well as against food and water, in the hope of gaining an earlier release. I tramped about the cell as I had done in March; the same old cell. The night wardress opened the door: 'You must not make that noise!' I knew that on one side of me was the staircase, on the other the lavatory and sink, but I took a blanket from the bed and threw it on the floor to deaden the sound of my steps lest other prisoners might be disturbed. Then I walked on. The gas light in the recess behind the glass, dim as it was, hurt my eyes. I covered it with one of the prison rule cards, but still the light of it made me dizzy as I turned. I watched the patch of sky through the heavy bars; a sombre grey, charged with sullen, yellow fire, the lights of the London streets. I stumbled over the blanket; it wrinkled and caught my feet. I grew sick and faint, and often sank to my knees, clutching the bed or the chair. Sometimes I slept an instant as I crouched there, for sleep seemed to be dogging me as I walked. It was cold, cold, and as morning came, colder still. The sky turned violet; a strange, brilliant, almost startling colour it seemed, between those heavy bars. Then it died to the bleak, grey white of early day. I still walked, but sometimes I could not forbear to rest on the hard wooden chair. Then my head would nod heavily to one side, and I would pull myself up and walk again. I was racked with pains, my legs ached, my feet were swollen and burning. I thought of the martyrs of the past who walked on red-hot plough shares for their faith. The pain in my back was overwhelming, my throat was parched.

On Wednesday I began to faint. I had pressure and noises in the head. I asked to see a Home Office doctor. He came on Thursday. On Friday I had fever; I knew it by my burning skin, and the cold shivers passing over me. I lay on the bed; there was no question of sleeping now. That evening I was released. It may be that by all the additional agonies I had piled upon myself I had not shortened my sentence by a single hour.

Indeed the Government was conditioning the punishment to the offence; to prisoners who kept quietly out of the way, the 'Cat and Mouse' Act might be a menace rather than a reality; to those who persistently repeated their offence the Act was merciless. Mary Richardson, asked by the prison doctor whether she would refrain from militancy on her release, answered: 'I shall be militant as long as I can stand or see; they cannot do more than kill me.' He told her: 'It is not a question of killing you . . . you will be kept till you are a skeleton, and a nervous and mental wreck, and then you will be sent to an institution where they look after mental wrecks.'

The words were denounced as a threat. In fact it was simply a warning; the doctor spoke the thing which he foresaw, knowing the intentions of those from whom he took his orders.

Unknown to me in prison, that Sunday's march on Downing Street had created a sensation. It was the first large-scale demonstration of real popular turbulence the Suffrage movement had shown. Nevinson expressed his opinion with emphasis:

. . . the barbarity of the 'Cat and Mouse' Act has struck very deep into the mind of the ordinary man and woman. . . . A great deal also is due to Miss Sylvia Pankhurst's action in throwing herself upon the genuine chivalry and good sense of the workers in the East End. I think that was a stroke of genius. We have all the working classes now, not only favourable, but zealous. After the battle of Valmy, when the national troops of the French Revolution held in check the hirelings of official Europe, Goethe said to his friends: 'To-day marks a turning-point in history, and we can say we were present at it.' We who were in the Square last Sunday can say the same.

Discounting something for journalism, and more for sympathy, the words were true enough, for the demonstration had been unlike all the old 'raids' on the House of Commons, in which a picked band of women, recruited from all parts of the country, had gone forward to struggle with the police, watched by a crowd mainly composed of sightseers. Now at last we had seen an entire crowd in action. Mrs Pankhurst, at the London Pavilion next day, expressed a similar view:

The fight is nearly over; the end is at hand—a few months more and the spirit of the crowd that followed Sylvia Pankhurst down Whitehall . . . will have found some definite expression which the Government will no longer be able to deny.

I did not see these or any such comments till long after. At that Monday meeting Annie Kenney had been recaptured, four other arrests being made in the struggle. Mrs Pankhurst had sold her 'Cat and Mouse' licence for £100. She had been released the previous Thursday. She had refrained from water during her four days in prison, and at the last had walked up and down until exhausted. She was in a jaundiced condition, a tendency which persisted for many years. It was erroneously reported in the Press that the operation of transfusion of blood from another person had been performed on her.

That same Monday (July 28th), Lansbury's appeal was rejected by three Judges of the King's Bench Divisional Court; on Wednesday he surrendered to his bail, and was removed to Pentonville Prison. He refused to eat and was released on Saturday. He has since revealed that he had begun his hunger strike some days before, in order to shorten his imprisonment. He was taken from prison to the house of Joseph Fels, in Cornwall Terrace, Regent's Park. A procession of 10,000 people, organised by the Poplar Labour Party, marched from the East End to welcome him. He was not re-arrested, though he gave no undertaking. He presented, however, a petition to Parliament asking for intercession with the Crown on his behalf, and representing that he was 'not guilty of any crime or offence, or likely to commit any crime or offence', though 'for particular reasons affecting his own personal honour' he did not 'feel at liberty' to find sureties. This petition was cited by the Government as an expression of his intention not to break the law, and as the reason of his non-arrest. Wedgwood had made in the House what was something like an apology, though Lansbury may not have been responsible for its terms.

Before his appeal was heard, Lansbury's connection, with Christabel and Mrs Pankhurst was already at an end; his temperament was too volatile; theirs too ruthless for its continuance. He soon abandoned the claim that the Labour Party should oppose all Government measures without exception. Indeed he forgot that he had ever made it. By the time he published his life story, in 1928, he thought he had simply demanded that the Party should move an amendment to the Reform Bill, and vote against the Bill unless women were included. Moreover, Christabel's cry had now definitely crystallised into: 'Wanted, a Tory Government!' Lansbury would not support the Tories; with all his vacillations, he preferred to go on working and waiting for a strong Labour Party. Christabel lacked both the patience and the sympathy with Labour ideals which could have made that course acceptable to her, short of clear proof that it could achieve immediate success. Yet for a brief period she had been attracted by Lansbury's Left Wing insurgence. So recently as June a by-election had occurred at Leicester. The Lansbury faction desired the Labour Party to contest the seat, the Party officials refused. It was alleged the Party officials had made a bargain with the Liberals to safeguard Macdonald in possession of the second Leicester seat. Lansbury and his *Daily Herald* thundered against such arrangements, and joined with the Social Democrat Federation in running Edward R. Hartley, an original member of the ILP. The WSPU enthusiastically welcomed this candidature, Christabel declaring in the *Suffragette* that it would 'lead the way in a great attack by Labour against a decadent Liberalism and all its evil works'. The WSPU canvassed the electors assiduously and excelled itself in pageantry, sending forth a procession led by children with rose wands and tableaux of 'woman bond and woman free' and forcible feeding. Hartley polled 2,000 votes, a remarkable achievement for an Independent last moment candidate, but failed to defeat the Liberal. Christabel henceforth declared the policy of running Labour candidates to be 'over-rated' and 'too sectional'. What was required, she said, was to mobilise the Labour vote in support of the Tories until the Liberal Government would agree to give women the vote. When Lansbury's faction ran John Scurr as Independent Labour candidate at Chesterfield in the following August, the WSPU gave no support. When Lansbury went to prison the *Suffragette* referred to the fact in distant terms: Lincoln's Inn House no longer invited his services as a speaker.

The Free Speech Defence Committee, of which Wedgwood was chairman and Keir Hardie a prominent member, had announced another Trafalgar Square demonstration on August 10th. Those of us who had been charged under the Act of Edward III were invited to speak. In conveying the invitation to me, Frank Smith asked for a pledge that I would not ask the people to march to Downing Street. I refused to accept this condition, and issued a leaflet: 'To Lovers of Freedom,' stating that after the 'Free Speech' meeting had done its talking, I should be in the Square to go with those who cared to Downing Street. The leaflet was scarcely out when Keir Hardie visited me. He had just returned from the International Women's Suffrage conference at Budapest, where he had received a great ovation. The Leicester and Chesterfield contests had focused unrest in the Labour ranks. F. W. Jowett in the *Labour Leader* was complaining that the Party's subservience to Liberalism was 'injuring the movement'; Snowden, in the same paper, had written that the Party could not take an independent line because four-fifths of its seats were dependent on Liberal votes. To many it appeared that the Labour advance of 1906 was being followed by a continual retreat. The Party's banner, I thought, was being dragged in the dust. I flashed all this out to Keir Hardie, and asked unhappily: 'Why do you allow yourself to be tarred with Macdonald's brush?' I told him of my answer to Frank Smith. I saw his dislike of it, though he said no word to dissuade me, and doubtless it was he who had insisted I should be invited. In spite of his gentleness it was almost a quarrel—on my part, not on his. I did not see him again till the following summer; indeed I had told him it was too painful, too incongruous he should come in the midst of the warfare waged against him and the Labour Party by the orders of my sister. I saw myself now in the position towards him in which I had so often see my mother; he trying to help her, she flouting his efforts. I did not want him to help me to get free, or even to try. It might have been better to leave the 'Free Speech' meeting alone—my manifesto had gone out; it was too late now to draw back.

Next day it was Mrs Pankhurst who came to my bedside. The Government was permitting a holiday respite to her and Annie

Kenney, it seemed; at any rate they had been at large for some time, and both had delivered speeches in public after the expiry of their licenses without any attempt at arrest. She complained that she had intended to visit me the previous day, but learnt that Keir Hardie was coming and feared to encounter him. She spoke as though he were a person a Suffragette should be ashamed to meet. So far had divergence of opinion on tactics, not on principles, destroyed her old friendship. I answered her reproaches with sadness: 'He will not come again.'

*   *   *

[FROM BOOK IX, CHAPTER IV: 'EAST LONDON
FEDERATION IS SEVERED FROM THE WSPU']

For some time messages had been reaching me that Mrs Pankhurst and Christabel desired to see me in Paris. I was loath to go, for as the ports were watched I was likely to be arrested on embarking, and I was unwilling to expend my energies in another hunger and thirst strike except as the price of a rousing struggle. I realized that, like so many others, I was to be given the *congé*. In November Elsa Dalglish had been persuaded at Lincoln's Inn House that her duty was to resign the honorary financial secretaryship of the East London Federation, and to 'concentrate' on the honorary secretaryship of the Kensington WSPU as the East End work was on 'wrong lines'. I was unwilling to argue points of view, which I knew would not be reconciled, unless by the development of events. I was anxious to avoid a rupture in the full impact of our struggle with the Government, and, as far as possible, to stand together in the fight. Yet so insistent were the messages from Paris, that a few days after my release, and as soon as the welcome meetings were over, I agreed to go. The arrangements for the journey were made by Lincoln's Inn House. I was smuggled into a car and driven to Harwich. I insisted that Nora Smyth, who had become financial secretary of the Federation, should go with me to represent our members. My uncle, Herbert Goulden, always kind and thoughtful, to my surprise appeared to accompany me to the boat. He knew, I suppose, the reason for which I was summoned to Paris, though we did not discuss it. I was miserably ill in body, and distressed by the reason of my journey. A small private cabin had been booked for us in an assumed name. I reached it without mishap, but my uncle came down to tell us that detectives were on the boat. So ill that I almost wished I might die, I was tortured throughout the night by the thought that I should be seized on emerging from the cabin, and dragged back on the return voyage next morning. The detectives, however, were not seeking me, but on the trail of diamond thieves, and I landed at the Hook of Holland unmolested. The journey, which in other circumstances would have been delightful, seemed only excessively tiring.

As soon as we reached Paris the business was opened. Christabel, nursing a tiny Pomeranian dog, announced that the East London Federation of the WSPU must become a separate organisation; the *Suffragette* would announce this, and unless we immediately chose to adopt one for ourselves, a new name would be given to us. Norah Smyth was known both to Christabel and Mrs Pankhurst. She had served as unpaid chauffeur to Mrs Pankhurst; she had been the companion of Helen Craggs at Newnham, and had assisted the WSPU headquarters in other ways. Dr Ethel Smyth said of her to Mrs Pankhurst in my hearing: 'She is just the class we want.' She happened, in fact, to belong to a distant branch of Ethel Smyth's own family. Having experienced both aspects, she had chosen to work with the East London Federation as the branch of the movement which appealed to her as most useful. Like me, she desired to avoid a breach. Dogged in her fidelities, and by temperament unable to express herself under emotion, she was silent. I said she had accompanied me to represent our members and to report to them. Therefore she should be told the reason for our expulsion. Christabel replied that I had spoken to Lansbury's Larkin release meeting, which was contrary to WSPU policy. Lansbury was a good fellow, of course, but his motto was: 'Let them all come!' the WSPU did not want to be 'mixed up with him.' She added: 'You have a democratic constitution for your Federation; we do not agree with that.' Moreover, she urged, a working women's movement was of no value: working women were the weakest portion of the sex: how could it be otherwise? Their lives were too hard, their education too meagre to equip them for the contest. 'Surely it is a mistake to use the weakest for the struggle! We wanted picked women, the very strongest and most intelligent!' She turned to me. 'You have your own ideas. We do not want that; we want all our women to take their instructions and walk in step like an army!' Too tired, too ill to argue, I made no reply. I was oppressed by a sense of tragedy, grieved by her ruthlessness. Her glorification of autocracy seemed to me remote indeed from the struggle we were waging, the grim fight even now proceeding in the cells. I thought of many others who had been thrust aside for some minor difference.

We drove in the Bois; Christabel with the small dog on her arm, I struggling against headache and weakness, Mrs Pankhurst blanched and emaciated.

We returned to our conversations. 'Moreover', urged Christabel, 'your Federation appeals for funds; people think it is all part of the same thing. You get donations which might come to us.' 'That is what *we* say!' Norah Smyth interposed at last; it was a practical point of interest to the financial secretary. 'We know people have sent money to Lincoln's Inn House on account of our big demonstrations, for which we have the bill to pay!' 'How much do you want? What would you think a suitable income for your Federation? You can't need much in your simple way!' Christabel challenged her. 'All we can raise for our work, like you!' 'Suppose I were to say we would allow you something,' Mrs Pankhurst interposed; she was obviously distressed by the discussion. 'Would you—?' 'Oh, no; we can't have that!' Christabel was emphatic. 'It must be a clean cut!' So it went on. 'As you will then,' I answered at last.

Afterwards, when we were alone together, Christabel said that sometimes we should meet, 'not as Suffragettes, but as sisters.' To me the words seemed meaningless; we had no life apart from the movement. I felt bruised, as one does, when fighting the foe without, one is struck by the friend within. My mind was thronged with the memories of our childhood: the little heads clustering at the window in Green Hayes; her pink cheeks and the young green shoots in the spring in Russell Square; my father's voice: 'You are the four pillars of my house!'

The Federation was unaltered. We had defended the WSPU against outside attack; we still would do so. Our place in the Union had been merely nominal: indeed the local unions were united by no tie of organisation, only by sympathy and support to Lincoln's Inn House. There was no real change, yet the sadness remained. Any resentment I might otherwise have felt, then and always, was allayed by commiseration for Christabel: how terrible to be away over there, giving the orders leading to imprisonment and torture for other women! I would not take that part. A thousand times easier to be in the struggle and share its anguish. I knew the call of a compelling conscience, stronger than all the shrinking of unwilling impulses, dominating the whole being, permitting no reprieve from its dictates. Under that force I believed she, too, was acting. When the War came I was glad of the 'clean cut' she had insisted upon.

Norah Smyth and I left Paris immediately. She had arranged with the others that we should travel by a circuitous route through Normandy, taking some days for the journey to give me time to regain strength before running the risk of arrest on touching English soil. I left it all to her. Provided with disguises procured on the journey, we landed unrecognised at Southampton, and were motored to London by a man supporter accustomed to carry Christabel's visitors. He had been notified by her messengers where to meet us in the town. On reaching London we at once summoned a general meeting of the Federation. The members at first declared they would not be 'thrown out' of the WSPU, nor would they agree to a change of name. I persuaded them at last that refusal would open the door to acrimonious discussions, which would hinder our work and deflect attention from the Cause. The name of our organisation was then debated. The East London Federation of the Suffragettes was suggested by someone, and at once accepted with enthusiasm. I took no part in the decision. Our colours were to be the old purple, white and green, with the addition of red—no change, as a matter of fact, for we had already adopted the red caps of liberty. Mrs Pankhurst, annoyed by our choice of name, hastened down to the East End to expostulate; she probably anticipated objections from Paris. 'We are the Suffragettes! that is the name *we* are always known by,' she protested, 'and there will be the same confusion as before!' I told her the members had decided it, and I would not interfere.

When the WSPU sent out a brief announcement of the separation, the newspapers jumped to the conclusion that a split had occurred, because the WSPU had resolved on a truce from militancy, which I had refused to accept. The *Daily News* observed exultantly: 'There could scarcely be a more crushing condemnation of militancy than its formal abandonment by all save one of its inventors and patentees.'

The WSPU protested:

There is no change in the policy of the WSPU . . . The statement already issued by the Union is a recognition of the fact which for a long time has existed—viz., that Miss Sylvia Pankhurst prefers to work on her own account and independently.

Christabel followed this up with a letter over her own signature:

The true position is that since the WSPU does not exist for the mere purpose of propaganda, but is a fighting organisation, it must have only one policy, one programme and one command. The WSPU policy and the programme are framed, and the word of command is given by Mrs Pankhurst and myself. From the very beginning of the militant movement this has been the case. Consequently those who wish to give an independent lead, or to carry out either a programme or a policy which differs from those laid down by the WSPU, must necessarily have an independent organisation of their own.

The subject was further developed in the *Suffragette*, coupled with a reference to a new organization for men and women, 'The United Suffragists,' which had just been formed, and in which it had been announced that militants and non-militants were to join hands: 'Now that something like fifty suffrage organisations have come into existence those who are connected with the WSPU . . . are determined not to have their energies and subscriptions divided and subdivided.' The attitude which led to such expulsions as my own and the denunciation of old supporters like Zangwill was upheld:

As victory grows nearer and the fight, therefore, grows sterner, distinctions have to be drawn and a stringency displayed which were less needful in the early days of the militant movement . . . the course becomes specially dangerous and careful piloting is needed. . . . The Suffragettes as the fighting force—the advance guard—necessarily stand alone. Theirs is glorious isolation—the splendour of independent strength.

In the following issue appeared a warning against 'Liberal intrigue':

It is as the result of Liberal intrigue and inner weakness that the Labour Party has come to naught and is today powerless and despised. Here is a tragic end to twenty-five years of effort and sacrifice, generously spent by those who brought the Labour Party into being!'

Strange that the woman who wrote thus should depart absolutely from the Suffrage movement on the outbreak of war. Yet in those days she appeared inflexible in that one purpose. To me it seemed that her isolation in Paris was the main cause both of her growing intolerance and of her sudden retirement. Yet, withal, one must say: she was the true begetter of the militant movement, though others bore a greater share of the physical suffering of its travail, and the labour of many equally devoted workers maintained its life. Carrying the majority of the WSPU membership with her, she had travelled far from its starting point in the ILP and her interest in the Women Textile Workers' Labour Representation Committee. Her early speeches had dealt almost entirely with the industrial status of women; her later utterances with the political tactics required, in her judgement, for winning the vote. She who had deprecated and shunned every mention of her sex, now hinged the greater part of her propaganda upon the supposed great prevalence of venereal diseases and the sex excesses of men. 'Votes for women and chastity for men', became her favourite slogan, elaborated in articles in the *Suffragette* and a collection of these called *The Great Scourge*. She alleged that 75 to 80 per cent of men become infected with gonorrhœa, and 20 to 25 per cent with syphilis, insisting that 'only an insignificant minority—25 per cent at most'—escaped infection by some form of venereal disease. Women were strongly warned against the dangers of marriage, and assured that large numbers of women were refusing it. The greater part, both of the serious and minor illnesses suffered by married women, including the vague delicacy called 'poor health', she declared to be due to the husband having at some time contracted gonorrhœa. Childless marriages were attributed to the same cause. Syphilis she declared to be 'the prime reason of a high infantile mortality'. The mutilation of a 'White Slave Traffic' Bill in 1912, the notorious Piccadilly flat case in 1913, cases of assault on young children punished with leniency by the Courts, were seized upon, week by week, to illustrate the text that 'Man is not the "lord of creation," but the exterminator of the species.' The injuries of women in the sex relationship were now put forward as the main reason and basis of militancy. The tremendously advertised *Great Scourge* was on the whole well received. The *Medical World* cast some doubt upon its statistics, which had been largely culled from American writers:

Were 80 per cent of the male population infected with gonorrhœa, the state of the country would be too appalling to contemplate . . . but even if there is some exaggeration, the figures are far too high!

The Royal Commission on Venereal Diseases, appointed in 1913, reported in 1915 a prevalence of such diseases which was certainly serious, but very much smaller than that asserted in *The Great Scourge.* Sir William Osler placed syphilis as fourth amongst the 'Killing Diseases,' and the Commissioners estimated that not less than 10 per cent of the population in large cities was infected with syphilis, congenital or acquired. Thirty to 50 per cent of sterility amongst women they attributed to gonorrhœa. Later researches suggest that even these estimates were exaggerated. Post mortem examinations of still-born infants by Holland and Lane Clayton showed 8.7 per cent of syphilis. Other investigators found from 8 to 18 per cent. In the British Army in 1912 a strength of 107,582 men showed an average of 593 men incapacitated from venereal disease.

How exaggerated was the alarmist view of syphilis as the prime cause of the high infant death-rate has been revealed by the great reduction in infant mortality which has happily been secured. The establishment of mother and infant Clinics and Welfare Centres, and other social improvements, did much to reduce the then terribly high rate of infantile mortality. Our East London Federation was subsequently to bear a notable part in this work.

Apart from any intrinsic merit, a great advantage of *The Great Scourge* propaganda in WSPU eyes was that, like the vote itself, it cut across the usual line of Party programmes. It did not offend the sensitive class consciousness of those frail hot-house blooms, the Conservative supporters of Women's Suffrage, whom the WSPU was eager to encourage. By its sensational nature, this propaganda encouraged the fevered emotions, and sense of intolerable wrong, required to spur women to the more serious acts of destruction. Christabel was now, in effect, preaching the sex war deprecated and denied by the older Suffragists. Mr Lawrence had often said he had thrown in his lot with the militant women in order that the Suffragette struggle might not become 'a sex war'. Not from the speeches of Mrs Pankhurst, who never lost her gift of sympathy with her audiences, but from the columns of the *Suffragette* the deduction was clear: women were purer, nobler and more courageous, men were an inferior body, greatly in need of purification; the WSPU being the chosen instrument capable of administering the purge. Masses of women, especially of the middle class, were affected by this attitude, even though they remained outside the ranks of the Union. The pendulum had swung far, indeed,

185

from the womanly humility of Victorian times. No matter; it must right itself.

The propaganda for sexual purity made strong appeal to the clergy and social workers, brought by the nature of their work into close contact with the sad effects of prostitution and the sexual abuse of girl children. Mrs Fawcett, always strictly temperate in her observations, testified to the fact that Votes for Women had made great advances amongst the clergy during the years 1913–14, the period in which the WSPU had shrieked this propaganda of 'chastity for men' in every key of vehemence and excitement. A number of clergy were ardent supporters of the WSPU, speaking from its platforms, contributing to its organ, hailing the militants as heroines and martyrs.

In the East End, with its miserable housing, its ill-paid casual employment and harsh privations bravely borne by masses of toilers, life wore another aspect. The yoke of poverty oppressing all, was a factor no one-sided propaganda could disregard.

The Home Front (1932)

[FROM CHAPTER II: 'WAR HARDSHIP DESCENDS
UPON THE POOR']

A great heaviness overwhelmed me. I saw our members and neighbours, women who loved and trusted me, grief-stricken that their husbands and sons had been torn away to the war, hungrily grasping at every shred of news and every breath of rumour, pathetic in their eagerness to believe the dictum, retailed with every news-sheet, that the war was needed and noble. Who, without quailing, could say to a mother: 'Your son is dead; he was sacrificed in a struggle evil and worthless?'

Stout old Mrs Savoy, the brushmaker, was on her doorstep, a throng of mothers around her. Despite her palpitations and her dropsy she was a leader amongst them, the cheeriest and jolliest woman in many a mile of streets. A young soldier, son of some friend or relative, had sent home his photograph in a daily newspaper, taken as he went riding on a pig, cheered by the laughing lads of his company. Excited, she hailed me, waving the journal with trumpetings of delighted pride, so confident in her pleasure that she did not observe my silence. I flinched from thrusting, so soon, the iron of resentment into the heart of this old friend and all her cronies.

Ruthless economic pressure supplied, with unpitying haste, the teaching my lips were loth to utter. Already before war had been declared, dealers had sent their emissaries to buy up commodities at the small shops, to make a corner in supplies. From day to day prices rose hugely. Reservists were called up, men enlisted, their families left without sustenance; for there were no separation allowances yet. Industry was dislocated, employers shut down their factories in panic, leaving their workers to starve, or enlist; to shift for themselves as best they could. Three hundred thousand people engaged in the manufacture and sale of goods imported by Germany were bereft of employment. The fishing industry was thrown into chaos. The weavers and spinners of Lancashire and Yorkshire were working short time. All sorts of clothing manufacture was brought to a standstill. The export of many foodstuffs was prohibited. The purchasing power of large sections of the people had dwindled to zero. To be workless then meant literal starvation. The small unemployment benefit obtainable under the National Insurance applied only to a few trades. It was an axiom of then Poor Law practice that relief, save the shelter of the Workhouse, must not be granted to the 'able-bodied' and their dependants. Even to the impotent, Poor Law relief was then but a meagre supplement, mainly in kind. The 'dole,' as it developed after the War, was non-existent. Even had Poor Law Procedure allowed it, the Guardians had not the funds to cope with this great wave of unemployment, though their expenditure actually rose to double its former rate.

Up and down the Old Ford Road under my windows, women were wont to hurry past, pushing the battered old perambulators of children, or packing cases on wheels, laden with garments for the factories. Now, with their little conveyances all empty, they lingered hopeless. 'Any work?' Always they asked each other that question; the answer, so obvious from the downcast face and the empty vehicle, was always: 'No'. I gazed on them mournfully, tenderly, feeling as though the wings of a great pity enfolded me. The absence of work, the cost of food—these were the burden of every talk, floating up to my window, passing me on the road.

Across a neighbouring street a rudely lettered calico banner hung:

Please, landlord, don't be offended,
Don't come for the rent till the War is ended.

Was it a product of our Suffragette call for a No Vote, No Rent strike?

Women gathered about our door asking for 'Sylvia'. They had followed and fought with her in the hectic Suffragette struggles; they turned to her now in these hours of desperate hardship; poor wan, white-faced mothers, clasping their wasted babies, whose pain-filled eyes seemed older than their own. Their breasts gone dry, they had no milk to give their infants, no food for the elder children, no money for the landlord.

Their faith in me seemed a sacred charge, their sorrows stirred me— I girded myself to fight for their interests. I had no thought, as yet, of collecting charitable donations for them. On the contrary, I wanted the need for such charity abolished, by the Community taking the responsibility for the well-being of its members; for the unemployed, not doles, but work at a living wage; for the men drafted away to fight, pay at least not worse than the best obtainable in industry; nationalisation of food to keep down prices and insure that the incidence of shortage should be equally shared; such measures as steps toward the goal of plenty for all by mutual aid.

In face of the hideous ugliness of war, good people of humanitarian aspirations yearned for compensation, weaving fond dreams of social regeneration. In the Press were fairy-tale stories of the great schemes afoot for manifesting national unity. Class distinctions were to be swept away. All the children of the nation were to stand as one, Austen Chamberlain perorated, and Parliament cheered him. Sidney Webb produced a pamphlet, The War and the Worker, giving forth glowing impressions of what might happen. Socialism was to advance, war-time was to be a period of national re-building. Lloyd George declared the country would be made a nation worthy the prowess of heroes.

A Cabinet Committee for the prevention and relief of distress was formed. John Burns was made Chairman of the committee for London; a seat was found for Mrs Sidney Webb. Both these appointments were calculated to appeal to progressive sentiment; for Burns had left the Government from opposition to the War, and Beatrice Webb had received more praise than any woman of her generation, for her authorship of the Minority Report to the Poor Law Commission of 1905-9. To many people the ideology of the Webbs was still the last word in Social regeneration. Of the first £100,000,000 which Parliament voted for the War a part was promised for civilian distress. Moreover, a National Relief Fund was inaugurated under the auspices of the Prince of Wales. It was to be administered by so-called Local Representative Committees convened by the mayor of each area. The Government promised £4,000,000 for the erection of working-class dwellings.

The machinery of succour might be preparing; but the people were hungry. I ran round to Lansbury's house in St Stephen's Road, to ask what plans he and the local Labour Party were making to stem distress and keep down prices. On the way I met little Rose Pengelly, one of our junior Suffragettes—out of work, like the rest. 'What are you doing in Ranwell Street?' I asked her, knowing the chronic poverty of that little alley.

'All out of work, all helping each other', she chirruped gaily, flashing a merry smile to me from her clear green eyes, her red plaits tossing. Yet I saw she was pale, and her gait not buoyant as usual.

Lansbury was hopeless of action, and advised me to get on to one of the relief committees which were being formed, 'to show what women could do.' He offered to nominate me. I told him women had always done that.

Already from Ireland, I had telegraphed Smyth to call our Federation Committee for August 6th. Its members were in a ferment. Mrs Bird, the wife of a docker earning 22s a week, and mother of six children, wanted the 'No Rent' strike to begin at once, for the people could find no money for the rent with food at its present cost. We adopted a programme of immediate demands, including the nationalisation of the food supplies; and arranged to run a campaign of street corner meetings, as though an election were in progress. Many organisations, stunned by the War, were suspending activities; to us the need of propaganda was intensified.

That first weekend of the War I went lecturing in the provinces, as I did constantly, to build up new branches of the Federation and extend the circulation of the *Dreadnought*. As always, I hurried back to Old Ford by an early train on Monday. Mrs Payne met me on the doorstep lamenting. A lady had telephoned that she was bringing milk from the country for distribution to the poor. Mrs Payne had hied her into the by-streets to gather a score of the neediest mothers. The news of the promised windfall reverberated through the streets. Hundreds of women came rushing from every quarter. The road was thronged. The lady arrived in her car; but, alas, she brought only a few pints of milk! Sad were the tears of the disappointed mothers, seeing the dear illusion fade which was to have succoured their starving infants. The poor old Payne, whose heart was too tender to witness trouble, wept in recounting, striving in vain to thrust from her the memory of those poor ones. 'Oh, Miss Pankhurst, don't let anyone bring them here like that again! I can't bear it. Oh them poor little babies! I can't lose the sight of 'em!' She sobbed on my shoulder, then looked up, smiling through tears, a confident hope in her loving gaze: 'Miss Pankhurst, couldn't you help 'em? Couldn't you get milk for 'em? Couldn't you do it?'

I wrote to the *Times*, describing the incident, as she told it; the misery of those hundreds turned empty away. I demanded attention for the distress. In immediate response came £10, to buy milk, from a Suffragette, Mrs Forbes of Kensington. Other sums followed. 400 Old Ford Road became a milk centre. The old house had been used as a school. 'There were cornfields around it when we were children,' the son of the owner told me. At the rear of the house a queer flat-roofed building, which served as our general office, communicated with a small hall, a poor mean edifice, its interior walls of unplastered brick merely brightened with a rough colour-wash. At one end of the hall was a low platform; at the other, a wooden archway, with niches holding plaster casts of Homer, the Venus of Milo and the Delphic Apollo. Here we held our meetings. Here, and in the passage through the house, the queue of distressed mothers extended: poor young mothers in their starving fortitude, with faces of ashen pallor, and sorrowful eyes, dark-ringed; beautiful in their fading as pale lilies in the moonlight, to those who had eyes for their mournful loveliness; divorced from the vigour of health, as is the night from day. Tidy, hard-working little women they were, even at the best of times, daily accomplishing a miracle of endurance and devotion, clad in their poor, ill-shaped clothing, dingy and drab; clean aprons over their shabby shirts, in respect for themselves and others. Some wore their hair closely braided, or screwed up in curling pins, to save spending time on it. Tragic mothers, anxious mothers, mothers with knotted, work-worn hands, and deep-lined faces, older in looks than women of their years in more fortunate circles; grandmothers, sad and sorrowing, a world of unmerited suffering in their patient eyes and drawn, white faces.

Already the babies were ill from starving; they could not digest the milk now we had got it for them. Moreover, the other members of destitute families all had their needs. A comprehensive organisation was necessary for dealing with hardship; yet still I did not contemplate that our Federation should undertake this; it was the workers' mate, through which women submerged in poverty, and overburdened with toil were finding self-expression, and a medium through which they could force their needs and aspirations upon the attention of those in power. I feared that organised relief, even the kindliest and most understanding, might introduce some savour of patronage or con-descension, and mar our affectionate comradeship, in which we were all equals, all members one of another.

Moreover, no private effort could cope with the great misery around us; it was the responsibility of the Community, of the State. In the *Dreadnought* of August 15th I published a paragraph headed, 'Our Duty,' urging our members to seek election to the Local Representative Committees for administering the National Relief Fund, and declaring that our main duty was to bring pressure to bear on the Government to secure the great needs of the people. I regarded our milk distribution as so temporary a stop-gap, that I made no mention of it in our paper then.

Yet public assistance tarried; the plight of the distressed weighed heavily on me. Under pressure of the need, daily confronting us, I announced an employment bureau, with Maud Joachim as secretary, and appealed for work for brushmakers, shoemakers and others. In the following issue I had thrown away reserves, and was pleading for funds to buy milk, for eggs to provide albumen water for infants too ill to digest milk, for other invalid necessities, and announcing that a nurse to advise mothers whose babies had fallen ill would attend every afternoon at the Women's Hall. Henceforth every week Dr Lilian Simpson was in attendance, and a regular clinic was established in the Old Ford Road, and soon at five other centres.

How could one face a starving family with nothing to offer save milk for the baby? Orders for the various sorts of home work our distressed people could do, we gave out, as they came to us, through the employment bureau; but these were miserably few, as compared with our numbers. Expectant mothers were unable to provide for their confinements. We purchased material, cut out garments for mothers and babies, and older children, and paid our starving applicants for employment to make them up.

From the first we laid it down rigidly that we should pay no woman less than 5d per hour, the district minimum wage of the unskilled labouring man. To pay a woman less, and call it charity, was to connive at sweating; and cost what it might, we were resolved not to depart from that standard.

We had now a systemised distress bureau. Already before the War we carried on a continuous house to house canvas of East End districts, to draw the women into our movement. Our canvassers returned to me now with piteous stories of misery accentuated, of hard lives rendered harder. I urged them to take notes of every case. From the canvassers' reports, and from the constant stream of distressed callers, who came at all hours to consult me in their despair, great shoals of misery were cast up to me, the very bowels of hardship were disclosed. To aid these unhappy souls one must deal with each case in detail, appealing, demanding, exhorting the Government Department, or the Board of Guardians, the landlord, the employer, the Trade Union appropriate to the case. Sometimes one must attend a police court to plead with the magistrate. Occasionally a lawyer's aid became necessary, and soon we had three firms of solicitors willing to act for us gratuitously.

People I knew as good comrades filed in with the rest to tell their troubles; mothers and fathers, pale and spiritless, with wasted children. The cry: 'Enlist or go!' was already raised; a knell of despair to many a father, cast on the streets with every door shut against him. Large families with eight and ten children were absolutely destitute, not a penny coming in from any source; or, at best, a child or two earning a paltry wage, from three to five shillings a week, too little even to pay the rent. One of the young fellows who had fought beside me in many a Suffragette tussle had come in with his little family. He was white to the lips from privation. Edith Jones, dark-eyed and serious, a young Suffragette from Holloway, come here to help us, took down particulars. 'Why do you not enlist?' Her question to him stabbed my heart with a pang. This war virus was everywhere! Tragic that even one of our own helpers should be urging these poor youths into the carnage toward which economic pressure was irresistibly driving them!

* * *

[FROM CHAPTER XIX: 'PEACE EFFORTS']

The War grew daily more terrible. The miseries of a winter in the trenches were followed by frantic efforts to break through the opposing lines, in which thousands of lives were lost without result. On the shores of the Dardanelles poor fellows were dying in attempting the impossible, the blockade was tightened—submarine warfare intensified. Behind the great offensive, Peace efforts were feebly striving. News filtered through that there had been a Truce in the Trenches on Christmas Day, that British and German soldiers had thrown down their arms to fraternise, exchanging little keepsakes and comforts, rejoicing in the respite from slaughter their mutual confidence had won for them, finding themselves as brothers in their adversity. This brief manifestation of human solidarity, banned from official reports, was never permitted to recur.

———

Vain efforts were being made to resurrect the Socialist International. The Dutch Socialists had given hospitality to the Secretary of the International Socialist Bureau, Camille Huysmans, a Belgian. It was their hope that on neutral soil he would be able to perform the difficult task of resuscitation. The difficulties were great, and Huysmans unequal to the task. The officials of the Majority Socialist Parties in belligerent nations maintained, until the end of the War, their refusal to meet the Socialists of the countries with which the capitalist Governments of their countries were in conflict.

The Socialist Parties of the northern neutral countries had met a Copenhagen in January 1915 and had issued a manifesto denouncing the War as a product of Capitalist imperialism and its secret diplomacy, and calling on the Socialists of the belligerent nations to be active for peace, and to work with renewed energy to conquer political power. The leaders who controlled the Socialist parties of the belligerent nations were in no mood to second such a pronouncement.

Under the auspices of the British Section of the International Socialist Bureau, a conference, which was supposed to represent the Socialist movements of Britain, France, Belgium and Russia, issued a declaration strongly supporting the cause of the Allied Governments, and declaring the Socialists of their countries 'inflexibly resolved to fight until victory is achieved.' When this manifesto was condemned at the ILP conference, J. R. MacDonald, who had been a party to it, characteristically replied that it was a compromise. He urged his critics to 'be very careful to remember the date on which it was passed.'

Across the ruins of the International came the voice of Karl Liebknecht, demanding on the floor of the Prussian Landtag the democratisation of the franchise and of foreign policy.

> Democratic control by the people would have prevented the War. . . . Away with the hypocrisy of civil peace! On with the international class struggle for the emancipation of the working class and against the War!

His words thrilled round the world, evoking the heartbeat of a multitude. Brave Karl Liebknecht!

Already on December 2nd, 1914, he had voted against the War Credits in the German Reichstag. No British Socialist was ready to follow his example. On March 10th, 1915, Leibknecht repeated his negative. We learnt with joy that on March 18th several thousand women, who had organised secretly with this intent, had appeared before the Reichstag, shouting for peace. Karl Liebknecht from a window in the Reichstag had addressed them. As punishment he was ordered to the Front—to his death his friends feared. He had been joined by Ledebour, Ruhle, Mehring, Clara Zetkin and Rosa Luxemburg in a manifesto calling for an immediate peace, without annexations, which would secure political and economic independence to every nation, disarmament, and the compulsory arbitration of international disputes. At Christmas Liebknecht had conveyed a message to the ILP in London appealing for a new Socialist International.

In March a conference of Socialist women, summoned by Clara Zetkin, the International Secretary of the Women's Socialist Organisation, and one of the leaders of the German Social Democratic Party, met secretly in Berne. It was attended by delegates from both factions of warring nations, who met in their old fraternity, to utter a call for the speedy ending of the War, and a peace which should impose no humiliating condition on any nation. Unheralded and unchronicled, little was heard of the event. Women Socialists of all countries had overcome the nationalist hysteria of war time, which held the male leaders of the International in its grip. Clara had planned this conference with Rosa Luxemburg. They intended to go together across the frontiers to visit the Socialists of the other nations. Then Rosa was arrested. Clara saw her in prison, then went to Holland, but was unable to pass the Belgian frontier. She sent couriers to Huysmans but he did not reply. Soon Clara was herself in prison for four months; she was ill when she came out, but she persevered with the conference. The Social Democratic leaders declared it an offence against the discipline of the Party and forbade their members to distribute the conference manifestoes.

Amongst women of another milieu a movement for peace was also germinant. At Christmas Emily Hobhouse, Helen Bright Clark, Margaret Clark Gillett, Sophia and Lily Sturge, Isabella Ford, Lady Barlow and Lady Courtney of Penwith had addressed a letter to the women of Germany and Austria, urging them to join in calling for a truce. Through Jus Suffragii, the organ of the International Women's Suffrage Alliance, whose editor, Miss Sheepshanks, bravely upheld its internationalism, despite very great discouragement from the majority of the British Suffrage Societies, a response was received from prominent German and Austrian women.

Dr Aletta Jacobs and other Dutch Suffragists now issued an appeal for a women's international congress at The Hague, to urge the belligerent governments to call a truce to define their peace terms; and to demand the submission of international disputes to arbitration; the democratic control of foreign policy; that no territory should be transferred without the consent of its population; the political enfranchisement of women; and the inclusion of women delegates in the conference of Powers which would follow the War. The conference was to cost £1,000; the Dutch Suffragists offered a third of the sum; the German Suffragists responded with a further third. The National Union of Women's Suffrage Societies under Mrs Fawcett, which represented British women in the International Suffrage Alliance, repudiated the Congress; but a group of seceders from that organisation met with other women's organisations, including our Federation, in conference at the Caxton Hall to answer the invitation from Holland. The delegates were enthusiastic. More than 200 of us volunteered to go to The Hague.

The Congress now began to receive tremendous publicity. The Press condemned it; prominent women assailed it. We who had agreed to go were execrated. Mrs Fawcett declared that to talk of peace while the German armies were in France and Belgium was 'akin to treason.' Mrs Cecil Chapman, President of the New Constitutional Society for Women's Suffrage, considered the time 'painfully inopportune' for members of the belligerent nations to confer. The WSPU which had been *hors de combat* and existing on occasional speeches by Christabel and Mrs Pankhurst, now burst into life to oppose the Congress. The *Suffragette* reappeared on April 16th, 1915, after eight months' suspension, declaring in its leading article that it was a 'thousand times more' the duty of militant Suffragettes to fight the Kaiser for the sake of liberty, than it had been to fight anti-Suffrage Governments. Nina Boyle, in the Women's Freedom League organ, *The Vote*, attacked *Jus Suffragii* for becoming 'the mouthpiece' of the promoters of the Conference, and protested that the Women's Freedom League 'refused to ask for more legislation—even reform legislation—until women could help to control and administer it.' She marvelled that there should be Suffragists 'who imagine it possible for them . . . to be an international power, and set in motion reforms vaster and more quixotic than any body of men with franchise, representatives, and Cabinet Ministers in their pocket, would venture to attack at the present moment.'

With such chilling and bitter sarcasm the ardent idealism of the pioneer is ever met; yet the true pioneers fling out their golden conceptions on the world, recking not of obstacles, serene in their faith.

From French Suffragists came equally emphatic denunciations. An American women who considered joining the Women's International Congress Movement sent a copy of its objects to ex-President Roosevelt: he condemned them as 'silly and base.'

Mrs Astor wrote to me that she would never have invited me to her house, had she known I would offer to attend such a Congress. She added that she had learnt we were paying £1 a week in the toy factory, instead of the 10s of the Queen Mary Rooms. Had she known it she would not have aided us. Many members of the Women's Social and Political Union, who during its inactivity had worked for our

Federation, now sheered off and left us. Some even of those who had professed internationalist and pacifist views now rallied to their old allegiance to Mrs Pankhurst and Christabel; some hesitated, uncertain what course to take. Many subscribers to our work for mothers and children withdrew. By every post came letters refusing further support. 'Subscribers are falling off like dead leaves at the end of the season!' I said to Smyth, but we held on, redoubling our efforts, that those who depended on us might not suffer. Many times, before and since, the choice came to me, whether for the sake of the work I was doing, to stay my hand and remain silent, or to speak and do what I believed to be right, knowing that through me, all else that I was prominently engaged in would suffer attack and perhaps extinction. I was guided by the opinion that freedom of thought and speech is more important than any good which can ever come of concealing one's views, and by the knowledge that in the hour of its greatest unpopularity the pioneering cause needs one most. Yet it was often hard to choose thus sternly, flying in the face of what seemed prudent, casting to the winds the result of laborious effort; hard, not on my own account; for I had shred all personal aims when I gave up painting in the years of the Suffragette struggle before the War; hard only on account of the work I was striving to do, and the people who looked to me for aid. On this occasion we weathered the storm. Smyth came forward as usual with donations and loans, writing off most of the latter, too, as donations, when she found, as financial secretary, they were too hard to repay. New workers and subscribers came gradually in to replace the departed.

The women of Russia, Germany, Austria, France and Belgium were permitted to proceed to the Congress; but the British Government, having directed the Press abuse of our mission, refused to let British women go. McKenna, at one point, conceded to Miss Courtney and Miss Marshall, who were conducting the negotiations, that passports should be issued to twenty women of discretion, whom he selected from the 200. Some of the chosen were quite flattered by his choice: such phrases as: 'They don't mind when they feel they can really trust you' fell from their lips. It is impossible to describe the atmosphere of repression which overhung the movement. Vain efforts at diplomacy attempted to parry opposition. In the *Dreadnought* I had written of the Women's Peace Conference at The Hague. I received a letter of protest from Miss Crystal MacMillan of the British Committee for the Congress:

British Committee of the
International Women's Congress

DEAR MISS PANKHURST,

It has been pointed out to us that in the *Woman's Dreadnought* you speak of this International Congress as a 'Peace Congress.' This is giving rise to a good deal of misunderstanding, as the Congress cannot fairly be so described. The definition of the terms of peace is the only point in connection with peace on which it expresses an opinion or makes a demand. To call it a 'Peace Conference' gives the impression that its object is to demand peace at any price. We shall be very glad, therefore, if you will do what you can to remove the false impression which has been created.

C. MACMILLAN.

Alas, for the caution and confidence of the chosen ladies; McKenna, for all his promises, did not permit them to sail. Miss Courtney, it is true, had been too sharp for him. When he assured her: 'Of course I should have no objection to issue permits to you and Miss Marshall,' she answered: 'I will take mine now,' and was allowed to proceed. The others were kept waiting expectant, until the eleventh hour. On one occasion McKenna assured them that he would have issued the necessary permits to them there and then; but the official whose duty it was to affix his signature to the documents had left the office for the night. It would be quite out of order for himself, or anyone save that particular official to sign. On their final visit he assured the chosen ladies that he would assuredly have let them travel at last; but, to his great regret, 'the boats had stopped running' on account of a great event of which they would certainly read in the Press. No notice of the event ever appeared. The ladies declared they had been tricked. The rest of us were curtly and frankly informed that no permits to attend the Congress were being issued. (. . .)

From the Women's Congress at The Hague arose a permanent organisation. A British Section, termed the Women's International League, was formed in the autumn. As at the preliminary Conference, all the women's organisations working for Peace were invited to send delegates: Suffragists, Socialists, Labourists and Quakers being thus represented. I was elected to the Executive. The majority of its London members were seceders from Mrs Fawcett's National Union of Suffrage Societies. The work, therefore assumed a cautious and moderate tone. Our Federation delegates were out-voted, when we proposed that the title should be the Women's International Peace League, and that women of foreign citizenship, resident in Britain, should be admitted to membership of the British Section. Mrs Swanwick opposed the proposition on the ground that 'a great deal of mud' would be cast at the organisation. Even the British wives of aliens were excluded.

The non-militant Suffragists felt the fierce opposition to our Peace efforts more sharply than Suffragettes and Socialists, who had already borne the brunt of championing unpopular causes.

The organisation was from the first overshadowed by the tremendous magnitude of its task. It worked many degrees below the high-keyed enthusiasm of the Hague Conference. It carried no fiery cross; but tried, in a quiet way, sincerely, if at times haltingly, to understand the causes of war, and to advance the causes of Peace by negotiation, and the enfranchisement of women. From time to time it expressed itself by resolution in careful phrases; from time to time it held a public meeting, from which notorious people were, as a rule, prudently excluded. All Peace work laboured under the weight of harsh adversity. The less could be accomplished, alas, the more lengthy, were the sittings of the Committee. They lasted from 10 am to 6 pm. It seemed almost like undertaking the labours of Penelope, when I essayed to induce the Executive to call a week's Conference to debate such international questions, then to the fore, as the Freedom of the Seas, Disarmament, the Self-Determination of Oppressed Nationalities and so on! Protracted as the task was, it was accomplished at length! When I returned to the East End after these lengthy sittings, to find myself obliged to cut out sleep, and work forty-eight hours, with scarcely a break, to cope with the arrears which had accumulated during my absence, I often told my East End colleagues I should prefer to resign from the WIL. 'Oh, do stay there and leaven them!' Norah Smyth and others urged me: but I did so reluctantly. In the East End we were equally powerless to stay the hideous progress of the War; but we could alleviate some of its miseries. To me it was essential to be able to voice my opinions spontaneously, and without fear or favour. To trim one's statements, in order to conciliate influential opinion, oppressed me with a sense of insincerity.

'In the red twilight'

[Selection from one of several hand-written drafts, in note book form, File 79, Pankhurst Papers, International Institute of Social History, Amsterdam.*] n. d., approx. 1935

SETTING UP THE PEOPLE'S RUSSIAN
INFORMATION BUREAU (PRIB)

The prophets of hope who come with promises of bright futures may be most adored, but the jesters are ever the longest loved, for life is too often sad and the world ways drear. In the days of adversity they can cheer alike, the faint heart and the careless, exacting no sacrifice and no labour, asking nothing save smiles.

The dreamer whom men and women have followed with hearts aflame is reviled or forgotten when the rays of hope grow wan and the glory which, near and so tangible, appears a vision fantastic and unreal. Thus they live lives of happiest tranquillity who choose for their goal one simple and near objective, not cutting sharply across the passions and interests of others, not demanding too mordant a sacrifice.

The comfortable do not care to be reminded too oppressively of the unhappy, nor the [unfinished]. For beauty and joy in the breasts of all of us is a great hunger, and they who espouse the cause of the poor and demand an egalitarian society must accept as their portion the antagonism of those who desire to find contentment by blinding themselves to the squalor and scarcity upon which our social edifice is based.

Litvinov's departure

Litvinov[1] asked me to come there to say goodbye. He was very friendly, very cordial, and urged me to come to Russia. 'You would have a big reception,' he said, smiling warmly.

He gave me a piece of paper in which was written the name and

---

* Note: some words were illegible and are marked [ ] in the text.
1 Maxim Litvinov, official Soviet representative of the Bolsheviks in London

address of Theodore Rothstein,[2] telling me that from that source I should receive information and a weekly donation to the funds of the People's Russian Information Bureau, which I had already taken steps to found. He told me it was his purpose to contribute £10 a week to the funds of the PRIB.(. . .)

Mrs Litvinov received me with great friendliness, commiserating herself that she saw only men with their perpetual talk of politics. With the phrase 'we women' on her lips, she seemed a feminist of a type then new and strange, even a little repellent to me. She would talk of sex, and impart her ideal and experiences, complaining that her upbringing had been to prepare her for the marriage-market and that an engagement to marry in her first London season had been expected of her. To me such matters appeared infinitely remote. A London season in her sense of the term would have been declined had it come my way. Moreover, they concerned only the leisured class in this society I believed ending; the multitudes had no part in them. Did this woman understand the meaning of the Soviet Revolution, its portent flung across the world to us? I was depressed by her talk, and surprised. How had she come to marry a revolutionist? I admired her beautiful child. She answered, without enthusiasm, yet I saw she was pregnant, wondering the while how a revolutionary had failed to interest his wife in the cause.

*　*　*

Rothstein's £10

The £10 did not go far. It had to be supplemented by the efforts of the Committee and officials. The half sent was to be Miss O'Callaghan's half salary—£2, Miss Cohen's £3 10s and a junior getting probably £1. At one time there were two juniors, a girl and a boy, for thousands of circulars had to be rushed out weekly. Numerous pamphlets were produced and proof-reading arrangements with printers, etc., had to be transacted.

Efforts to obtain offices for anything connected for the Soviets had failed. I proposed that I should take a city office for the *Workers' Dreadnought*, and sub-let to the Information Bureau. S. [Silvio Corio] hunted the city and discovered two light offices at the very top of 152

2　Theodore Rothstein, Litvinov's successor and one of the leaders of the British Socialist Party

Fleet Street, up a dark narrow stair above Alderton's, the Tailors, entered from Bolt Court, with a heavy, old sliding door which became the cause of many humorous, but provoking, incidents. If, as often happened, the little wheels on which it ran came out of the worn slot in the ground, it could neither be locked or unlocked and the help of two or three burly policemen had to be requisitioned to test their strength on it. One might by no means go home and leave the recalcitrant door unfastened, for if one did, the police would bring the unfortunate manager of the tailor's shop from his bed in a distant suburb to lock it up. If one were locked inside, as many times happened, it was a case of telephoning here and there and signalling for aid, to a deserted city, from those terribly high windows. On one occasion, a nimble young lady climbed over roofs and obtained aid from a neighbouring building.

I was all zealous for the Information Bureau, but Miss O'Callaghan was not inclined to the rapid methods which, in my opinion, the situation dictated and for which Rothstein clamoured. We published from the *Dreadnought* on October ninth, but operations at the Bureau hung fire. [As] the editor of the *Dreadnought* and the Secretary of the Federation, I could rush things forward as fast as my energy would drive them; but Miss O'Callaghan was manager of the Information Bureau and, albeit the treasurer, I did not feel I could supersede her. Driving was never in my line and she was wrong; it was urgent to get ahead with things.

It was only a couple of weeks or so—yet how the delay irked me and how humiliating I felt it to have to take the subsidy from the discontented Rothstein!

Then we were inundated by the influenza epidemic. At Old Ford Rd half the staff was laid low. In the Bureau and the *Dreadnought* offices everyone was struck down. I brought from Old Ford Mr Young, a conscientious objector permitted to us from an employment scheme organised by the Quakers, and, with the aid of some casual volunteers pressed into the service, produced both the *Dreadnought* and the first bulletin of the People's Russian Information Bureau. Rothstein had sent a paragraph; I added some others collected from various sources.

I was sorry for Miss O'Callaghan and the staff, but what a weight of miserable oppression was lifted when I got a free hand to get the bulletin started! After that, they did not cease; it was a law inexorable that they must come out like the *Dreadnought*. If Rothstein failed with his matter we must cull it from other sources.

I was scribbling an article on the bus on my way somewhere when a voice spoke to me: 'You have energy!' It was Rothstein, with something of the cordiality of that first meeting. It had evaporated so rapidly. S. proved invaluable. He took over the Parliamentary notes which lately had been done mainly by Miss O'Callaghan, with some interpolations by me, for I did not cease to read *Hansard*. He imported a fresh humour and an insight which were enlivening. He declared we needed humour, and introduced me to Z. A. Motler, a writer of real talent. He had edited, during its brief existence, a clever little periodical, a new departure in proletarian journals, all fun and pictures, many of them excellent, notably those by 'Rodo', a Frenchman, and the son of the great Camille Pissarro, whose numerous clever offspring all elected to work under other pseudonyms lest their father's works of genius should be overcast by less good work under the same name. Motler, who was employed printing tram tickets, wrote with a caustic and racy humour which made me laugh over his proofs in spite of myself. (. . .)

There were many late nights for me and many a long, weary tramp to the East End, but I cared little for that, even though it was a hard struggle to manage the last third of the journey.

When the paper and bulletin were safely gone, S. would come in with good suggestions for the new issue. It was delightfully stimulating to have someone to plan with whose knowledge of world socialist movements was older and wider than mine, who had read all that mattered of socialist writings and manifestoes from Marx to Kropotkin and the literature of all the parties, from the Right Wing to the Reformists to the Anarchists. (. . .)

Before the paper was out, I was off to Glasgow to speak in the John Maclean[3] election campaign. Enthusiasm at the meetings was high, though we were barely touching the fringe of the electorate. John Maclean had been forcibly fed in Peterhead Jail since July, until recently twice a day. He had now abandoned the hunger strike and was eating the food provided. Yet forcible feeding was still continued once a day, as officially stated in Parliament, for what reason, unless to punish and intimidate, it was difficult to conceive. Police reporters

3 John Maclean, leader of the 'Red Clyde' shop stewards' movement in Glasgow

appeared at the meetings. The audience howled at them and would have hurled them from the hall, but the jovial Gallacher[4] from the chair called on them to desist, saying that the police would retaliate by sending reporters who could not be recognised, if the plainclothesmen who were known to us were turned outside.

Glasgow was bleak and cheerless. I never saw it more dingy and grime-laden. I stayed with Agnes Aiton. By my bed side was a portrait of Keir Hardie, his mother and large family of step brothers and sisters. I thought with mingled happiness and sorrow of his dear memory.

4 Willie Gallacher, also of the shop stewards' movement

Part V

Anti-facism and Ethiopia
1936–53

Pankhurst re-entered active politics in the early 1930s when she joined several pacifist organisations including the Women's International League for Peace and Freedom, the International Women's Peace Crusade and the Women's World Committee Against War and Fascism (of which she became treasurer). But the issue which proved to be the greatest catalyst, and reorientated Pankhurst's politics for the rest of her life, was the 1935–36 Italian facist invasion and occupation of Ethiopia, which until then had been the only independent African state.

Her opposition to fascism was not new; as early as November 1922, Pankhurst had published in the *Workers' Dreadnought* an article on the tactics of the *fascisti* in Italy (reprinted in the *Reader*) and also drew attention to Hitler's activities in Bavaria, in 1923. In 1932 she had also formed the Women's International Matteotti Committee to try to protect the widow of Giacomo Matteotti, who as a moderate opposition leader had been murdered by the Fascists. But her greatest anti-fascist campaign was the one she launched in May 1936, when she inaugurated another newspaper, *New Times and Ethiopia News* (*NT&EN*), to publicise the plight of that country and its exiled leader Emperor Haile Selassie, and to expose the apparent acquiescent attitude of the British Government to Mussolini's colonial ambitions. The subtitle of the first issue was 'Remember—everywhere, always, fascism means war' and she turned her attention later that year, in 'Three Great Powers Betrayed Us' (reprinted here), to the League of Nations for lifting sanctions imposed on Italy after the invasion. She mourns in particular the retreat by Soviet Russia from its opposition to Italian fascists who, she predicts, will unite with

205

Hitler's nazis to 'make common cause against the democracies of the world'.

The paper also gave her the opportunity to publish, in serial form, a history of fascism in Italy (from 5 August, 1936), and a similar record of Hitler's rise to power (between October 1938 and February 1939), which she intended to publish as a book, *Fascism As It Is*. However, the unpublished manuscript remains among her papers in Amsterdam. A chapter on women under fascism is reprinted here.

The defeat of the Italian fascists in Ethiopia in 1941 did not signal the end of Pankhurst's championing of Ethiopian liberty. She used the *NT&EN* to oppose various British proposals, whether they were to dismember the country or establish extra-territorial rights over it. She argued that as the victim of an unprovoked aggression, Ethiopia was entitled to its liberation without the imposition of any such arrangements. In particular, she denounced the Anglo-Ethiopian agreements of 1942 and 1944, as a result of which the country was treated, she argued, as a virtual protectorate, and vehemently protested against continued British military occupation of several parts of the country.

The other important political campaign Pankhurst conducted after the defeat of Mussolini was to try reunite Eritrea, occupied by the British from 1941, with its Ethiopian 'motherland', countries which were historically linked prior to colonial intervention in the nineteenth century. This she firmly believed to be in the best interests of both countries. Her arguments were put forward in most detail in one of her many books dedicated to Ethiopian politics, *Ethiopia and Eritrea* (1953, with R. K. P. Pankhurst), a short section of which is reproduced as the last item in this section.

She was active in the reconstruction of Ethiopia after the war and helped to raise funds to build the first modern hospital in the country. Pankhurst emigrated to Ethiopia in 1956, launched another paper, the *Ethiopia Observer*, which she edited for the last four years of her life, and was buried in Addis Ababa as an honoured patriot in 1960.

'Our policy [on the invasion of Ethiopia by fascist Italy]'

[*New Times and Ethiopia News*, 9 May 1936
– first issue]

OUR POLICY

New Times and Ethiopa News appears at a moment when the fortunes of Ethiopa seem at their lowest ebb; the greater need then for an advocate and a friend. We know that the difficulties facing her are grave, but we do not falter, either in faith or determination that they shall be overcome.

The cause of Ethiopia cannot be divided from the cause of International justice, which is permanent, and is not determined by ephemeral military victories. As friends of Ethiopia we most solemnly and most vigorously protest against the attack on her millennial independence; we condemn the atrocious barbarities employed against her, the bombing of her undefended villages, the use of poison gases, by which thousands of innocent women and children have suffered agonising death.

The Italian victories were inevitable, her victim being virtually unarmed. We utterly deny that these or any military successes furnish a title to annexation.

We uphold the principles of international justice and denial of annexation by conquest, on which the League of Nations has been formed.

In the words of Sir George Paish:

We cannot permit a situation to arise again such as that which resulted in so great a sacrifice of life in the Great War.

The only way to prevent such a catastrophe is for the nations to stand at all costs for the new system of international law and justice for which the adoption of the Covenant of the League of Nations by so many countries stands.

That all nations are not members of the League, and that certain Governments have broken their Covenant, is greatly to be deplored. But this does not diminish the need, or the value, of the system. On the contrary, it increases its need and its value. Just as a national system of law and justice is of still greater moment if and when the law is broken, so an international system is of increased value if any nation is breaking the law or threatening to break it.

It is only by enforcing the law that order and justice can be maintained either nationally or internationally.

Moreover, only by enforcing International law will there be any possibility of preventing another and more dangerous world war from breaking out and destroying vast numbers of people in all countries, either in the conflict or through the resultant collapse of the world structure.

It is vital, therefore, to the present and future welfare of the people of every country—including the Italian people themselves—that the new system of international law and justice should prevail, and that the authority of the League of Nations should be maintained now and for all time.

Even were Italy to succeed in conquering Abyssinia; in spite of her pledges under the Covenant, and in spite of the opposition of the League, the eventual result must be disaster to the Italian people in common with the peoples of all other countries.

The Fascist Government and its hired propagandists in all lands have already launched an intensified propaganda to secure the lifting of sanctions, and to justify the conquest of Abyssinia, or at least the retention of the occupied territories. We shall set ourselves resolutely to combat fascist propaganda, to secure the continuance and strengthening of sanctions, which in fact are only soon beginning to exert serious economic pressure. We shall strive to induce measures by the League to resist the Fascist usurpation, and to aid and defend Ethiopia, and will persistently urge that Britain take the responsibility of initiating an active League policy on these lines.

We shall urge also that Britain shall herself individually give aid to Ethiopia (. . .) Thereby some partial atonement may be made for the cruelly unmerited suffering to a defenceless people which has been caused by the long inexcusable failure to obey the Covenant of the League. Sir John Maffey's Report reveals clearly that our 'National Government' must bear a serious share of responsibility for the tragedy in not having laid the matter of Italy's intended aggression before the Council of the League.

We shall urge, in season and out, that the facts of the Italo–Ethiopian war and the reason of League intervention therein be broadcasted in all languages to inform all peoples thereon, and especially those of Italy where free information is denied.

New Times is opposed to the conception of dictatorship. It under-stands that fascism destroys all personal liberty and is in fundamental opposition to all forms of intellectual and moral progress.

We draw a profound distinction between the Italian Fascist Government and the Italian people, who are enslaved to-day, but whose freedom is slowly but surely being prepared by the martyrdom of thousands of heroic men and women, guardians of an inextinguish-able faith, murdered, tortured, imprisoned, exiled in poverty and sorrow, they keep high and untarnished the ideal of justice.

Millions of people in Italy fervently cherish that same distinction between the people of Italy and the Fascist Government. When Mr Anthony Eden made it at the League of Nations even to the smallest, remotest Italian villages far from the railway the news travelled and was joyfully received.

THE WITHDRAWAL FROM ADDIS ABABA

The arrival of the Italians at Addis Ababa changes nothing; it has long been forecasted by the progress of the war, in which inevitably the Italians were victorious, because of their superiority in arms. Our demand that Italy shall receive not a yard of territory, not a single economic or political advantage as the reward of conquest remains unchanged. The burning by the Abyssinians of their capital, whether official or unofficial, occasions no surprise. The Russians, in face of Napoleon's victorious advance, similarly burned Moscow.

For the deaths and injuries which followed the departure of the Emperor and his Government, we feel deep regret and we offer sincere sympathy to the injured and to the relatives of the dead. No blame for these sad events is attached to the Abyssinian Government. It withdrew under the pressure of superior forces commanded by a ruthless foe, who by persistent and flagrant disregard of the more chivalrous usages of civilised warfare, had but too clearly indicated the terrible fate which would have overtaken the Emperor, his family and his Ministers had they permitted themselves to fall into the power of the Fascist Government.

It was the right and the duty of the Emperor and his Government to take such steps as seemed best to them in the interests of their people, their country, and the struggle for independence they will certainly continue.

Having regard to the high-minded and able manner in which they have dealt with each stage of this awful conflict, we do not doubt that they have taken the course which was wisest under the appalling circumstances in which they were placed. Life has been lost, but there can be no doubt that had they remained to meet the Italians, the loss of life to all in the city would have been infinitely greater.

MR EDEN AND THE EMPEROR

Mr Eden has disclosed that the British authorities in conceding the Emperor's desire for safe conduct to Palestine laid upon him the condition that he should take no part in continuing the resistance of his people to Italian aggression. We enter our protest against this condition; so far from imposing it the British authorities should render the Emperor and his people all assistance in their fight.

What we demand of His Majesty's Government and of the League of Nations is that the Emperor of Abyssinia and his colleagues shall be treated as loyal and honourable allies in the struggle to uphold the Covenant of the League against the treaty-breaking aggressor. The proposal that Ethiopian Enclaves on British African Territory shall be offered by the British Government to the Emperor and his people assumes an urgent and immediate importance, in view of the present position.

That such Enclaves would have to be offered under conditions which would involve no loss of dignity or prestige to the Ethiopian Government and people is evident. It must be made clear that acceptance of the Enclaves would entail no agreement, expressed or implied, to refrain from any measures to recover from Italy the whole of Ethiopia as it was before the war. There must be no question of abating the efforts of Britain and of the League to annul the Fascist conquest.

We should prefer that the Fascist attack on Ethiopia be terminated by League action, but so long as the League fails to shoulder effective responsibility to defend the victim of aggression, the victim must be permitted, nay aided to defend herself.

Hospitals, schools, training and experimental centres could be preserved and built up in the Enclaves secure from war. The reforms of the Emperor could continue there when peace is restored and the sympathy of experts be capitalised in service.

'Three great powers betrayed us'

[*New Times and Ethiopia News*, 11 July 1936]

Three great Powers have betrayed Ethiopia and the League. Three great Powers have betrayed Democracy. That is the sad truth we have to face to-day.

The responsibility of our own 'National' Government is heaviest because it gave the lead in the great retreat from principle, because it professed to have assumed the leadership in defending the Covenant and the small State menaced by aggression, and had accepted the plaudits of the world and the grateful confidence of Ethiopia for this supposed service to truth and justice. Britain's responsibility is heaviest, too, because of the vast African populations under her rule, her great possessions, her enormous Navy, and because her huge command over sources of raw material and her large Mercantile Marine gave her a greater power than any nation or group of nations to make economic sanctions effective or the reverse. Her control of Egypt gives her control of the Suez Canal, which has been the vital crux of the whole question as to whether the Italian aggression was to be helped or hindered by League Powers. The other nations knew that if Britain withdrew from sanctions they would be of no effect.

The blame for lifting sanctions and abandoning Ethiopia to the aggressors rests heaviest on the British Government, because the British people, from the General Election onwards, have given their mandate in every way possible under our constitution for defence of Ethiopia and the Covenant. The National Government has betrayed the definite pledges it gave to the people when it appealed for their votes.

FRANCE

Yet the betrayal of collective security by M. Blum and his 'Popular Front Government' has proved the deepest disappointment of all to the people of most countries outside France, and, we believe, also to those of France itself. Had he broken with the old methods of Laval, and boldly declared for intensified sanctions immediately his majority was secured, the British 'National' Government could not have deserted Ethiopia. Had the 'National' Government attempted such a betrayal, with France standing true, the Government would have been overthrown by a tempest of popular indignation which would have forced even the most subservient House of Commons to keep faith with the public.

The Regional Pacts proposed by Mr Neville Chamberlain, and accepted by M. Blum, are but another word for the old alliances which led to the last great war. They represent the national selfishness of the Government of the great Powers.

The great betrayal of today is excused by the thought that liberty and justice for an African people do not matter. When national policy enters upon that inclined plane, betrayal of principle follows betrayal, till the only straw grasped at is supposed national self-interest.

In this case the national interest of France, as well as the international need of the world, was to secure a resounding defeat for Italian Fascist aggression. This would have given pause to the German Nazis and the Japanese militarists. We declare, as we have done from the beginning of this hideous contest, that the only safe course for the world was to prevent the success of the Fascist aggression. A reverse in this costly African adventure would probably have meant the downfall of Fascism in Italy, the greatest thing which could have happened at the present time to safeguard the peace of the world.

It has been said that to maintain sanctions now would have been purely punitive, but punitive sanctions are precisely what is required. No honest upholder of the Covenant can deny that, on calm and candid reflection.

The Popular Front government has been chosen by the people of France as a bulwark against Fascism in France, which is threatening the national liberties of France. Fascism in France is supported and aided by Fascism in Italy. That the Popular Front Government has refrained from punitive sanctions against the Power which has nourished and aided the Fascist movements throughout the world is a gross betrayal, which, alas! will not escape the consequences of such betrayals because it has arisen from political incapacity and lack of clear decision and purpose.

RUSSIA

That Mr Litvinov joined the betrayal of the Covenant, led by Britain and followed by France, will be a grave sorrow to millions throughout the world who hoped that they could rely upon the Soviet Government, which has spoken so much of peace, for more altruistic policies than those which obtained under the old diplomacy. Mr Litvinov's own expressions of opinion, in conveying the decision of his Government, will not assuage the grief of his Italian friends who suffer under the Fascist regime.

The result will undoubtedly be disastrous from the Soviet point of view. Fascism throughout the world has been strengthened by this surrender. By far the strongest weapon of international Fascism, in its contest against world democracy, is the cry that Fascism is saving the world from the dictatorship and expropriation of Communism. The moderate democrats who fear the Communist always fall victims to the terrorist outrages of Fascism wherever it obtains power, but whilst Fascism is struggling for the ascendency, it endeavours to justify its existence in the eyes of the moderate democrats, as well as in those of the frank reactionaries, by furious attacks on Communism. There is very little doubt the Russians are justified in their fear, that unless Hitler–Fascism receive a check, it will ere long attack Russian territory; the great mistake of the Russian Soviet Government and of the French Democratic 'Popular Front' Government is the absurd belief that they can count on the support of Italian Fascism to protect them against the Fascism of Germany. These two barbarous super-militarist forces will undoubtedly make common cause against the democracies of the world. The politician who is not able to perceive that truth is a public danger in every democratic country to-day. (. . .)

THE ETHIOPIAN GOVERNMENT

The pretence that there is no Ethiopian Government and that the Ethiopian people have accepted Italian rule is false and dishonest. It is manufactured purely to condone the Italian aggression, and to excuse the refusal to combat it. The Ethiopian Government exists and will continue to exist. The members of the British Government who stated it to be non-existent must unfortunately be convicted of expressing a wish which was father to the thought.

We are able to state that British advisors to the provincial Governments of Ethiopia received telegrams from the Foreign Office in London when Addis Ababa fell, stating that the Foreign Office was opposed to their remaining in Ethiopia. We know that at least some of these British advisors informed the authorities in neighbouring British territory that it would be a mistake to weaken the existing Ethiopian administration in the territories not occupied by Italy, and that, on the contrary, this administration should be assisted by arms and money to maintain its authority, and to keep order under the difficult circumstances.

MR EDEN SHOULD KNOW

Mr Eden should be aware of these communications; he should know positively that the Ethiopian administration has never ceased to function, despite the appalling difficulties which the Italian aggression has cast upon it.

The gallant Ethiopian Government is worthy of all our help. It has behind it the moral forces of all clear-sighted internationalists; if we all refuse to admit failure, Ethiopia and justice will be vindicated in the end. Other cases have suffered days of adversity and have come through to victory; so shall it be in this case.

'The fascist world war' (Ethiopia and Spain)

[New Times and Ethiopia News, 1 August 1936]

We are in the world war of Fascism against Democracy. The Italian Dictator's other term for this war already in full swing, is the war of the 'Dissatisfied Nations' against the 'Satisifed Nations.'

This war began in Ethiopia; now it has spread to Spain, where the Government democratically elected by the Spanish people, in constitutional form, is being attacked by the Fascists, who were defeated at the ballot box. The Spanish Fascists would already have been defeated in the test of force which they have chosen, were it not that they are being assisted by the Fascist powers outside. Italy and Germany are assisting them. (. . .)

THE AIR ARM

It is the air arm which counts in Spain, as it counted in Ethiopia, and there is evidence that the Italian dictatorship is supplying its Fascist ally with aeroplanes, and that the German ally is supplying cash. One of the first to publish the news was the Antwerp correspondent of the Paris newspaper *Populaire*, which reported that the Spanish Fascist leader, General Franco, had made an important transaction in gold at Hamburg to buy twenty-four aeroplanes from Italy.

What more natural, given Signor Mussolini's often-declared determination to create a Fascist International for war on the rest of the world? Italy has the planes accumulated for exterminating Ethiopians immobilised by the rains of that much tortured country: therefore she is able to lend them to her Fascist ally!

PEOPLE STOOD BY

People stood by while Ethiopia was vanquished: this is only Africa; this is not a White Man's country. They listened to the Italian propaganda; these are primitives, their customs are barbarous. Now people stand by again; they do not like Spanish politics; these are a disorderly people, fighting amongst themselves; they are Anarchists, Socialists, Reds, strikers; it does not matter to us.

Meanwhile the Fascists consider it does matter and are supplying all they can to their own side.

It was the same in Italy when Fascism started the civil war there: the Christian Democrats of Don Sterzo's Popolari, the old Liberals of Giolitti, the Free Masons, the old, tolerant type of Conservatism, all said: it is only the Socialists and the other Reds, the Trade Unionists and the Co-operators, who are attacked; then, one by one, each of them went down before the bludgeon, the rifle and the repressive antics of Fascism; their organisations were suppressed, their leaders imprisoned or compelled to flee. (. . .)

DIVIDE AND CONQUER

The policy of the Fascist government is based consistently on the old maxim: 'Divide and Conquer.' To the conservatives of France, Britain and every country, it represents itself as the Party which opposes Bolshevism, and organises and disciplines the disorderly and selfish ranks of labour. Hence on the French Bourse spirits rose, and prices ascended with a rush for Spanish securities when an unfounded rumour flashed through that Madrid had fallen to the rebels. Hence, too, we find certain Members of Parliament becoming indignant at the notion that this country might perhaps be supplying arms to the Government of Spain which has been elected by due process of electoral law and is now fighting a life and death struggle against the Fascist International. All this despite the fact that the Spanish Fascists have promised assistance to Germany in case of world war should they get into power. It is on class and party prejudice that the Spanish Fascists rely when they broadcast appeals for help in their rebellion to the British, German and Italian Governments. (. . .)

THE PEOPLE OF SPAIN

The people of Spain have rallied with amazing spontaneity against the rebel lawbreakers. Let pressmen and detractors say what they will, the photographs published in every newspaper record uncontrovertibly the fact that men and woman have rushed to the barricades by the thousand, to defend their liberty at the risk of death. They are no embittered fanatic groups, these crowds of men and women, old and young; they are the average people, who have left their work and play, their domestic joys and cares to defend a cause which to them over masters all.

'Our policy [on the democratic ideal]'

[*New Times and Ethiopia News*, 17 October, 1936]

In these days when the flag of the League's great Covenant is humbled to the dust and a deadlock faces all its larger purposes, enabling progress to continue only in matters of detail, we state again the policy of *New Times and Ethiopia News*.

We appeared when the then capital of Ethiopia fell to the invader. Our purpose was, and is, to champion and to give news of the brave little nation who, by her fidelity to League principles and by the wanton aggression she has suffered, has become the symbol of the world-embracing movement to secure international justice, the peace of humanity in the reign of law.

We have chosen advisedly the prefix *New Times*; for we desire to be no mere chronicle, uncritical and without purpose, but to take an earnest part in building the hopeful edifice of the future.

We lay firmly hold on certain great principles: respect for the human personality and the freedom of the human spirit.

This respect involves the basic principles of democracy; the golden rule: do unto others as you would they might do to you; the absolute right of free opinion and the free expression of it so far as the rights and the happiness of others are not thereby unjustly invaded or curtailed; the right of every man and woman to participate in making the conditions which govern our lives, the laws we must obey and which are designed for mutual protection, the right of fair trial by our peers if we are charged with an offence.

All this is embodied in democracy, and more than this; democracy has the essential aim of giving to everyone of us, wherever we may have been born and reared and under whatever circumstances, safety against aggression and oppression, safety from starvation and famine and preventable disease, liberation from want and stultification of mind and body, opportunity to develop to the highest of which we are capable.

Humanity has been struggling since before the dawn of history at this desirable condition of life. Our early forbears, who gathered round the moot hill or the sacred tree, when those who were distinguished by service made proposals for the management of the affairs of all and the assembled people were called to give or to withhold assent, were working towards this ideal. In one form or another the struggle has never ceased. Ceaselessly striving towards this ideal, we have built up such ancient basic Acts as Magna Charta, the liberties of the free towns and the abolition of serfdom in the middle ages, and in more modern times representative Local Government, and Parliament with a Government responsible thereto, with adult manhood and womanhood suffrage and vote by ballot, the factory acts with their safeguards for mothers and children, popular education, a host of social services, in the administration of which anyone may share who is freely chosen by his or her fellows as fitted for the task; no citizen is debarred by reason of sex, race, opinion or faith. We have built up safeguards and liberties, assured by which men and women may freely profess their views and faiths and publish them abroad from pulpit, platform or Press.

These are no small things; they are so great that all our lives are influenced by them. To the fool who cries: 'Democracy can do nothing!' we answer: all the best of our life today has been fashioned by and through democracy, albeit it is imperfect still.

To crown the edifice of democracy and democratic right, the structure of a League of Nations has been created to preserve world peace by assuring the justice between nations which the peoples have won for themselves under democracy within their national frontiers.

It is the States where democracy has been overthrown within the national frontiers which today present the great obstacle to the functioning of the League.

The two most powerful of the Fascist dictatorships stand today aloof from the League; the small Fascist States in fact belie their own theories by participation in an organisation which is essentially democratic in principle, and a denial of the basic Fascist doctrines that force alone shall be the test of the right to rule and that government shall not rest upon the consent of the majority subject to protection of minorities against oppression.

'The conspiracy against world peace'

[New Times and Ethiopia News, 2 October, 1937]

There is a conspiracy against the peace of the world by the dictatorships which dominate Italy, Germany and Japan. They are at war with the rest of the world and will carry their war as far as they dare.

Peace-loving people find it hard to face this. They would like to believe that by moderation and friendliness on our own part this will pass like an evil dream. Many in this country have convinced themselves that by generous sacrifice on the part of other nations, particularly our own, the war spirit in these dictatorships can be arrested. They would rather think of Mussolini and Hitler as the leaders of unfortunate peoples who are arming and attacking, only because their economic position has become too hard to endure.

On the ground of this economic hardship they excuse the Fascist aggression in Abyssinia and refuse to believe that the war there was prosecuted with terrible atrocities and that inhuman cruelty and repression are still visited on the unfortunate population.

The aggression of Japan against China they condone in the same way, declaring that this is all a phenomenon of poverty and malnutrition, and if only there could be a great share-out of colonies, and if tariff barriers were down, then all would be well.

The answer to all this is that these same dictators have shown no mercy to their own people, no charity towards the land hunger of peasants, the economic pressure upon the unemployed, the small wage-earner and businessman. They have employed against the people of their own countries pitiless and widespread terror. They have used imprisonment, violence, torture, murder, without even the form of legal process, to suppress every sign of discontent, every expression of desire for measures to alleviate conditions, however legally, however temperately expressed. They have persecuted the inhabitants of their own country for their opinions, for their party affiliations or those of their relatives, for the unavoidable accident of their race, even that of their remote ancestors.

To believe that oligarchies of that type are the upholders of international justice, and have only to be met with generosity to behave as good and generous men, is pure moonshine. The problem of peace-loving peoples and governments faced by the will to war of these dictatorships is undeniably difficult.

THE LEAGUE—WHITHER?

The League of Nations, so far as concerns its primary purposes of preserving justice between small Powers and great and providing mutual security against war, is in a moribund condition; it literally hangs between life and death. (. . .)

If only one could have forgotten the agonised cries from Ethiopia, Spain, China, if only one could have forgotten the ever-accelerating race of armaments.

Those cries cannot be silenced. The conspiracy against world peace cannot be evaded; it must be faced. Steps must be taken to encourage and sustain the victims of aggression and to discourage the aggressors. The letter of the Emperor of Ethiopia to the League was not read to the Assembly, as was its due, but it was officially circulated. There has been thus far no discussion of Ethiopia's case. The Council and Assembly ought not to dissolve without applying themselves to this cruel problem which lies in the plain path of their obligation.

Every State delegate receives at the League a copy of this paper week by week. To the conscience and responsibility of each and all of them we make a direct appeal.

The emissaries of Mussolini have been busy in the ante-rooms, the corridors and hotels endeavouring to secure a decision by the League that Ethiopia is now Italian East Africa, and that on the strength of this inhuman aggression Italy has become an Empire. (. . .)

CHINA AND JAPAN

We are in the presence of a great fear, and be it said frankly, a great moral collapse. The Dictatorships have fallen into a moral abyss so profound as to have reduced the entire world level of international morality. Statesmen have grown hardened to injustice and wanton cruelty seeing it practised so constantly and so arrogantly. Moreover, war has become so terrible that governments and peoples surrender to panic, cowering under the shroud of cowardice and flinging all courage and chivalry to the winds with common prudence.

Most painful indeed was the scene in the League Commission for intellectual co-operation when the aged Professor Ly Yu-ying, venerable in his grey hairs and stricken with deepest sorrow, read a telegram just received from his colleague, the president of the Chinese Commission for Intellectual Co-operation, Shu Shi-Fee, the doyen of Chinese intellectual life, recording the systematic destruction of centres of education and learning by the aircraft of Japan.

Not a word of response followed his intensely moving recital of these grievous destructions. The Commission went on to discuss indifferent things. Only M. Herriot, the rapporteur of the

Commission, later replying to the discussion, observed that if the commission agreed, he would add to his report an expression that in any hostilities care should be taken not to injure the monuments of art and culture—not a word of the actual situation—not a reference to Japan.

When, as was inevitable, the question of the hideous attacks on civilians and non-combatant organisations and institutions came before the League's Advisory Committee on Far Eastern questions, to which Japan's aggression against China had been referred, the attempt to avoid imputing blame to Japan was again made and, be it noted, by the British delegation.

We protest very strongly against this action by the representatives of Mr Chamberlain. We are convinced that it is dramatically opposed to the wishes and the feelings of any but a small minority of the British people in Britain and throughout the Empire. Despite this ignominious attitude on the part of the representatives of the strongest Power in the world, the Committee insisted in placing the blame for the atrocities squarely upon the shoulders of Japan where it fully belongs.

The League Assembly, when the resolution of the Far Eastern Committee of twenty-three was brought before it, adopted the resolution by the vote of fifty-two States and without a vote of dissent.

Be it noted that Italy and Germany have been invited to sit on the Far Eastern Committee. Our respected contemporary, the *Manchester Guardian*, has most surprisingly, in its leading article, expressed regret that those dictatorships did not feel able to accept the invitation. Even Satan, we understand, has at times a sense of the proprieties and refrains in the more glaring instances from rebuking sin. How, indeed could Italy, who has bombed open towns and villages in Ethiopia and is still doing it there, and Germany, who has joined the Italian dictatorship in doing the same thing in Spain, condemn Japan for following their example in China? Japan's aggression in Manchuria was ugly, but Japanese aggression having acquired the latest terrors from Italy and Germany is a thousandfold uglier on this occasion. Even Japanese militarism has not gone so far in cruelty as Fascism in Ethiopia; it has not, like Fascism, yet taken to extermination by poison gas and the deadly rain of yperite! (. . .)

'Fascism As It Is'
(n.d., approx. 1940)

[Chapter 39, 'Women under the nazis', unpublished
manuscript, File 150(c), Pankhurst Papers,
Institute of Social History, Amsterdam.]

Women, according to the dictum of Hitler, must return to the three
K's, *Kirche, Kinder* and *Kueche,* to which the last century opponents
of women's enfranchisement desired to confine them. According to
Goebbels 'whilst man masters life, woman masters the pots and pans'.
The German *Financial Times,* January 1934, observed: 'The self-
supporting woman injures man, not only by being his competitor, but
also by depriving him of his pride of being the family's bread winner.'

The Nazi advent to power meant the immediate exclusion of
women from the Reichstag, and from the provincial Parliaments and
all local legislative bodies to which they had been elected in
considerable numbers after they won the rights of citizenship in the
revolution of 1918. Women had been members of all the political
parties except the Nazis, which refused to admit them. Therefore when
all Parties except the Nazis were forbidden, and their elected members
driven from office, no elected woman remained.

All the women's organisations were dissolved, including the
German branches of the International Women's Suffrage Alliance,
the Women's International League for Peace and Freedom, which
flourishes here and of which the late Jane Addams, of the United
States, was then still International President, the Catholic Women's
Peace Society, the Association of War Widows and Children, and
many more. Their officials have either fled abroad or have been flung
into concentration camps. The arrest of Frau Zihetmeier, of the
Catholic League of Peace, a high-school teacher, is characteristic. The
women's patriotic societies, like the women's Steel Helmet League and
the Queen Elizabeth Society, have been forcibly absorbed into the
women's Nazi organisations, which are themselves autocratically ruled
by the men's Nazi Party.

A determined move was at once made to exclude women from
all employment by public bodies, Government departments, local

councils, hospitals, and as far as possible, even schools. All women under thirty-five years were made ineligible for Government employment, and over that age, were debarred if married to husbands in employment, or to men of non-Aryan stock. The law of June 30th, 1933, provided that married women were to be dismissed from all employment if their superiors considered them sufficiently provided for, and unmarried women were also to be dismissed if it were held that they could be supported by parents, brothers, or even sisters. Without waiting to pass any law, the Nazi Government had already removed thousands of women from public offices, which they had occupied with great dignity and competence during the Republic.

Among the earliest dismissed were Dr Gertrud Baeumer, Inspector of Girls' Schools in Prussia, Emmi Becker, Inspector of Girls' High Schools in Hamburg, Susanne Engelman, Director of one of the largest girls' schools in Berlin, Professor Wunderlich, head of the Berlin Pedagogical Institute, Dr Menter, Chief Librarian at the University Library of Cologne, and Professor Vaerting from the University of Jena. Frau Trapp from the Women's Section, and Frau Albrecht from the Trade School section of the Ministry of Labour, and from the Ministry of Education, Frau Heinemann, of the Girls' High Schools Department, and Frau Ermler, from the Kindergartens, were among the many obliged to leave. The Home Office dismissals included Anna Meyer, from the Health Department, Frau Hirschfeld, from the Pensions Ministry, and Hilde Oppenheimer, from the department dealing with economic questions.

Among the women eliminated are the very people who, since the Revolution in 1918, have actually created Government Departments dealing with infants' welfare and the education of girls and women. Kaethe Kollwitz was excluded from the Academy of Arts, Ricarda Huch from the Prussian Academy of Poets. Anna Seghers, who had won the Kleist Prize, was forced to leave Germany. Emmi Neother, Helene Ziegert, Elizabeth Blochman, Anna Deynahl, Marianne Kunze, Gerda Simons, Bertha Kiesa and Melitta Gerhardt, and many more, were deprived of their professorships. There is no question here, either of race or political view. Women are excluded on the clear basis of womanhood and that alone. Many famous actresses like Elisabeth Bergner, Fritzi M. Massary, Elisabeth Lennartz, and Greta Mosheim, can no longer appear in Germany either because of Jewish race or political opinion, but many hundreds of medical women have been obliged to renounce the practice of their profession simply because of their sex.

For twenty-five years, German women had possessed the right of admission to the Universities, and to the practice of professions. Today only ten per cent of the women students who pass the Baccalaureat are permitted to enter the University. The immensity of this injustice can be gathered from the fact that out of 10,500 women who passed this examination in 1930, only 1,000 are permitted to study at the University. To all save ten per cent, even of the ten per cent who are allowed to enter the University, the right of practising their professions is absolutely refused! Moreover, even to them the right is not guaranteed. Whatever may be the number who qualify, only seventy-five women a year are allowed to enter the medical profession. The official doctor's organ has announced: 'The woman doctor is a hermaphrodite who offends the natural and healthy instinct of the people.'

Scientific studies are rigorously reserved to men. In the words of an official communication in the *Cologne Zeitung*, January, 1934, 'Women must recognise that scientific work is specifically masculine . . . Woman must never think in a theoretical manner, her brain ought not to occupy itself with abstract things'. Strange sayings these in an age which has produced Marie Curie and Maria Montessori.

As teachers, women may only fill subordinate posts. The organ of the Prussian teachers observed: 'The men teacher's aversion to women superiors is in keeping with the healthy instinct of man.' Jewish women, of course, have been ruthlessly driven from all professions.

Women previously employed in responsible and skilled public and professional work have been drafted into the compulsory labour corps for work on the land. Civilisation has for many generations made steady progress in the elimination of women from heavy agricultural labour. Under Nazi rule, Germany compels her most intellectually gifted women to such work, under conditions approximating to slavery! Everywhere the effort has been to drive women from skilled to unskilled labour, in domestic service, on the land, and in factory war work, particularly in the making of poison gasses and explosives, where they are employed at dangerous and debilitating processes in dark rooms by red or blue light.

The wage of women in industry is ordinarily sixty per cent below that paid to men, but masses of men, taken on to replace women, under the phrase 'double income' have been obliged to accept the woman's wage. At a Wuppertal textile factory, the entire female staff was turned adrift for men paid at the women's rate. Women so dismissed are denied unemployment pay. In the cigar industry at Hamburg, women were threatened with the concentration camp if they did not leave voluntarily. In hospitals and other institutions, all the women cooks have been replaced by men.

Another means of removing women from their employment were the State marriage loans up to 1,000 marks (about £50) to brides who had been in employment at least six out of the previous twelve months, on condition of their undertaking not to go to work unless their husband's wage should fall below 125 marks (£6 5s 0d) per month and the loan had been repaid. This loan is paid, not in cash, but in coupons for the purchase of furniture or household equipment, and must be paid back in not less than eight years. By March, 1934, the conditions were changed, and the women must pledge themselves not to take work unless the loan had been repaid and their husbands were obtaining the unemployment dole, the last a condition difficult to satisfy, because makeshift seasonal land work and work camps are used to evade the payment of unemployment insurance. Thus, for a loan of 1,000 marks, the wife probably loses an income of some 900 marks a year.

Unemployed women are drafted to camps, where they wash, mend and clean, and must undertake to do all work in house, stable, garden and field, and attend the lectures in Nazi philosophy after their labour of ten to twelve hours a day is finished. Receiving no wages, with bad food, crowded together in sheds and barns, sleeping on straw, they live under an iron discipline, and are liable to severe punishment. If one of them be dismissed, the fact is stated on her certificate and is a bar to obtaining other work. If thereafter her parents dare to receive her, the father loses his right to unemployment benefit, should he fall out of work. Large numbers of women, from factories and offices, schools, Universities and Government departments have been thus drafted, in city clothes and high-heeled shoes, working in the muddy fields for ten to twelve hours daily, often obliged to sleep with the men labourers. Many young girls have returned to their homes pregnant after this sad experience. At first only single women were sent to the camps, but afterwards also the married, their children being sent to orphanages.

Note Hitler's declaration that the children of Germany must be trained whilst very young to be what Germany desires; if their parents are 'still old-fashioned people, who cannot move with the times, we shall take the children away from them.'

Some of the unemployed are sent to unpaid domestic work. In Wuppertal, where unemployment was great among women, owing to large-scale dismissal from the textile factory, they were paraded through the streets with brushes, pans and ladles, and placards: '1,000 girls seek work', but there was difficulty in placing them, though the Council offered forty-five to sixty marks to employers taking a domestic pupil without wages for six months.

For girls between the ages of seventeen and twenty-one, there is compulsory labour, which is equivalent to men's military service. Some are congregated in concentration camps for both domestic and military aid work. Others are drafted to compulsory domestic work.

It must be emphasised that though the employment of German women in the labour market had changed, the number of women industrial workers actually increased by 9.1 per cent during the first nine months of Nazi rule. Dr Ley, in *Voelkischer Beobachter*, observed: 'It is quite erroneous to think that women in industrial work have their health impaired . . . we get both healthier and fresher women, since they have again entered a life of employment'.

Though driven from public work, women are not spared either the insult or the violence the Nazis visit upon opponents. Five cruel examples are typical of many more: I have before me the photograph showing terrible contusions from the beating given by the Nazis to the Socialist, Maria Jankowsky, aged forty-six years, well known and widely respected for her Municipal and social work in Koepenick. This act of marked brutality received the approval of Alexander Bogs, head of the Scandinavian section of the Nazi Press Department, who said: 'If ever a Communist or a Socialist deserved such a hiding, it was Maria Jankowsky'. In the small hours of March 21st, 1933, she was taken from her dwelling by fourteen armed men to the temporary Nazi premises in the Dorotheenstrasse, where there were six other men, making twenty in all. They showed her the Republican flag, and invited her to call it a foul name. When the brave woman still refused, she was stripped naked, laid on a table, and while one man held her head, four others belaboured her with canes and sticks. After receiving at least a hundred strokes, she rolled bleeding from the table, but was dragged to her feet with a violent blow in the face. Only when she at last agreed to recant her Socialism, and report regularly to the Brown House was she taken to St Antonius Hospital in Karlshorst, where she told all that had happened. Her death was subsequently reported.

Betti Suess, having been seen in the company of a Jew, had her head shaved, and was dragged round the streets and cafes with a placard round her neck bearing the words: 'I have offered myself to a Jew'. From this terrible experience she became mentally affected, and had to be sent to a home at Erlangen.

Madame Schwalbach was arrested after returning from abroad, where she had been to visit her husband who had escaped from Germany. She has been thirteen months in prison. Her mother has also been arrested and interned in a concentration camp at Moringen.

Francisca Kessel, an ex-Communist Member of the Reichstag, was condemned to three years' imprisonment and found hanging in her cell in the prison at Mainz. She was said to have committed suicide, but her friends believe she was murdered.

Fanny Planck, a young working woman, was arrested whilst pregnant and incarcerated in the women's prison at Atach. She gave birth to her child, which remained three months with her in the cell, and was afterwards removed to an orphanage, where the officials stated that the child was in a terribly emaciated condition.

One of the early acts of the Nazi Government was to abolish compulsory unemployment insurance for female domestic servants, on the ground that by reducing the cost to the employer more servants would be employed. Taxpayers were granted remission of tax for every maid employed. Women who had for years paid into the insurance fund were deprived of benefit.

The German woman today has fallen to the position from which the women of the world struggled for a century to free themselves; they are liable for every punishment, but entitled to no privileges under the State.

Marriage is to come under rigid control. Love and natural selection are to give way to Nazi dictation, in the interest of health, man-power, and political obedience. Women, mere breeding machines in the warrior State, are to be divided before marriage into four classes. In the first class, comprising about ten per cent of the girls of marriageable age, are those deemed capable of producing desirable children. The second class, subdivided into A and B classes, are considered fit for marriage, but will receive less consideration. The third class will be allowed to marry only if they undergo sterilisation. The fourth class will not be allowed to marry, either on account of tainted antecedents, or because they are themselves infected with venereal disease, consumption or other serious illness. In the Nazi State, poor women not judged fit for child-bearing will have a miserable lot indeed!

To obtain authorisation to marry, it is necessary to prove physical and mental health, and absence of any 'hereditary taint foreign to the race'; that is to say, any admixture of Jewish, Negro, or other undesired alien blood.

German women are not to mingle their blood with that of Jews or foreigners. Divorce at will is opposed to the Fascist conception; but annulment of marriages between Germans and aliens is desired, and non-Jewish women married to Jews are often subjected to fearful persecution. Women who have had children by Jews, or other non-Aryans, may not subsequently marry; they are held to be contaminated.

A certificate from the Social Insurance Bureau must be presented, showing that neither party to the intended marriage is receiving any assistance from the public funds. This means that, if the law be obeyed, an unemployed woman who has been receiving any sort of public assistance cannot even marry a man who is in work. The tremendous drive to remove women from all skilled employment and professions has, of course, placed an immense number of women in this position. One can scarcely believe that a provision so widely exclusive can be fully applied, but it can always be used against opponents. If applied, it means the debarring from marriage of thousands of the most intelligent women, who will be forced into exclusively menial occupations.

Proof is also required, as a condition of marriage, that neither party has been condemned to imprisonment during the previous three years. This debars thousands of people who were incarcerated at the time of the Nazi rise to power.

As in Fascist Italy, Germany has now made birth control a penal offence.

Adultery by a woman is punishable, though winked at in a man, for the dual moral code of the fighting Middle Ages is the Fascist ideal. Adultery with a foreigner is more heavily punished than with a person of German race; for this even a man may be made to suffer, though not so heavily as his woman partner; she will be sent to prison, he to compulsory labour. The woman, however, may evade punishment by confessing to the police and disclosing the name of her partner; a terrible invitation to blackmail and intimidation.

Children born out of wedlock have little claim for maintenance upon their father. To enforce any claim for support, it is necessary, according to the law, to demand absolute proof of the paternity, including tests of the blood of the mother, the father, and the infant. As such tests often give negative results, the possibility of proving the paternity becomes a slender one. In any case, the law strictly dictates that the maintenance payments must be very small, and only such as will aid in providing the child with an education such as can be given by mothers of humble rank. It is also insisted that no payment can be exacted from the father which would interfere with the 'other obligations which his rank imposes upon him'. These conditions, of course render evasion of payment exceedingly easy.

The Nazi Government proclaimed through the Press that 40,000 German inhabitants are mentally unfit, and that progeny is not desired from them.

Compulsory sterilisation is decreed in the case of persons suffering from hereditary diseases, including congenital feeble-mindedness, mania, melancholia, dementia praecox, or schizophrenia, hereditary epilepsy, hereditary St Vitus' dance, blindness, deafness, bodily malformation and habitual alcoholism. Hundreds of infants born of German mothers and foreign fathers have been sterilised.

A person may propose himself for sterilisation, or may be compelled to submit to it if he has been declared incapable of managing his own affairs. The demand may also come from Medical Officers of hospitals and sanatoria, and from Governors of penal establishments. The proposal goes before a Court of Eugenics, composed of a magistrate, a Medical Officer of Health, and a doctor specialising in the study of hereditary hygiene. The proceedings are secret, but one may appeal against the decision to a 'Higher Court of Eugenics'. When this law was passed, 1,700 Courts began to examine people recommended for sterilisation, together with twenty-seven Appeal Courts. Two hundred and thirty-six Tribunals for the defence of the purity of the race, with power to order sterilisation, were subsequently set up.

Sterilisation when ordered by the Court, can be carried out against the will of the persons concerned, and by the assistance of the police.

229

Persons taking part in these operations are bound to silence, on penalty of imprisonment or fine. Given the present state of Germany, one need not emphasise the highly dangerous character of this order, which came into force on January 1st, 1934. The spirit in which it is employed may be gathered from such observations as those of Dr Dietrich, President of a Civil Court, reported in the *Deutsche Juristen Zeitung*, as follows:-

On medical grounds, all acts performed by a doctor on the body of a patient are perfectly justified; he can kill the child in the womb of the mother; he can deprive a person of his freedom of movement in case of mental alienation. It is the same in what concerns national interests, which can justify a series of similar acts. Infliction of corporal punishment, deprivation of liberty, assassination, are methods which the State is justified in using. The radius of action of the national interest is very vast, and in this category one may add destruction of property and arson. All these acts maybe justified by national interest.

Dr Wellguth, in the official organ of the German doctors, was still more explicit:

To destroy weeds several methods can be employed. On flower-beds we gently take out the weed with two fingers and throw it away; in the vegetable plot where weeds are more numerous, we take the spade; in the field the peasant passes the plough and buries the weeds. We are now in the position of the peasant; we must destroy weeds wholesale.

The same doctor is of opinion that sterilisation should be applied to all persons living by aid of the State (probably war cripples as well as the unemployed) and all Jews, Negroes, Mongols and non-Europeans resident in Germany. According to Von Papen, whose views are evidently not so far removed from those of Hitler as some people believe, those who are deemed unfit for the struggle of present-day social life, include men, 'who after the Great War, abandoned their military uniform, and are now a dead-weight on Society, because they have proved, by such action, their incapacity for the struggle of life.'

As usual when repressive measures are adopted, the first to suffer are those who can offer least resistance. Many Jewish women were at once sterilised in hospital without their consent, the Nazi doctors took advantage of their position when they had them under an anaesthetic for some other operation.

Ethiopia and Eritrea. The Last Phase of the Reunion Struggle, 1941–1952 (1953)

(with R. K. P. Pankhurst)

[FROM CHAPTER XV: ASMARA AFTER 60 YEARS OF COLONIAL AND CARETAKER GOVERNMENT]

While the British Administration was tearing down the splendid buildings in the ports, poverty reigned in Eritrea. This chapter describes the conditions in its capital while the identity of its future administration was yet unknown.

Asmara (Forest of Flowers), capital city of ex-Italian Eritrea, is usually described as 'a lovely modern city.' Few of its visitors, however, have really seen Asmara. The majority have seen only a gay, illusive mask which has hidden from them the true Asmara with the cankerous misery and pollution at its heart.

In fact Asmara might aptly be described as two cities, quite separate and distinct, yet interdependent. The 'lovely modern city' is purely the European town, with its government palaces, hotels and restaurants, shops, cinemas and tennis courts. It seems to belong to another world than that of the 'native' city where the Eritrean people, descendants of the ancient Ethiopian owners of the land, exist in conditions of misery which beggar description. (. . .)

Already in the market area we enter what seems another world, though we have not yet penetrated the inner recesses of the Eritrean town. The mean shops and dwellings here contrast painfully with those of the gay European city. The dusty and stony unpaved roads, devoid of pedestrian sidewalks, in the Eritrean area make a still sadder impression in contrast with the splendidly surfaced roads and neat stone pavements, perfectly maintained by the British authorities in the European town, because here we are compelled to notice a discrimination by the authorities against the defenceless people of the land. The Municipal Offices, whereby the collection of taxes is operated, are to be found in the Eritrean as well as in the European area.

To comprehend to the full the cruel heart disease of the Eritrean city we must penetrate to such wretched quarters as Abba Shiaul, Gheza Berhanou and Gheza Banda. They are situated on a rocky hill, almost devoid of earthy covering, so that little of it could be cultivated, even if the congestion of its population did not preclude it. On this unpropitious terrain many thousands of hovels are huddled together. No ground has been levelled, no roads have been cut. In want and poverty a crowded warren has been erected of stones roughly hewn from the mountain with poor tools, of battered sheets of iron or whatever material the poor folk could discover whereof to build their dwellings. Mean as the hovels were when first erected, lack of material to repair them during the past leanest of lean years has rendered them increasingly miserable; a number have entirely collapsed.

Every man builds and maintains his own dwelling in this part of Africa; municipal housing is unknown. Timber is scarce; the land all around Asmara is gravely eroded by reckless felling and failure to replant. In consequence the Eritreans are forbidden to cut living wood by an Administrative Order specially applied to them, though they were by far the smaller consumers on account of their poverty. The prohibition of wood cutting, of course, renders building the more difficult.

As far as their means permit these poor folk make the best of their small dwellings; the walls of many are coated with earth plaster, the making of which is an old Ethiopian craft. Some dwellings are also whitewashed.

The hill is as densely packed as space permits with small dwellings, built in rows, as far as the uneven ground will allow. Some of the alleys are barely three feet wide.

The dwellings consist in most cases of one room, only six to eight feet square, or less, in which the family must sleep and crowd for shelter in the torrential rains. There are no windows, only a doorway, through which light and air are admitted. If the ground on which the house stands permits a small space to belong to it at the back, there will be an aperture also at the rear through which some light and air can enter, probably only a trifle, the whole hill being so densely congested. A woman washing clothes in one of the houses had only a space about two feet deep at the rear in which to dry the clothes. At night the doors are shut, or if there is no door, they are barricaded;

even the poorest of the people possess something they fear to lose; to the unemployed multitude starving in Asmara, the most meagre belongings may offer temptation.

During the not infrequent curfews proclaimed from time to time by the 'caretaker' Administration in the course of the recent troubled years, families have been cooped up in the exhausted air of these hovels for twelve or more hours at a stretch.

The steep alleys by which the people reach their hovels are hard to climb, being of the rude, unlevelled rock. During the rainy season they are scoured by torrents. In one or two places a trench has been hewn in the solid rock to make a passage for the flood-water to pass to lower levels.

Asmara, however, has only one rainy season; each year there are many months of drought. The piped water to the houses is reserved for the European city. There are two street fountains on the hill to serve Abba Shiaul, Gheza Bernahou and Gheza Banda, and two in the road below to serve the lower part of the hill and Haddis Addi and Edaga Arbi. The horror of this wretchedness was increased by the fact that to economise water in the dry season, the two fountains at the foot of the hill were turned off, though baths and showers were still available in the European town.

Women, and often quite small girls, are obliged to queue for hours in the hot sun to be able to fill an old petrol tin with water and to climb with it slung on the back up and down the steep rocky alleys.

As in Italian times, water-carts thread the wider streets of the Eritrean town, selling this vital necessity of life and health.

Needless to add, no light is supplied to the dwellings of the native quarter; the electric lighting system is reserved for the European town. There are three street lights, raised high to cast a glimmer of illumination which may aid the police to make arrests or enforce a curfew.

With the exception of some truly appalling street latrines for men in the centre of the main road, there is no sort of sewerage for the Eritrean town. The people are ordered to tip their refuse, including human excrement, on ground close to the houses. A foul stench rises from these dumps, one of which is beside the main road through the 'native' town.

Bitter poverty has been growing for years in the Eritrean quarter owing to widespread unemployment resulting from post-war depression.

During the whole period of Italian colonisation, the administration of Eritrea had never been self-supporting; it had always depended on a subsidy from Rome. An ephemeral prosperity was created for Asmara by the Italian aggression in Ethiopia, with the commerce in goods imported from Italy, and the transport, hotel and amusement industries which flourished on the passage of soldiers, workmen and officials to and from the war, and 'the Empire' subsequently proclaimed. All this collapsed when the British troops victoriously entered Asmara in the spring of 1941. Thousands of Italians were now without means of support.

Large numbers of Eritreans, to whom the crumbs of Italian prosperity had meagrely descended, were also rendered destitute. The British Administration supplied relief to the Italians, on a regular scale and assisted them to adjust their lives to the new circumstances, encouraging them to build up agricultural and industrial enterprises in Eritrea which, incidentally, have increased their hold upon the territory. When the war ended, those who desired to return to Italy were repatriated.

For the destitute Eritreans there was no relief, or assistance to enable them to surmount the hardships which the policies of their foreign rulers had brought upon them. There was only the suggestion that they might benefit indirectly by the increasing prosperity of the defeated rulers against whom they had been asked to co-operate during the fighting. Small wonder that bitterness entered into the hearts of young men and women who had grasped with eagerness the leaflets distributed by British military aircraft promising liberation and reunion to the Ethiopian Motherland, and had cheered the British troops as they marched into Asmara!

In the years of depression a large proportion of Eritreans have suffered unemployment. This, accompanied by rising prices, accentuates the misery of the congested slums they were compelled to inhabit under Fascism. Any possibility of moving to a more salubrious neighbourhood is prevented by their poverty, even were room to be found elsewhere.

The nights are cold in Asmara; frost during the night and early morning is not uncommon, strange as that may appear to the untravelled European. Even the days are chilly out of the sunshine at certain seasons, and the winds at times are keen. Yet, owing to the great poverty prevailing, the single tattered cotton garment of many a little child covers less than half the small, frail body. Pneumonia is one of the common diseases on the plateau; its toll of death is high. The women and girls endeavour to preserve an appearance of neatness and modesty. Destitution renders difficult even the purchase of needles and soap—but those who are able wear beautifully white shammas even in these wretched surroundings.

One of the saddest sights in this sad area is that of the starving people avidly seeking in a vile dump on the outskirts of the native quarter for broken and discarded refuse, men with picks and shovels feverishly hacking and digging, children scratching with their tiny fragile fingers. Every bit of broken glass, every scrap of wood or metal is seized and hoarded to be sold. The glass will be carried to the glass-blower; the wood will be sold for fuel; the metal will go to the scrap merchant, probably for export abroad.

Mothers tramp across country to seek in the fields a few tiny discarded potatoes and onions for sale at their doors. Some walk far to gather the fine wild grasses used for basketry. These they dye in varied colours to sell in the market along with pot-herbs dried and torn into fragments ready for cooking, cotton cleaned and spun by their industrious fingers and other small wares. Market dues absorb half their small gains.

*   *   *

[FROM CHAPTER XVI: AWAITING THE TRANSFER OF POWER]

Note: The United Nations appointed a Commissioner for Eritrea in 1951 to federate the country with Ethiopia. The new Constitution was passed by the recently elected Assembly of Eritrea in July the following year.

Ratification by the Emperor Haile Selassie I followed on September 11, 1952, at the Menelik Palace in Addis Ababa. After signing the historic document the Emperor went out on the balcony and addressed the enthusiastic populace. Giving thanks for the happy end to twelve years of struggle, he thanked the United Kingdom, the United States of America, France, and the many other members of the United Nations who had lent their assistance to Ethiopia during the long search for the solution that had been reached that day. He explained that during seven years, from the moment he had issued his first statement on the Eritrean question, his Government had defended the principles which had now been accepted, rejecting all offers incompatible with respect for the sacred principle of the self-determination of peoples and remaining steadfast to the cause of justice. Not only would Eritreans constitute and participate in their own local government, but they, Christians and Muslims alike, would receive the fruits of self-determination and freedom through the fullest participation in all branches and at all levels of the Imperial Ethiopian Government. This association would make for the prosperity of the area and give the Federation access to the sea. The Ethiopian Empire, now grown larger, would not lose sight of its international responsibilities, but would contribute to the furtherance of the ideals embodied in the Charter of the United Nations:

> Ethiopia stretches out her hands unto God in thankfulness for the wondrous work of justice which He has vouchsafed to His people of Ethiopia and Eritrea, now liberated and joined in common brotherhood. Let this day be remembered throughout our history as a day of national rejoicing in the farthest reaches of our Empire.

In presenting the Federal Act for signature, Ato Aklilou said: 'At this solemn moment in the history of our three-thousand-year-old Empire, it is not without deep emotion that, as Minister for Foreign Affairs, I humbly inform Your Imperial Majesty that the aspirations and the fate of millions of human beings await your decision.'

Ato Tedla Bairou, the Unionist leader, now Chief Executive of Eritrea, declared:

> To-day we see the happy conclusion of the 67th year of our struggle. The rebirth of Eritrea testifies to the glory and greatness of Ethiopia. It is not necessary to elaborate the fact that Your Majesty and the Ethiopian Government struggled effectively to bring about this end. This I will leave to the pages of history. It is my duty to inform Your Majesty of the will of the Eritrean people to accept the Federal Act proposed by the United Nations.

When the ratification ceremony was complete, the Minister of the Pen, H. E. Tsehafe Taezaz Wolde Guiorguis, took up his position at the head of the stairway in front of the balcony and publicly announced that the Federation of Eritrea and Ethiopia was an accomplished fact. A salute of sixty-seven guns was given to denote the years of separation from the Motherland which Eritrea had suffered.

During the twelve years of Ethiopia's final struggle to regain her ancient access to the sea, and to liberate from the colonial yoke her lost province, an immense change in the international status of this cause had been effected. When the Council of Foreign Ministers first met to discuss the future of the former Italian colonies, the representatives of defeated Italy were alone invited to be present to state their claims, Ethiopia was refused even the right to be heard, her Government being curtly informed that they might present their views in writing. The American and French Governments at that time considered the former colonies should all be returned to Italy; the British Government had hardly advanced beyond the conception of a European Trusteeship.

By the unswerving patience and persistence of the Emperor Haile Selassie and the Ethiopian Delegations at international conferences and discussions all this had been changed. Now that success had been achieved, the Red Sea ports regained, Eritrea federated to the lost Motherland, a host of powers offered their felicitations on the great event. The Doyen of the Diplomatic Corps in Addis Ababa voiced the general congratulations. Telegrams poured in from Heads of States.

Queen Elizabeth of Great Britain sent her 'cordial greetings'. The British Foreign Secretary, Mr Anthony Eden, expressed his 'particular pleasure' in congratulating Ato Aklilou, the Ethiopian Minister for Foreign Affairs, on the part which he had 'personally played in facilitating this settlement of Eritrea's future.'

From the United States President Truman cabled to the Emperor:

It is deeply gratifying to me to send You congratulations on this important and historic occasion of Eritrea's Federation with Ethiopia under Your Sovereignty and to extend to You and Your subjects new and old the best wishes of the American people.

Patience and wisdom are bearing their fruits to-day and the occasion justifies the confidence of all those who have sought a settlement of Eritrea's future through the United Nations. I feel certain that under Your guidance Federation will be the means of bringing together the people of the area in co-operative effort leading to their greater welfare and happiness.

From France President Auriol expressed his warm wishes for the happy future of the Federation.

On the day of the ratification of the Federal Act the Emperor addressed a Proclamation to the people of Ethiopia and Eritrea, 'now joined together as brothers'. He recalled that in the message he had given to them, which had been distributed throughout the land by British aircraft on his return to Ethiopia in 1941 at the head of his army of liberation, he had stated that the people of Eritrea would 'henceforth dwell under the Ethiopian flag.' The promise had now been kept, but twelve years of struggle, sacrifice and abnegation had separated its utterance from its glorious fulfilment. Though one of the first territories to be freed during the World War, Eritrea was the last to receive liberation. Exactly seven years before he had addressed to the four Great Powers meeting in London his first communication in defence of the ex-colony. Foreign political obstacles and intrigues had delayed the just settlement; it had been left to Ethiopia alone to lead the struggle for justice for the brothers of Eritrea and Ethiopia. As head of the Empire of Ethiopia, he had always firmly adhered to the great principle of the self-determination of peoples, and had resolutely rejected all suggestions of political bargaining in conflict with this sacred right. In conformity with this policy he had been among the first publicly to proclaim attachment to that principle for Libya, and to express his conviction that its people profoundly desired independence. The Ethiopian representatives at the United Nations had supported every resolution and amendment tending to that end. In their struggle for the freedom of Somaliland, Ethiopia had been the sole country to vote consistently for that solution.

Four days later, on September 15, nearly 40,000 clapping, rejoicing Eritreans watched the Chief British Administrator, Mr Duncan C. Cumming, in a shining black top hat, lower the Union Jack in Asmara. A few days later it became known to the people that the British had exacted a sum of more than £900,000 from the Ethiopian Government for stores they had decided to leave in Eritrea—a sad finale to the British Administration.

Appendix

BOOKS AND PAMPHLETS (P) PUBLISHED BY E. SYLVIA PANKHURST

The Suffragette. The History of the Women's Militant Suffrage Movement 1905–1910 (Sturgis and Walton, New York, 1911)
Soviet Russia As I Saw It (Dreadnought Publishers, London, 1921)
Writ on Cold Slate (Dreadnought Publishers, London, 1922)
The Truth about the Oil War(P) (Dreadnought Publishers, London, 1922)
India and the Earthly Paradise (Sunshine Publishing House, Bombay, 1926)
Delphos The Future of International Language (Kegan Paul, Trench, & Trubner, London, 1927)
Poems of Mihail Eminescu (translated with I. O. Stafanovici) (Kegan Paul & Co., London, 1930)
Save the Mothers. A Plea for Measures to Prevent the Annual Loss of about 3000 Child-Bearing Mothers and 20,000 Infant Lives in England and Wales and a Similar Grievous Wastage in other Countries (Alfred A Knopf, London, 1930)
The Suffragette Movement. An Intimate Account of Persons and Ideals (Longmans, London, 1931)
The Home Front. A Mirror to Life in England during the World War (Hutchinson, London, 1932)
The Life of Emmeline Pankhurst. The Suffragette Struggle for Women's Citizenship (T. Werner Laurie, London, 1935)
British Policy in Eritrea and Northern Ethiopia (P) (New Times and Ethiopia News (NT&EN), Woodford Green, 1945)
Italy's War Crimes in Ethiopia (P) (NT&EN, Woodford Green, 1945)
The Ethiopian People: Their Rights and Progress (P) (NT&EN Books, Woodford Green, 1946)
Education in Ethiopia (P) (NT&EN, Woodford Green, 1946)
British Policy in Eastern Ethiopia, the Ogaden and the Reserved Area (P) (NT&EN Books, Woodford Green, 1946)
Ex-Italian Somaliland (Watts & Co., London, 1951)
Eritrea on the Eve (P) (NT&EN Books; Woodford Green, 1952)
Why Are We Destroying the Ethiopian Ports? With an Historical Retrospect 1557–1952 (P) (NT&EN Books, Woodford Green, 1952)
Ethiopia and Eritrea. The Last Phase of the Re-Union Struggle 1941–1952 (Lalibela House, Woodford Green, 1953). Co-authored with R. K. P. Pankhurst
Ethiopia. A Cultural History (Lalibela House, Woodford Green, 1955)

UNPUBLISHED MANUSCRIPTS

Fascism As It Is, published as articles in New Times and Ethiopia News, August 1936–September 1937. Manuscript in Pankhurst Papers at the International Institute of Social History, Amsterdam.
In the Red Twilight, handwritten notebooks of third volume of autobiography, Pankhurst Papers (ibid.)

Appendix

NEWSPAPERS FOUNDED AND EDITED BY SYLVIA PANKHURST

The Woman's Dreadnought, 18 March 1914–21 July 1917
The Workers' Dreadnought, 28 July 1917–14 June 1924 (renamed: *Workers' Dreadnought,* 31 January 1920)
New Times and Ethiopia News, 9 May 1936–5 May 1956
Ethiopia Observer, 1956–1960

SELECTED BIBLIOGRAPHY OF WORKS ON SYLVIA PANKHURST

Biographies

Patricia W. Romero, E. *Sylvia Pankhurst. Portrait of a Radical* (Yale University Press, New Haven and London, 1987)
R. K. P. Pankhurst, *Sylvia Pankhurst. Artist and Crusader. An Intimate Portrait* (Paddington Press, New York and London, 1979)
David Mitchell, *The Fighting Pankhursts. A Study in Tenacity* (Macmillan, New York, 1967)
Barbara Castle, *Sylvia and Christabel Pankhurst* (Penguin Books, Harmondsworth, 1987)
Rita Pankhurst, 'Sylvia Pankhurst in Perspective. Some comments on Patricia Romero's biography' (*Women's Studies International Forum,* XI, 1988),

Pankhurst as an artist

Hilary Cunliffe-Charlesworth, 'Sylvia Pankhurst as an art student', in Ian Bullock and Richard Pankhurst (eds), *Sylvia Pankhurst. From Artist to Anti-Fascist* (Macmillan Academic, Basingstoke, 1992)
Jackie Duckworth, 'Sylvia Pankhurst as an artist' in Bullock and Pankhurst (eds), *Sylvia Pankhurst*
Lisa Tickner, *The Spectacle of Women. Imagery of the Suffrage Campaign 1907–14* (Chatto and Windus, London, 1987). Only a short piece on Pankhurst, but very good for the context of her art.

Pankhurst and socialist–feminism

Les Garner, 'Suffrage and socialism: Sylvia Pankhurst 1903–1914', in Bullock and Pankhurst (eds), *Sylvia Pankhurst*
Barbara Winslow, 'Sylvia Pankhurst and the Great War', in Bullock and Pankhurst (eds), *Sylvia Pankhurst*

Pankhurst and revolutionary communism

Barbara Winslow, *Sylvia Pankhurst: Suffragette and Communist 1912–1924,* PhD, Washington University, USA (to be published by Temple University Press)
Ian Bullock, 'Sylvia Pankhurst and the Russian Revolution: the making of a "left-wing" communist' in Bullock and Pankhurst, (eds), *Sylvia Pankhurst*
Mark Shipway, *Anti-Parliamentary Communism. The Movement for Workers' Councils in Britain, 1917–45* (Macmillan, Basingstoke, 1988). (A chapter)

Pankhurst as a writer

Jane Marcus, Re-reading the Pankhursts and women's suffrage', introduction to Jane Marcus (ed.), *Suffrage and the Pankhursts* (Routledge and Kegan Paul, London, 1988)

Appendix

Pankhurst, anti-fascism and Ethiopia

Richard Pankhurst, 'Sylvia and *New Times and Ethiopia News*', in Bullock and Pankhurst (eds), *Sylvia Pankhurst*

The Pankhurst archive at Amsterdam

M. Wilhelmina H. Schreuder, 'Sylvia Pankhurst's papers as a source', in Bullock and Pankhurst (eds), *Sylvia Pankhurst*

Index

Index

Index

Index